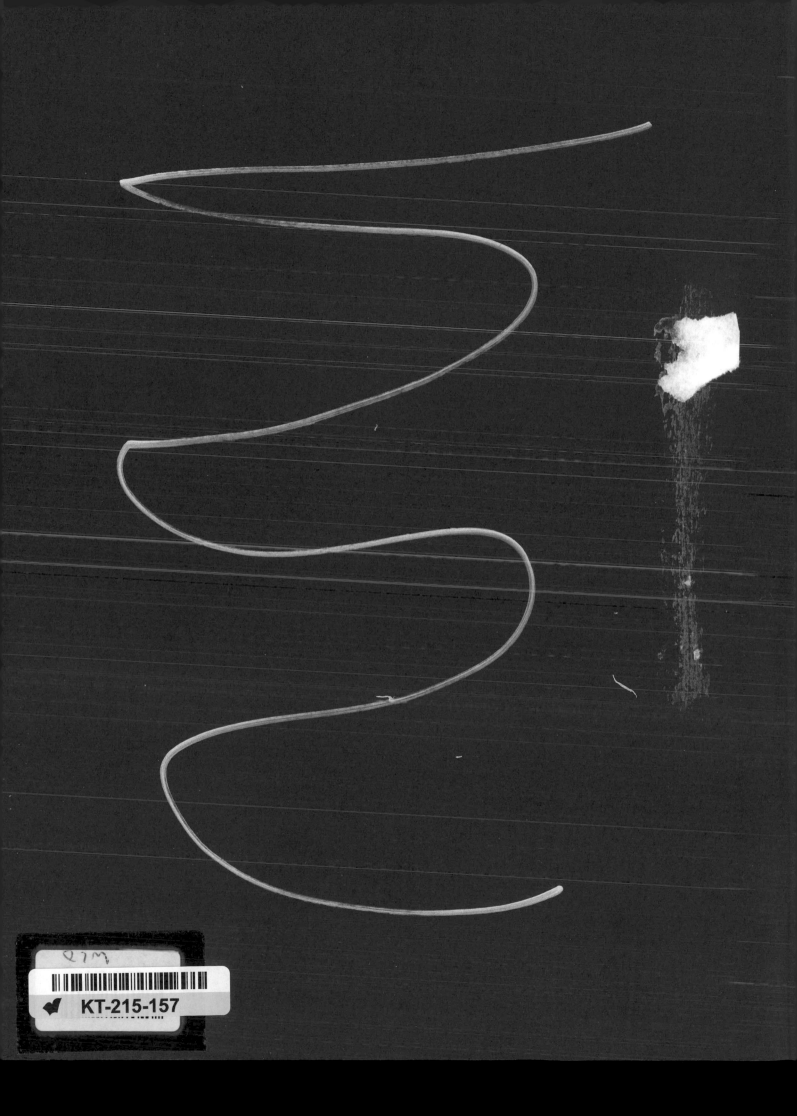

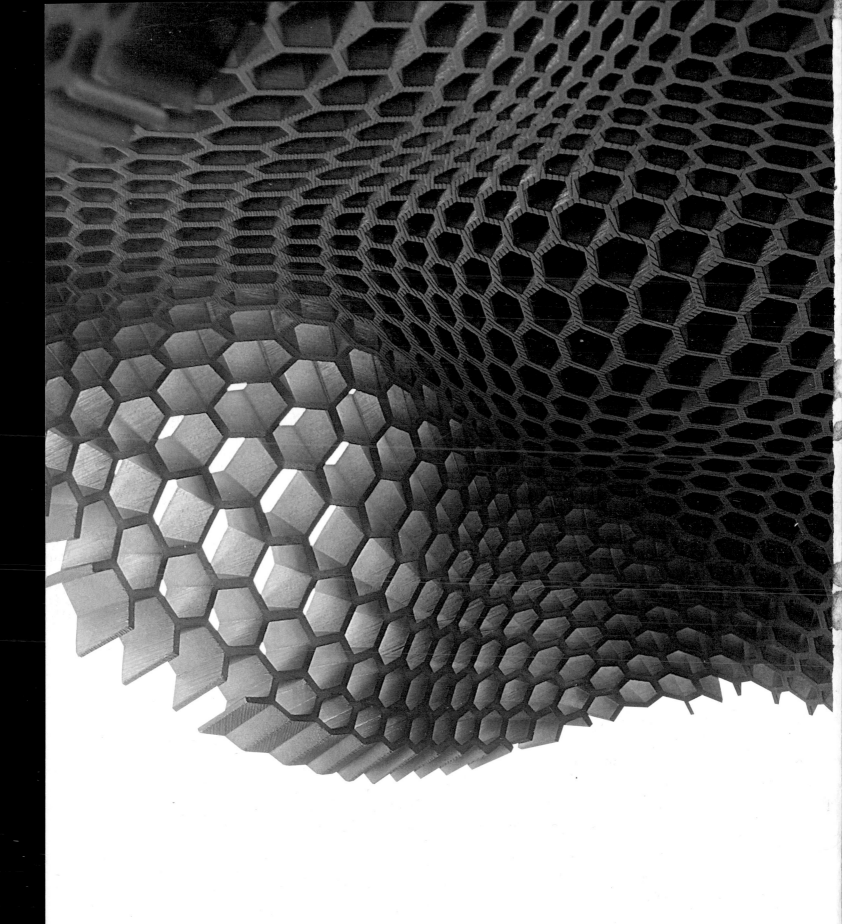

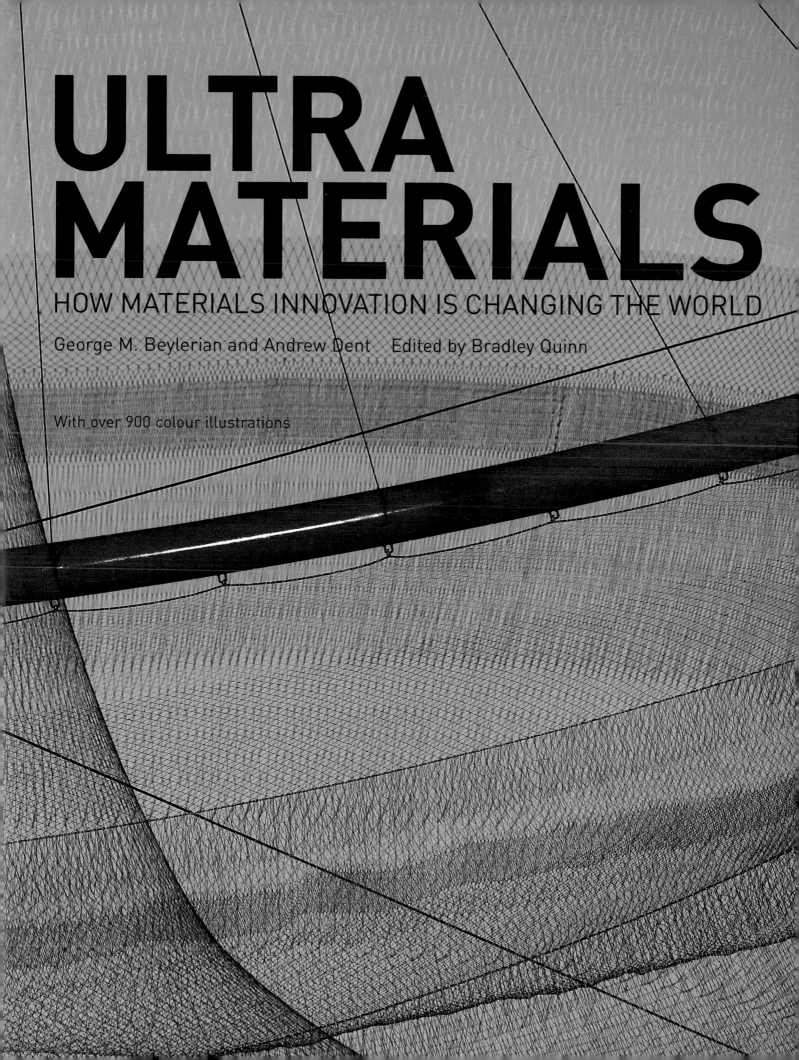

ULTRA MATERIALS

HOW MATERIALS INNOVATION IS CHANGING THE WORLD

George M. Beylerian and Andrew Dent   Edited by Bradley Quinn

With over 900 colour illustrations

First published in the United Kingdom in 2007
by Thames & Hudson Ltd, 181A High Holborn,
London WC1V 7QX

www.thamesandhudson.com

British Library Cataloguing-in-Publication Data
A catalogue record for this book is available from
the British Library

ISBN 978-0-500-51382-8
02137377
Printed in Singapore by Tien Wah Press

CONTENTS

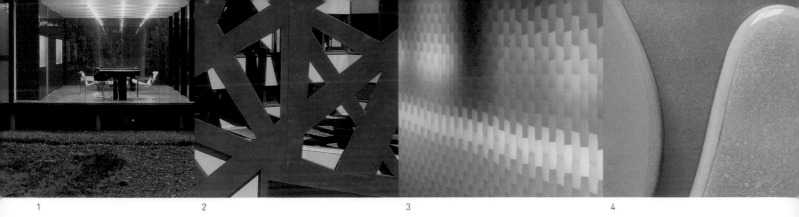

1   2   3   4

INTRODUCTION

BRADLEY QUINN

Materials have become hip at last. Until recently, specialized knowledge of materials was an area normally left to experts or scientists, but today materials have become a source of interest and inspiration for us all. High-tech techniques, smart substances, intelligent interfaces and sensory surfaces are radically redefining the world we live in. As today's generation of materials breaks new ground, many are able to anticipate and respond to changes in the environment. Now dynamic and interactive, materials have the power to change how the human body is experienced and how the urban environment is built. Combined with the new potentials they create for industrial design and medical science, they have the capacity to transform our way of life more radically now than ever before.

Our world is becoming stronger, faster, lighter and smarter; unbreakable gossamer fibres can hoist a satellite into orbit, yet remain soft enough to be worn directly on the body. Super-strong materials are engineering immersive webs and structural networks, and their ability to interface with the built environment has resulted in a fresh wave of product design as well as a novel paradigm of interwoven architecture. As materials assimilate technology, many of them also integrate software, communication devices and information exchanges. High-performance substrates are synthesized to make these materials flexible and even wearable, and imbue them with eye-catching optical effects and textures that appeal to our tactile senses.

This unique moment in material research is truly cutting-edge, yet at the same time it is nothing new; the quest for durable materials is almost as old as humanity itself. Whole civilizations have been categorized solely by the materials they used. Wood, stone, bone and earth were essential to humankind's survival for several millennia, and historians argue that the success of the Roman empire was partly due to the Romans' ability to build sophisticated structures that surpassed those of the peoples they conquered. Then, much as now, precious materials underpinned currencies and mediated global economies, while raw materials formed the basis for craftsmanship and the creation of luxury items. As materials continue to bridge creative production and commercial manufacturing, they preserve time-honoured practices as they strive towards future forms.

Most of the materials we consider to be modern today were born in the early part of the 20th century, mainly created by engineers, metallurgists and scientists. The study of polymers advanced rapidly after the Second World War, gradually leading scientists to conceive of a new interdisciplinary field that became known as material science. The study of materials developed in parallel with industry, and many of the materials-based professions were reinvented. The impact of technology and the burgeoning aerospace industry generated a new awareness of materials, and those with a capacity to function as media created new possibilities for architecture and design. The 1980s are remembered for metals research, culminating in the

5   6   7   8

development of 'superalloys' that combined upwards of thirteen different metal additions. The 1990s addressed ecological issues and introduced a wide range of sustainable materials, and subsequently generated a renewed appreciation for craft traditions. Today, textile design, metalwork, ceramics and glass are advancing dramatically as material science identifies new techniques and uncovers cross-disciplinary potentials, yet the touch of the human hand still remains as important as ever. As material science continues to broker even more interdisciplinary exchanges, the boundaries between science, technology, craft and design blurs even more.

Right now, materials are regarded as one of the richest sources of innovation. No longer intended for practical use alone, materials are playing an important role in taking aesthetics forward. As they imbue design with extravagance, imagination and symbolism, they also make space for brilliant colours, rich textures, unexpected finishes and lavish motifs. Whereas 20th-century materials evolved as high-tech solutions, the materials of the 21st century have emerged as a style-oriented phenomenon. As these materials build the world around us they also fashion the face we show to the world. They are what separate us from the street – and perhaps what make us human.

This book opens precisely at this definitive moment in the long evolution of materials. It is divided into two sections. Part 1: Materials + Design explores the theme of material innovation, outlined in five chapters in order to reveal applications in architecture, design, fashion and art. Chapter 1 offers an overview and introduction to the subject of materials innovation, while Chapter 2 highlights developments such as biomimetics and the new generations of biological materials that are forging fresh directions for the creative industries. Chapter 3 features some of the most ground-breaking products and projects of recent years, bringing the work of designers and practitioners into focus, and Chapter 4 features a compendium of interviews with leading designers and architects, each of whom outlines the diverse roles that materials play in their projects. In Chapter 5, material experts explain, in their own words, what the most important challenges for material science will be in decades to come.

Part 2: Reference and Information begins with encyclopaedia-like synopses of four hundred new materials, underpinned with references to aerospace, the military, architecture and the other design disciplines. The text reveals how engineers, technologists and scientists have masterminded most of these materials, but many were conceived and developed in collaboration with designers, architects and artists. Part 2 concludes with a comprehensive source book section providing an extensive glossary including the relevant terms mentioned throughout the book, as well an index to many of the practitioners, associations, publications and academic awards and fellowships that are transforming the materials of the past into fresh inspirations for the present, and signposting new directions for the materials of tomorrow.

1 The design for this 20x20 House by Chilean architect Felipe Assadi was based on the typical 20 x 20 cm (7⅞ x 7⅞ in) dimensions of a ceramic tile.
2 The Command and Training Centre of the Professional Fire Brigade in Cologne, Germany, was designed by BFM Architects. It comprises a circular building surrounded by a lattice of red concrete, which houses the fire brigade, and an elongated section which accommodates offices and a school.
3 This translucent honeycomb sheet 'pixelates' the transmitted shadow or image from behind it. It is used in the construction of curtain walls, room dividers, cabinet doors, work surfaces and shower surrounds.
4 Volcanic lava requires additional processing in order to be used in the home. But after processing and glazing, this stone is available in a range of thicknesses, and there are over forty colours to choose from.
5 Ross Lovegrove's Liquid Triloba table is a perfect example of combining technology and materials to create a uniquely organic approach to high-tech furniture design.
6 Using an oximeter sensor, Mathieu Lehanneur's 'O' device monitors the oxygen levels in the environment around it.
7 Enkatherm is a unique thermal and moisture barrier for buildings. This sheet incorporates a non-woven matrix of 3-D nylon, is adhered to moisture protection building paper, and provides continuous ventilation and moisture evacuation. It can be used with stucco, EIFS, vinyl and brick.
8 Jürgen Mayer received the Mies van der Rohe Award in 2003 for his Stadthaus Park, a municipal building in Ostfildern, near Stuttgart, Germany.

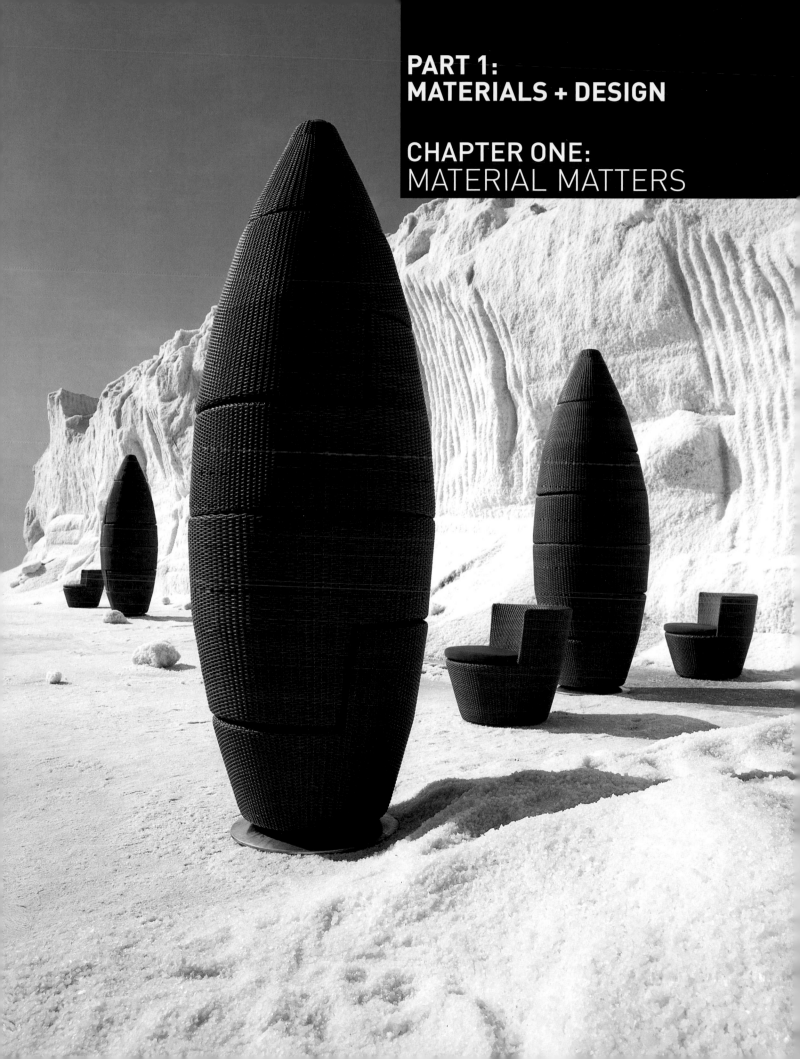

MATERIAL MATTERS

GEORGE M. BEYLERIAN

PREVIOUS PAGE This wicker 'obelisk' (the material is a polyethylene-based, extruded and vat-dyed synthetic fibre) by Dedon breaks down into tub seats and a table.
1 For the Ornamental and Architectural Ironworkers Training Facility, Daniel Goldner Architects used copper, stainless steel, glass and granite flooring.
2 Sandy Chilewich creates accessories from materials usually found underground.
3 Chris Lehrecke's Augie chair is based on a design by his son and was created with a special lathe capable of turning the log.
4 Belgian Peter Traag created his Mummy chair for Edra from a basic beech chair with padding and a 'mummy' wrap.
5 Mathias Bengtsson made this chair from 254 individual layers, producing a 3-D object from a series of 2-D ones.
6, 7 + OPPOSITE Lord Norman Foster's Swiss Re Tower is also known as 'The Gherkin'. Developed on the precedents of green architecture, its shape minimizes reflective surfaces, allows for reduced interior support leading to more natural light penetrating the structure, and creates external pressure differentials that draw air through the building, thereby reducing the need for traditional HVAC systems.
8 Christa Winters of Stuttgart uses poly-chromatic finishes, first initiated by Craig Kaufman in the 1960s.

Sensuous, exuberant, sexy and sublime: the colours, textures and shapes found in the material world have a unique presence. Whether crafted into furniture, everyday objects, high-tech hardware or tactile textiles, the beauty and versatility of the materials used today can help to showcase the mysteries of nature and the magic of science. From the warmth of harvested wood to the unsurpassed strength of solid stone, materials and their capabilities have moulded the built environment for many millennia. Just as alchemists once endeavoured to synthesize gold, modern scientists are now in pursuit of miracle materials. Perhaps because they stimulate our senses and fashion our existence, materials will always fabricate our world and continue to transform it for the better.

In the early part of the 20th century, stamped steel revolutionized the automotive industry, providing elegant and resilient car bodies. But the introduction of strong, lightweight plastics that can replace steel allows today's manufacturers to build lighter, more fuel-efficient cars without sacrificing safety. Likewise, when the International Style came into our vocabulary, characterizing a form of early 20th-century European avant-garde architecture which eliminated all arbitrary decoration inside and out, materials other than concrete, glass or steel took a secondary place in architecture. This scenario, which created 'default' materials, allowed two completely separate paths to emerge between those architects who embraced the new visual style and who chose to bring novel materials to it, and those who explored the amazing range and versatility of the limited set of material options promoted by it.

1

2

MATERIALS AS THE BASIS OF IDEAS

Material innovation has revolutionized both the construction methods and the design of products in almost every aspect of our lives and will continue to do so: in the late 19th century, high-strength iron and steel replaced bricks and mortar as the structural components of buildings, allowing architects and engineers to construct towers that rose higher than ever before. More recently, Peter Testa, an LA-based architect, proposed the construction of a forty-storey building made entirely from carbon fibre. If built, it would be the lightest and strongest of its kind.

The cycle is – and should be – endless, just as long as there are people looking for better, more efficient and less wasteful ways of doing things. Sometimes it is that quest to improve on an existing material or process that drives such progress on, but at other times inspiration (and innovation) can strike out of the blue. At such times, materials and processes emerge that answer no specific need or question, but exist merely as a statement.

Innovation, however, does not always emerge from a high-tech background or from new technologies: it can also develop from older ideas that continue to hold their own in the fast-paced world of design and architecture. When new technologies and materials are created, time and effort must be spent on 'practising' their application. As such, Gehry's Guggenheim Museum in Bilbao was the first building to make use of titanium 'scales' in its outer cladding after many prior experiments.

Yet experimentation in new materials, new technologies and new processes is much simpler when the scale is small – for example in product and furniture design – and when the application and usefulness of the product is more reasonable for the producer and consumer alike. The more exotic and experimental the piece, however, the more it becomes a work of art. Many interesting items can still look very 'experimental' material-wise, or else are either too costly to develop or too 'creative' for mainstream marketing. However, they are often the significant forerunners of things to come.

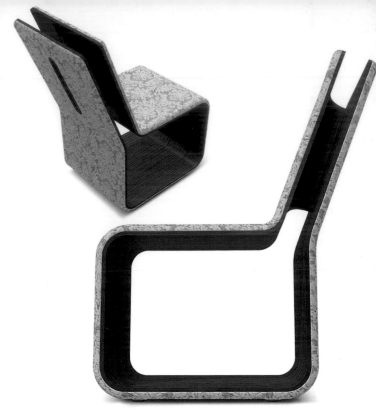

1   2

1 Alon Langotsky created this table for the design group Chista from a naturally formed teak root, finished to reveal the irregularities of the material and to draw attention to the beauty of the material.
2 Creativity and technology inspired James Owen to create this chair using a combination of bent plywood, urethane foam padding and brocade upholstery.
ABOVE Bathsheba Grossman designed a number of spectacular lamps for Materialize MGX, one of the pioneers of stereo-lithographic technology. Remarkably, despite their delicate appearance, the shapes formed by the process are quite durable.

For instance, when Dupont first introduced Corian® it was hailed as a unique material with very distinctive qualities: it was a durable, solid surface material. Unfortunately, the research and development cost was substantially reflected in the high selling price and so, while the product was widely appreciated, it was not a big seller. Yet several years later, with competition in full swing, the material is now on its way to becoming more mainstream, with acceptable price levels and availability. This type of evolution of a material follows a typical research and development pattern.

In addition to materials, processes are also the protagonists of new technology. As the costs of operating high technology drop, it has become a more viable option in the creation of medium-scale objects such as furniture. Computer Numerically Controlled (CNC) milling and stereolithography, as well as other rapid prototyping methods, are emerging as innovative tools. In the CNC process, a computer controls a robotic arm that routs or mills a block of material. Capable of achieving tolerances far tighter than any human could, time and time again, this process allows designers to create bespoke pieces in multiples.

Stereolithography is another process that is changing all the rules. Originally created as a way to form rapid prototypes, this three-dimensional printing process is one of those technologies that gives an astonishing amount of power to designers: if any object can be rendered on a computer, it can be produced: the designer's imagination becomes the final frontier. While there are a number of different processes involved, the basic premise of the stereolithography process is to build a product, layer by layer, using a range of materials. Eliminating moulds and skilled hand assembly production methods, this process has advanced the production of complex shapes more than any other. The materials used in this process include polymers, metals and ceramics and are continually being improved to provide better strength and surface finish. As a result, this process has been exploited for the creation of larger pieces such as stools and chairs, and for critical mechanical pieces in assemblies.

3

4

From science students to corporate scientists, there are countless individuals working on the next generation of materials, processes and tools that will allow us to design and build. Material innovation is clearly necessary if we are to solve the problems and the needs of the future, especially now that we must be concerned with ecological issues, a shortage of materials, progress in motion features, comfort, speed and nanotechnology.

MATERIALITY MEETS GLOBAL DESIGN

In *The Elements of Design* by Loan Oei and Cecile De Kegel, a richly illustrated world of patterns, textures and colours is revealed, including dots, crossing lines, planes and circles, all of which have supplied us with much visual excitement over the years. Our world is full of symbolism, and, looking at the myriad examples that demonstrate art imitating nature or one hemisphere taking inspiration from another, it is evident that the evolution of creative design is infinite. With so much richness in non-advanced materials and old-fashioned techniques, it is important to remember that we do not always need to look for answers in technology. Putting up skyscrapers of 100 storeys and higher is no longer the zeitgeist of innovation, whereas buildings that use material innovation make a truly artistic and individual impact compared to the backdrop of other less interesting buildings. Likewise, reducing the size of electronic components in products can only encourage technological advances so far: Apple has pioneered the development of high-tech electronic components, but by focusing on design and materials (most notably on its design for the casing for the iconic iPod) it has spawned legions of followers and created one of the most recognizable visual identities and brands of today.

We often seem attracted to those who can create new ideas, new applications, new installations, new fashion or new buildings. Yet in the context of material innovation, the term 'new' is most obviously applicable to those who can think laterally and apply their imagination to developing new vistas where materials, blended with creativity, can produce new 'products'. If this can also be extended to creating new solutions to an existing model, or a completely new invention, that is even better.

3 Italian artist Massimiliano Adami has created functional objects called 'Modern Fossils'. Various empty plastic containers and assorted plastic items are thrown into a mould and agglomerated with polyurethane foam to become 'drums' or 'tables'.
4 Jeroen Verhoeven used drawings of 17th-century furniture to make his industrialized wood table based on traditional forms. Using a computer program, he converted views of the table into a 3-D design in order to manufacture it on an industrial scale.
BELOW Patrick Jouin collaborated with Materialize to create this elegantly sinuous chair using the stereolithography process.

CREATIVE INDUSTRIES

In order for progress to continue, for people to truly 'create' something new, there must be a balance of technology, materials and human inspiration. The many ingenious thinkers, artists, architects and designers who manage to combine all of these considerations into their work are to be applauded for their initiative to pursue new ideas as well as their ability to implement them. Any project that is materially sensitive can boast the distinction of being a leader in the field of creativity.

Materials are the core of the built environment: everything we touch and smell, and most of what we see and hear, is based on a material of some kind. Design is the practice of making those materials into products and environments that, hopefully, meet the needs and desires of the consumer. If a practitioner is creating designs based on a limited knowledge of materials, the designs themselves will in turn be constrained. We all use tools to accomplish our work: some might use a computer while others use a pencil; many use both. It is the understanding of what each of those tools brings to a task that is ultimately important. Knowing the materials available is to know what tools are available. In this era of seemingly endless programmes of building development, materials serve a critical purpose in helping to differentiate one product from another. By simply changing the material of virtually any product, without altering any other aspect of its design, one can change it from a commodity product into luxury goods (or vice versa). Choose the right material and a designer can make this transformation without altering the unit cost of the product. That kind of knowledge is obviously extremely powerful.

Materials can transform design, and design therefore has the power to transform our lives. We have high expectations in terms of the places in which we live, the clothes we wear and the products we use in our daily lives: we seem to be looking for things that comfort, inspire and create a relationship with each of us as individuals. In order to create that personal relationship, a designer needs to be aware of all of the options available to work with.

OPPOSITE The material covering the Bayer Chemical Company's headquarters in Leverkusen, Germany, is a high-tech printed netting that serves excellent purpose as a temporary cover during renovation while also reinforcing the company's brand.
ABOVE Somewhere between art and function, urethane inspired Eelko Moorer to create a tongue-in-cheek bear rug.
BELOW This Nest chair by Charles Brill (see also page 4) emerges from being a functional item into an artwork.

1

2

1 The Saunabox by Castor Design was constructed using a Cor-ten steel shipping container, combined with other materials such as steel, glass and cedar and pine wood.
2 Claude Cormier covered this tree – which was a diseased tree slated for removal – with 75,000 blue Christmas baubles.
BELOW The designer John Houshmand uses nature 'as it is' in his screen, and so each piece is an individual work of art.

ART + INNOVATION

Within the realm of innovation, creative artists are almost always fascinating. Admittedly they are freer to express themselves generally in whichever form or materials they want, unless of course, it's a specific project they have been commissioned to deliver. Pulling materials and ideas from thin air with such impact is usually a thrilling experience for viewers. The artist sees, thinks and transforms – what the artist sees is a material, followed by the thought process 'I can do this' or 'what is seen here is an opportunity to convey...' and lastly comes the process of transforming the material into the ultimate phase of its existence: the finished art piece. Artists are also able to explore and utilize materials for purely aesthetic reasons, especially where performance is of no particular concern to the consumer. Finishes and surface treatments form part of the materials universe, and many artists have become leaders in understanding and applying this field to their work. Moreover, they are leaders because they are eager to experiment and are able to immerse themselves in a single material to 'see where it takes them' rather than concerning themselves with the outcome and seeking only the routes that will lead them there.

Going back almost half a decade, the design world experienced the real 'handling' potential of materials when they were mutilated, bonded and burnt – a sadomasochistic trip that explored materials as art. Such widespread experimentation around the world has provided a significant source of newly constituted materials that play a leading role not only in design and architecture, but also in the world of art.

Material experimentation today can blur the lines between art and function. Yet this transition between the two applications is proof that materials can often provoke the design possibilities of 'either/or' and a piece might easily become a 'functional/non-functional' art object. In these cases, the work is not quite finite: the artist is sometimes more anxious to play with the material than to create an object for commercial reasons.

3

4

Cross-utilization is an area that is of great interest to designers all over the world, and especially to Material ConneXion, mainly because it supports the benefits of cross-fertilization between the fields of design, architecture and art, encourages the economies of usage, and ultimately makes pure economic sense. For artists, who often have no interest in the physical properties of a material, they are free to use those materials that appeal to them on a purely visual level. Tensile strength? Not a problem, but look at the way it catches the light! In other disciplines of design, this can also be effective.

Sandy Chilewich, for example, is an expert in tracking down cross-utilized materials for use in her work. Having become a fan of vinyl fibres – usually seen in screen doors – when she created her Plinyl™ flooring and other woven pieces, Chilewich continued to mine the rich visual world of industrial materials. One of the more interesting outcomes of this search was a line of accessories made from polymer geotextiles. Usually found underground, these materials are used to prevent soil erosion and maintain vegetation growth in areas with significant water run-off.

Retroglo, a reflective yarn made from a 3M Scotchlite™ reflective material laminated on to a polyester film for added strength, is another example of such a crossover material. First developed as an innovation for road signs and markers, Scotchlite™ has made a huge impact on various industries, primarily in the sportswear arena where reflectivity is an important attribute to clothing worn by runners.

Inspiration can also come from places where it is least expected, or where the territory is completely new and unknown. As we will see in the following chapters, materials are mainly developed for specific use in a wide range of industries and products, and are often entirely unheard of by those outside these arenas. However, that is not to say that these specific materials cannot venture outside their specific role. Indeed, the cross-utilization of knowledge and materials will be one of the most important features of future developments in materials art and innovation.

3 To celebrate World Environment Day, Hector Serrano transformed discarded inner tubes into an architectural element, using them as a material to depict black clouds over the viewers' heads.
4 Handmade from a variety of textiles (including recycled fabrics), this clothing by Nathalie Chanin aims to preserve both environment and tradition. She uses local quilters to stitch and embroider the pieces.
BELOW Using tyres from dismantled shanty towns, artist Akemi Adrienne Tanaka created a humorous artifact for a community playground in South Africa, while adhering to sustainable principles.

1

2

1+2 On the West Side Highway in New York, Frank Gehry has used a fritted ceramic coating on the exterior glass of the new AC/InterActiveCorp headquarters, creating a unique appearance that transcends the shape of the structure. In this particular shape, Gehry has evoked a multi-masted sailing vessel: appropriate for a building that looks out onto the Hudson River.
3+4 This house by Kevin Daly and Chris Genik shows how perforated aluminum can provide a range of differing degrees of enclosure and shade. In the evening, light is emitted through the perforated holes, creating a magical effect.
OPPOSITE Felipe Assadi has brought a whole new interpretation of the International Style to Chile. In this building, the same glass material is used on three sides, along with one entire face of outdoor ceramic tiles. These tiles serve to shield the occupants from the intense heat of the sun.

TRENDSETTERS + PIONEERS

There is something special about the pure power of the human hand coupled with imagination, versus the awesome power of technology and innovation. While the pursuit of innovation seems to be one of life's primary drivers, the result of impressive technological advances can often fail to connect with us on an emotional level: very few people swoon over the latest computer chip or V8 engine.

Yet time and time again, we find ourselves moved, elated, transported even, by the results of nothing more than a creative mind in full bloom: the sensuality of a piece of handmade fashion or a simple wooden bowl turned on a lathe. Where technology appeals to the rational being in all of us, it seems that it is creativity that stirs our emotions and brings us true aesthetic satisfaction.

This creative mind is at the heart of human civilization and is at the root of the kind of innovative thinking that began many centuries ago. From the creation of the pyramids to the building of a titanium museum, these ancient and modern wonders of the world are living proof of how the minds of individuals have driven them to create. From Leonardo to Le Corbusier, and from Norman Foster to Herzog & de Meuron, it is that same mind, centuries later, with added layers of acquired knowledge and experimentation, which has allowed us to create and to design for the future.

3

4

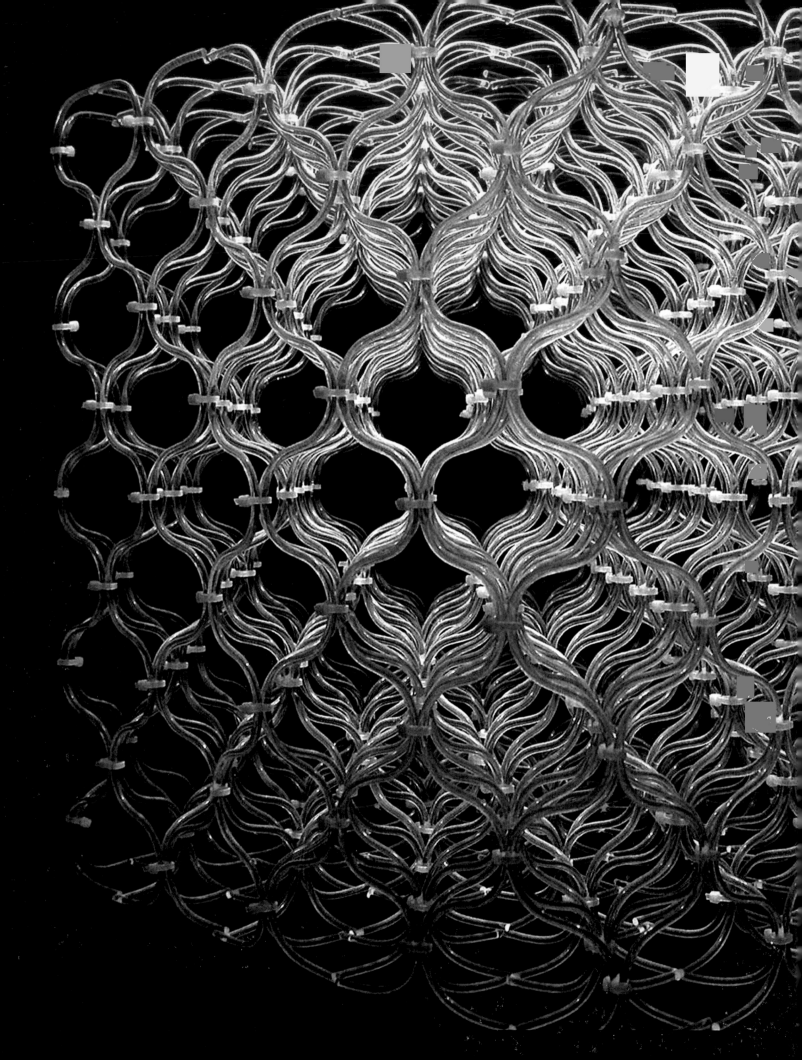

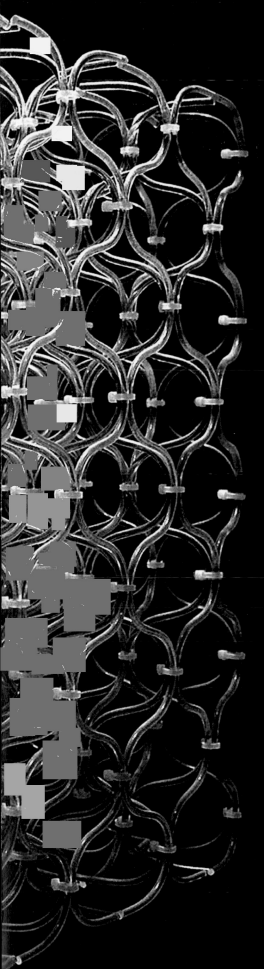

1   2   3   4

MATERIAL OVERVIEWS

ANDREW DENT

Covering the entire world of innovative materials is perhaps beyond the scope of
any one book. What were once individual disciplines have become endlessly and
increasingly subdivided as we learn more about substances and discover new ways
of processing them. However, thanks to new discoveries, breakthrough inventions
and on occasion, good marketing, certain trends in material development can be
determined within this vast industry. These trends often cover more than one material
category, as is the case for sustainability, where available solutions include all
material families.

Considering past trends or hot new topics, a number of examples stand out from
recent decades. High temperature superconductors became a white-hot area for
development following the now-infamous 1987 meeting in New York of the American
Physical Society where the research was first presented. The drive for better
commercial jet aircraft then led to the apex of super alloy development in the 1980s
and early 1990s, and these new metal alloys often contained up to fifteen different
metals, such as hafnium, rhenium and platinum.

Only a few years ago, the design world was enamoured of gels, those brightly
coloured, low-hardness, semi-liquid polymers that could be used in seating, consumer
electronics and sportswear, and were touted as the new generation of sensorial
surfaces. Similarly, as we have seen, Frank Gehry's use of titanium as the metal
cladding for the Guggenheim Museum in Bilbao was suddenly de rigeur, and as
a result found its way into laptops, golf clubs, ice-climbing equipment and even wallets.

So what are the hot topics of today? This chapter covers what promises to be the
defining trends in materials innovation at the start of the 21st century. Some, like
fibres and textiles, have been around for thousands of years, but are currently at
such a state-of-the-art developmental stage that they warrant special consideration.
Others, such as nanotechnology, are in their infancy, and it is still too early to tell
if the discipline will revolutionize materials or simply remain as a footnote.

5   6   7   8

FIBRE TECHNOLOGY

One of the easiest and least expensive ways to improve strength and stiffness in a material is to add short, stiff fibres to the mix. Whether it is a carbon fibre added to epoxy for bicycle frames, silicon carbide (a ceramic) added to metals for F-16 landing gear or bast fibres added to soy resins for Mercedes fender parts, incorporating fibres to a material makes it stiffer. Of course the type, length and surface compatibility of the fibre all have an effect on properties, and have enabled fibre-reinforced products to achieve strength-to-weight values unparalleled in the world of materials.

Fibres used to strengthen can usually be categorized by material. Glass, carbon and polymer fibres are the most widely used, each with their own advantages. Glass is inexpensive and versatile, carbon fibre is the highest performing and polymers tend to allow for engineering of specific properties that can be tailored to an individual application. There has been a constant increase, however, in the use of natural fibres in certain lower-performance applications, due to their abundance (most are a waste product of the agricultural industry) and sometimes even their aesthetic appeal.

For short fibre reinforcement, a good combination of strength and stiffness is necessary. When longer filament or even yarns are used, tensile strength becomes the dominant factor, and other issues such as flexibility, energy absorption and fracture morphology come into play.

Although significant advances in polymer research have led to the development of super-strong plastic filaments such as Spectra® or Dyneema®, carbon fibre still comes out on top with a tensile strength of a filament 1 mm (⅟₁₆ in) in diameter sufficient to suspend the weight of a car. To improve on this it is necessary to look to nature: the material used in spider silk offers even greater strength than that of carbon fibre and recent studies have shown the possibility of isolating the relevant protein to allow for its production on a larger scale.

Carbon fibre may currently be the strongest filament, but shoot a bullet at a woven vest made of the material and it becomes clear that tensile strength isn't everything.

ABOVE Fibre reinforcement is an essential technique in creating mechanisms with high strength and low mass, such as the landing gear of this military jet. Silicon carbide, which is a ceramic, has been added to some of the metal components.
OPPOSITE No chemical binder agents are used in the fabrication of this spun-laid, non-woven fabric: the bonding takes place with heat and pressure alone. The open uniform structure has good tufting abilities, and tufting can be done without elongation or a compromise in strength, due to a new fibre design of the product.

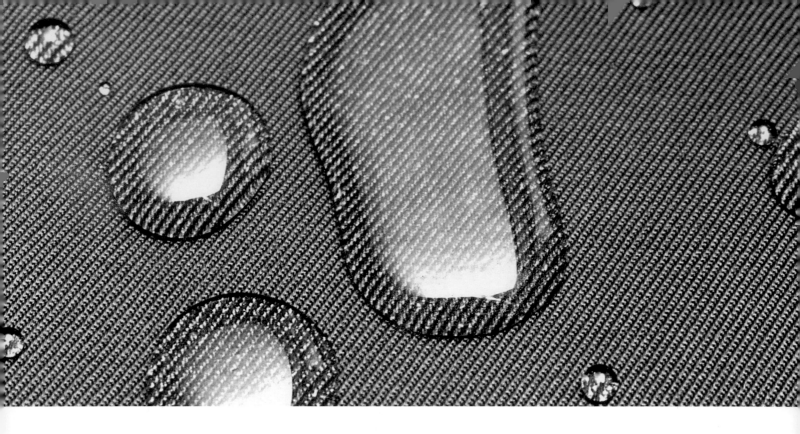

To make a successful ballistic-proof material, both strength and toughness are required. Carbon fibre is likely to shatter on impact but a polymer fibre, such as Kevlar®, will give, absorbing the impact energy and saving lives. This aramid fibre (currently available only in yellow) has proved uniquely suitable for this application, with few equivalent alternatives currently available. Indeed, other polymer fibres like high-tenacity oriented polyethylene are stronger, and as such are the filament of choice for haulage ropes used on tugboats and ocean liners. But they are unable to absorb as much energy on impact as the magic yellow yarn.

Improvements in fibre technology are not limited to the performance arena. In both apparel and upholstery, the stigma of 'synthetic fibres' is being overcome, as issues of texture, odour and stain protection, and wicking and wrinkle resistance are steadily resolved in polymer textiles. Microfibres are a good example of this, offering lighter, softer and more durable materials (such as faux suedes and furs as well as performance textiles for sportswear) than would be possible with naturals. Stain resistance has also taken a quantum leap in performance with the advent of the nanotech engineering of individual fibres to repel liquids. By altering synthetic fibres on a molecular level (rather than coating the surface as used in Teflon® stain resistance), a liquid-repelling property can be maintained throughout repeated washing without being abraded away.

Sometimes, however, the ability of a fibre to absorb liquid is a good thing. Super absorbent fibres are used for spill containment and are a significant improvement over foams. Absorbent fibres are also being developed for medical uses, but their true innovation is an ability to discharge their cargo at a particular rate after a specified time. This enables controlled drug delivery for sutures and wound dressings, according to predetermined changes in temperature, pH scale or time.

The new developments in fibre technology can be directly translated to textiles. Added to a woven textile, a short, long or a continuous-length fibre will provide incremental improvement in toughness, stiffness or strength. Simply put, using a woven textile,

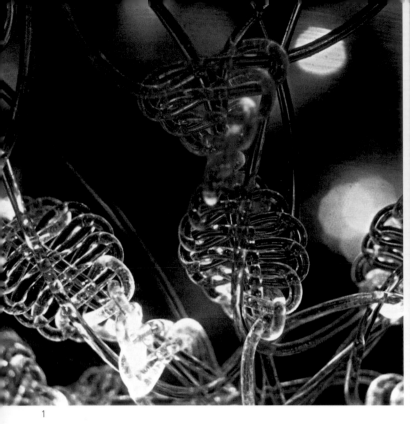

1

2

1 This is a close-up image of a knot made with fibre optics. This process weaves plastic fibre optics together in order to create textiles and objects, as well as signage. The woven fibre optics are gathered at one end and receive light from a small LED source that can change colour. Forms as complex as lingerie or decorative costumes may be woven using this process, though the robustness of such garments is limited.
2 This 3-D spacer textile is used in upholstery applications. The textile incorporates a 3-D woven structure that is warp-knit on a Raschel machine in a single knitting sequence, producing two face fabrics independently constructed and connected by 'spacer yarns'. The fabric properties for each face can be independently selected, and the spacer yarns grouped into rows to create a ribbed effect.

or adding one to your material, will improve performance in almost every category save transparency (and that is being worked on). An obvious example of this is the use of woven fibre composite materials in aerospace engineering, car racing, sports equipment and architecture.

Even after thousands of years, most of us are still wearing woven garments. The build up of individual flexible filaments into a warp and a weft enables any abrasion, tensile or crushing to be accommodated by the filaments, dissipating the effect on any single filament. As such, woven fabrics are a superbly simple and effective system and continue to be at the forefront of materials innovation. Perhaps one of the biggest advances in textiles in recent years has come from an innovation in knitting rather than in the materials themselves. Typically produced on a Raschel machine, spacer fabrics or three-dimensional fabrics, offer a new dimension in textiles: depth. Predominantly used in cushioning, these spacer textiles are better than foams, especially when used in sneaker, sportswear and car manufacturing, and avoid the need for an additional decorative top textile layer or adhesive. Moreover, they are easier to clean and recycle, and are also more durable. Synthetics such as nylons and polyesters can be used, as well as cottons and other natural fibres. Whereas textiles are often seen as flexible forms of a specific length and breadth, the addition of a customizable thickness of up to 5 cm (2 in) and variable from area to area, enables us to think about textiles as blocks of material that have volume.

Surprisingly, the production of non-wovens far outstrips that of wovens and knits in terms of volume. It's just that most non-wovens usually find an application in medical, chemical, construction and agriculture. Easier to manufacture than wovens, they are typically produced from polymer resins that are extruded at high speed (much like Silly String) onto a substrate where they bond with each other and solidify into a thin mat of entangled fibres. Though still a long way from the feel and strength of woven or knitted textiles, they can be used for insulation, as disposable wipes for liquid absorption, as spacers and linings and for cushioning. They may be easily

3

4

coloured, perforated, textured and bonded (by heat or sonic welding, stitching or gluing), and act as efficient filters. They have also found application as touch-sensitive pads for smart textiles where the randomness of the fibre orientation acts as an effective conductor for electricity.

Touch-sensitive textiles developed by companies such as Eleksen have typically been used in outerwear as touch controls for MP3 players or mobile phones. Likewise, the commercial use of 'smart shirts', to monitor vital signs and message them back to the wearer's physician in order to ensure real time assessment of the patient's health, has also been developed. The US military is conducting research into this technology in order to create more interactive uniforms for soldiers. Mainly developed at the US Army Soldier Systems Center in Natick, Massachusetts, researchers have also looked at woven structures that contain a substance that is highly flexible under normal conditions, but which stiffens on impact from a bullet or other projectile, hopefully stopping the object.

Thin and flexible polymer display screens can now be sewn into any garment for specialist use (although the limited durability of the material means they cannot yet be washed in the hot cycle of a washing machine). In an attempt to make soldiers less of a target, chameleon-like woven surfaces are also being investigated such that the colour of each thread can be controlled by an electrical impulse. Though still at a prototype stage (due to complexity and cost), this offers some idea of where fashion may be going in the future. A soldier accustomed to wearing heavy and uncomfortable armour, or a patient who is aware that a garment may save their life, is willing to put up with the addition of often cumbersome technology to their apparel. General acceptance, however, will probably only come when technology forms an integral part of the fabric and cannot be seen or felt. This is what researchers are currently working towards.

In conclusion, it is worth noting here the successful application of the first human-made annually renewable, melt-processable fibre. This fibre, woven into textiles and also available as a non-woven, is used in bedding and casual apparel as an alternative

3 Used as a thermal and moisture barrier for buildings, this sheet comprises a non-woven spacer matrix of 3-D nylon made of polyamide (nylon) filaments joined at the intersections. Ninety-five per cent of the matrix is open space, and the matrix is adhered to a moisture-protection building paper, providing continuous ventilation.
4 This moulded sheet is a 'cleaner' alternative to Velcro. Using regular, moulded shapes on the gripping surface, this system eliminates both unwanted attachment to fabric surfaces, and the presence of a backing that can absorb moisture. The interlocking fastening system includes low-profile, self-aligning islands which interlock when engaged but are easily disconnected by peeling, providing a strong, durable, non-grabbing, easy-to-use system.

to cotton or polyester. Synthesized from corn (the same raw material now being used to create E85 ethanol, the gasoline alternative), sugars from this plant are transformed into lactic acid and then polymerized into polylactic acid. This breakthrough offers an alternative to the oil-based polymer textiles such as nylon and polyester. Moreover, the textiles are industrially compostable, and eventually break down into harmless biomass when introduced to actively managed compost. This material offers a real and sustainable alternative to existing polymer textiles at a competitive cost and performance.

SUSTAINABILITY

Sustainability can seem an overwhelmingly daunting prospect. Simpler concerns of recyclability or use of natural resources have been superseded by the need to understand the entire lifecycle of a material, from creation to disposal, or more hopefully, from creation into something else. Tracking materials in this way requires information about extraction, synthesis, production into product, use as product, disposal and eventual re-use. In addition, it is necessary to factor in transport between all phases of production, to consider whether the product will use significant energy or other resources, and whether or not it will affect other products/materials in its use. Simply put, sustainability encompasses the total combined impact of a material on its surroundings and attempts to ensure that this material can be used again and again with no adverse result on the environment.

For creative professionals interested in lowering their impact on the environment, there are several promising attempts to create databases in order to help determine the total environmental impact of a material or product (typically referred to as LCA: Life Cycle Assessment or Life Cycle Analysis). LEED (Leadership in Energy and Environmental Design) is a US-based non-profit organization that uses a consensus-based assessment of materials and systems for construction, awarding points for individual products that can enable the assessment of an entire building.

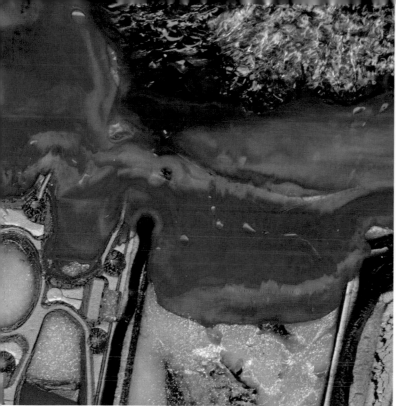

2

3

Though it currently stops somewhat short of complete LCA, the rating system is a step in the right direction and provides what no other organization has yet been able to do; a fair and scaleable system that is accepted industry-wide.

The product design industry is not so lucky, partially because such a wide range of products are possible to produce: heating, ventilation and air conditioning (HVAC) systems are reasonably similar in most buildings, whereas parts to be used in a child's toy are unique to that product and are not replicated in, say, shoes. It is also the case that often each moulded part of a product is made not only from resin, but also including five or six different additives, sometimes with pigments for colour, UV-resistance, plasticizers and even volume-increasing fillers. If designers are not careful, they can start with the most sustainable resin available but go on to contaminate it with toxic additives.

One of the most promising ideas for assessing sustainability in products is through the Cradle-to-Cradle system. Initially developed by architect and designer William McDonough, and materials chemist Dr Michael Braungart, and presented in a book of the same name, this system attempts to classify all materials as either technical or biological nutrients. The advantage of this approach is that synthetic materials are not discounted: in many cases they actually turn out to have less of an impact than those derived from natural resources. All products for which an exact chemical composition is not known (such as when a textile for a sports shoe has been purchased from another supplier) are tested by combustion and by analysis of the gases emitted. For any product that emits chemicals toxic to the environment, a change to a more benign additive is required before Cradle-to-Cradle certification can be granted.

So where are sustainable products right now? Some industries have taken a more proactive approach than others. Certainly the interior design and furniture industries have understood that they have an important role to play, and significant improvements in the sustainability of these products have been developed as a result. Upholstery fabrics and office chairs that pass Cradle-to-Cradle certification,

1 These polymer sheets are created from recycled scrap and waste materials such as coffee cups, CDs, production scrap, old bank notes and toothbrushes, which are added to small amounts of high density polyethylene. Each scrap type (in this case old mobile phones) imparts a distinct and non-uniform colour to the sheet. The boards can be processed like composite wood-based boards (like MDF) including drilling, cutting, milling and thermoforming.
2 Corn has been a multi-purpose food for years, producing everything from sweeteners to flour. Now, companies are using corn starch to produce a new type of polymer that has the same qualities – or better – than traditional petrochemical polymers, and has the added benefit of producing compostable products.
3 These sidewalks are made from 100% recycled rubber with a binder and a colouring agent.

1

2

1 Bamboo can be used for scaffolding construction, pipes, textiles and much more. Here, simple peeled bamboo is used to create attractive tableware.

2 Likewise, this woven rug is made from used (note the red patch) bicycle inner tubes. The inner tubes comprise one direction of the mat with a high-tenacity synthetic yarn in the warp to hold the tubes together.

OPPOSITE The designers at SEED have created this easily assembled chair from recycled paper tubes and plywood. The tubes can be easily replaced if damaged, and multiple chairs can be linked to create benches of various lengths.

alternatives to VOC-emitting (volatile organic compounds) formaldehyde resins for MDF office furniture, as well as non-vinyl wall coverings have all shown that being green is neither financially prohibitive nor aesthetically unappealing. There have been a number of forays into sustainable design by footwear manufacturers with mixed results, thanks mainly to the issues of adhesives and the complexity of construction for most modern sport shoes. Consumer products can often prove to be more difficult to ensure sustainability for, due to limited lifespans and the number of parts used in the construction process. At least in the EU there has been legislation to remove all hazardous heavy metals such as cadmium and mercury from electronics, and to force manufacturers to list all chemicals used. Product packaging, however, has been one area to demonstrate significant improvements, with a number of manufacturers rethinking their primary and secondary packaging in order to reduce waste, allow for composting and remove toxic additives.

Compostability on an industrial scale has proved to be an equally important issue. Under the larger umbrella of biodegradability, it allows products to have a complete lifecycle with little or no loss in performance, but also ensures they will break down into harmless biomass when subjected to particular compositing conditions. Resins that fit into this category include PLA (polylactic acid) resins as well as some of the newer bioresins that are not yet available commercially.

Perhaps one of the most noteworthy new ideas to come out of sustainable design is the general move towards simplicity in design. A reduction in the number of materials used in design, a refining of the complexity of construction (avoiding glues, complex fasteners etc) and an avoidance of unnecessary clutter has inevitably led to more sustainable and improved products. Making an office chair entirely from plastic so that it can be easily recycled is better than using combinations of metal and plastic. Enabling a product to be taken apart for disposal makes it more likely to be recycled and reused. Simplicity in design is harder to achieve, but no one said that being green was going to be easy.

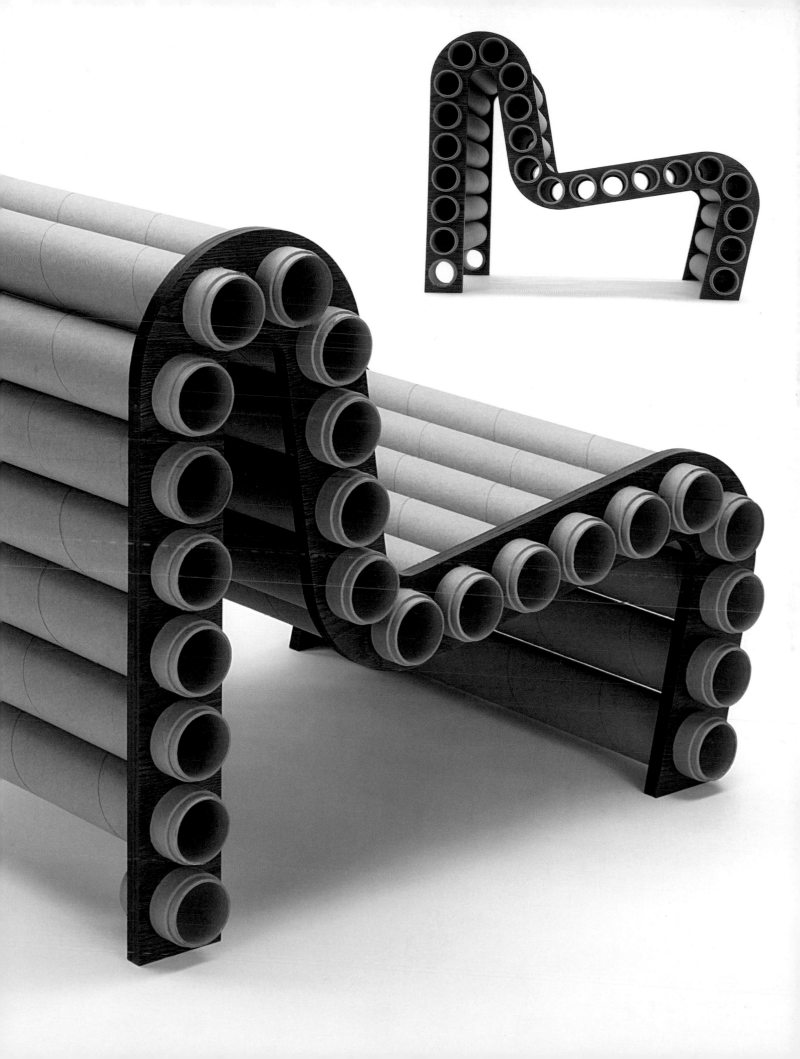

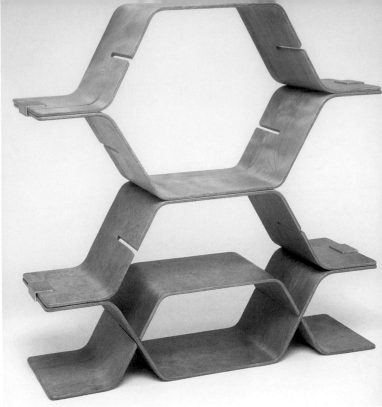

1

2

BIOMIMICRY

Mussels are not one of the most exciting animals in the underwater kingdom. They hardly even move. But that is exactly what caught the attention of Kaichang Li, a science professor at Oregon State University. During a trip to the Oregon coast, Li became fascinated by the impressive staying power of these shellfish, which clung to their subaqueous homes in currents that swept most other small animals out to sea. This observation led to research on waterproof adhesives with a view to replacing traditional, carcinogenic formaldehyde-based adhesives. In response to his discovery that the strength of the mussels' grip relies on secreted proteins known as byssal threads, Li created a mimetic adhesive made from soy proteins. Extremely water resistant, this new, soy-based adhesive outperforms formaldehyde-based alternatives and is comparable in cost. Kaichang Li's mussel-inspired adhesive has been licensed to Columbia Forest Products, the largest producer of decorative plywood in the US, and all Columbia Forest's plywood products will use the soy-based adhesive by 2006.

Taking inspiration from natural phenomena is hardly a new concept – it can be traced back to the ancient hunting techniques of indigenous peoples – but this innovative strategy, which in a less technology-obsessed era, might have been called 'common sense', has been recently dubbed 'biomimicry'. Janine Benyus, author of *Biomimicry: Innovation Inspired by Nature*, defines biomimicry as 'the process of learning from and then emulating life's genius.' A range of examples are already available as commercial products. The lotus leaf's ability to stay clean in muddy environments has inspired a range of self-cleaning exterior house paints. Like the lotus leaf, which emerges from the earth without a speck of dirt on it, the paint has a rough, hydrophobic surface. Though not detectable to the eye, the texture effectively forces water droplets to roll – not slide – off the leaf. As they roll, the droplets pick up any dirt, mud or small bugs in their way, much as a snowball accumulates mass as it tumbles down a hill. Applied to house paints, the hydrophobic surface allows a wall to be easily washed clean with just a spray of water.

1 Electronics contain many metals, some of them precious, which often find their way into landfill sites. Significant efforts are being made to reclaim these materials for reuse, and developments have been made to find replacements for the silicon boards on which the circuits are constructed.
2 This shelving system from SEED adapts to the needs of its users. The one simple shape can be combined to create openings large and small, and it can grow or shrink to accommodate new locations or needs.

3

4

One manufacturer also copied nature to create a more environmentally friendly food and liquid packaging product. The humble egg, its engineers realized, stores food beautifully and photodegrades like a charm: just the qualities they desired. Duplicating the chemical makeup of eggshell by combining calcium carbonate (chalk) and polyolefin entails forty to sixty per cent less polymer usage than making conventional food packaging films. Moreover, when left in sunlight, the eggshell films slowly decompose into silica (sand). This human-made packaging material improves on the original by being recyclable, printable and available in a variety of colours.

Beyond specific products, there is a common, broad category of materials whose structure is inspired by nature. To develop composites, which include fibre glass or carbon fibre, scientists studied the physical makeup of wood and then worked to optimize certain properties, such as increasing tensile strength or decreasing weight. Wood fits the definition of a composite material because it is made from two basic and distinct parts: a fibrous structure and a binder that holds the fibres together. In the case of wood, the fibrous structure is cellulose and the binder is lignin. In composite materials, materials as various as vegetal matter, glass, polymer or carbon (depending on the properties desired) can provide the fibrous structure. The binder can be any material that will hold the fibrous structure together. Again, the binder material is chosen based on its inherent properties.

Composites are used whenever there are specific performance requirements that monolithic materials cannot satisfy. One company creates structural composite forms for fence posts, ship masts, fishing rods, tent poles and tool handles. The structural forms are made by pultrusion: a process in which glass fibres are pulled through a liquid resin matrix to make a structural form that has excellent tensile strength and toughness. The resulting material surpasses wood in strength by improving on its composite structure.

Beyond benefiting the environment and solving tricky design problems, biomimicry can inspire sale-boosting aesthetic decisions. Notably, designers at Interface, a US

3 Scientists used inspiration from mussels to create an improved adhesive for plywood. Using a protein-based adhesive, the shellfish is able to attach itself to surfaces at the waterline where it endures tremendous impact from the pounding waves. The researchers recreated this adhesive to create a non-formaldehyde glue that leads to a far more responsible material.
4 Lotus plants (and others) keep themselves clean through what is known as the 'lotus effect'. Tiny hairs that protrude from the surface of the leaves keep dirt from adhering to the leaves. When any rain falls on to the plants, the suspended particles are washed away easily. This surface has been recreated in paint products for exterior use.

1

2

1 Comprised of melamine resin, decorative and core paper, and aluminum, these multi-layer, structural solid surfacing sheets have high structural strength, allowing thin sheets to withstand high loads. The sheets may be cut, drilled and milled and the edges of the sheets may be detailed by lipping, curving and milling.
2 The physical makeup of wood provided scientists with important information as they worked to create composite materials. Wood is made up of two basic component parts, cellulose fibres and lignin as a binder, much like modern composites which include fibrous materials (glass, carbon and polymer) chosen for their properties and joined with synthetic binders.

carpet tile manufacturer, analyzed naturally occurring ground covers and applied what they learned directly to their product. They noticed that a forest floor is not laid out in a grid: it presents instead a visual amalgam of unpredictable yet complimentary patterns. Translating the controlled imperfection of the natural world into carpet resulted in Entropy, a modular tile system composed of non-identical tiles arranged randomly. Despite being composed of disparate parts, taken as a whole, the carpeted room appears as one piece. At the same time, the irregularity makes repairs easier and less wasteful, as no exact matching is necessary.

For the past 3.8 billion years, nature has experienced rigorous development under countless extreme circumstances. As a consequence, the world today offers the designer a treasure trove of unpatented ideas that provide fresh insight into ways of approaching structural, environmental and aesthetic problems.

NANOTECHNOLOGY

Over the last fifteen years, nanotechnology has become one of the most hyped and least commercially realized of all the 'breakthrough' technologies. But we are still a long way from realizing the original premise of nanotechnology, posited by physicist Richard Feynman in 1959. In a lecture presented to the American Physical Society entitled 'There's plenty of room at the bottom', Feynman suggested that if we could control the movement of small parts of materials (to the order of ten to a hundred atoms), we should be able to completely change the properties and performance of things. This ability to manipulate materials on a molecular level in order to control properties is still only possible in nature (think of the way your skin protects and heals once cut). Even over the last decade we have witnessed incredible advances in certain industries using nanotechnology. Where we have seen real improvements as a result of nano research in materials, however, is in stain resistance in textiles, strengthening of plastics and in protective coatings. There have been other developments, particularly in the field of biotechnology, but these are beyond our scope or remit to adequately cover here.

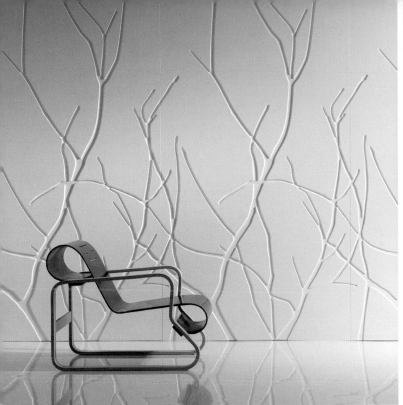

3

4

Stain resistance achieved through the molecular alteration of fibres has been discussed earlier as part of the section on fibres. But the strengthening of plastics as well as the advancements in protective coatings is based upon the dispersion of nano-sized particulates that enable proportionately greater property enhancements compared to standard size additives. An addition of only two to three per cent by volume of nano particles is needed compared to ten to fifteen per cent for regular sized additives. Though the particles themselves are not particularly revolutionary (a clay called montmorillonite is used for stiffening plastics and alumina platelets are typically used for protective coatings), it is the ability to disperse these tiny flakes within the host that is hard to do.

A major nanotechnology issue is centred on what actually happens when such small sizes are used; the physical attraction between individual particles (known as van der Waal forces) is enough to overcome gravity. Thus, trying to separate clay platelets is like trying to separate iron filings. But once separated, they become a lot easier to work with. One other notable property of these particles is that when they get to be only five nanometers thick, they are transparent to visible light. This is essential in applications such as protective coatings for clear glass and plastic surfaces, including protective screens on portable electronic equipment, ski goggles and spectacle lenses.

We have also seen advances in electrical and thermal conductivity, as well as impact energy, using carbon nanotubes (CNT). These comprise hollow cylinders of pure carbon about 50,000 times narrower than the finest human hair, but stronger than steel. The structure takes the form of a single-walled, long, slim cylinder closed at both ends. The diameter of a carbon nanotube is about 10,000 times smaller than its length. They offer considerable improvement in rigidity compared to ordinary carbon fibres, and are already used for their immense strength when added to materials such as polymers. In addition, they can both conduct or insulate depending upon their structure, leading to potential applications in nanoelectronics.

3 Shown here behind Alvar Alto's Paimio chair, these decorative panels are created from MDF with (or without) a laminate surface, and are available in various different relief patterns inspired by people, places and design movements (including 'Hitchcock', 'Versailles' and 'Helvetica'). The company offers a range of coloured laminate, or a paintable laminate, and the panels can be used for interiors only.
4 Seemingly simple materials can provide remarkable solutions. Certain clays, for instance, are utilized in nanocomposite materials and contribute significant strength, electromagnetic-interference (EMI) shielding, and even the ability to control the release of medicines from these compounds.

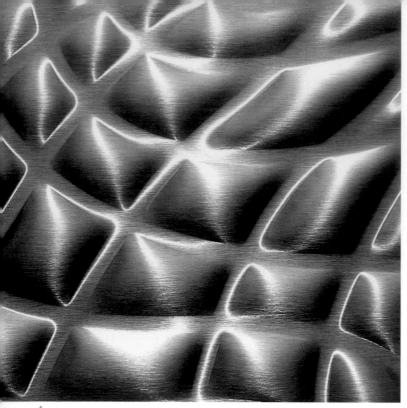

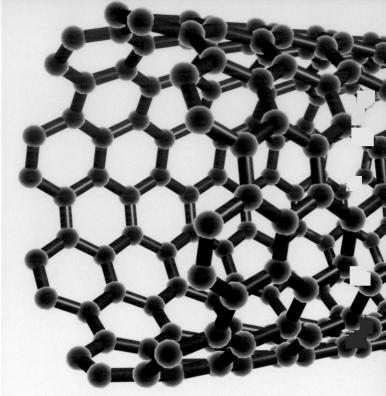

1 This metal sheet was formed by a process that uses high pressure fluid. Aluminum or steel sheet may be drawn to create patterns, either as a 'positive' or 'negative' surface. The pattern is created by the nature of the object over which the metal is drawn (ball bearings, rods or geometric objects), but the edges of the sheet around the pattern remain flat and undeformed.

2 This is a diagram of a carbon nanotube. Created from a one-atom-thick sheet of graphite, this cylinder constitutes a nanostructure where the length-to-diameter ratio exceeds 10,000. These structures exhibit extraordinary strength and unique electrical properties, and are efficient conductors of heat, making them potentially useful in a wide variety of applications including electronics, optics and other fields of materials science.

3 Here is another example of stereo-lithography, this time with a light-hearted rather than a lighting approach. In his 'Alcatraz', Guillaume Delvigne created this form with no discernable entry or exit.

OPPOSITE These office chairs feature bent aluminum shell components that form the basis of a novel modular system. Designed by Hadi Teherani, Hans-Ullrich Bitsch and Ulrich Nether, the 'Silver Chair' is strong, lightweight and durable.

Multi-walled carbon nanotubes were first discovered in 1991 by Japanese scientist Dr Sumio Iijima and are the basis for the single-walled nanotubes that are causing such interest today. Recent developments have also led to additional shapes such as 'nano-horns' (single-walled carbon cones that have remarkable adsorptive and catalytic properties), and 'nano-test-tubes', which can be opened and filled with a variety of molecules, including biological material.

So we see that our efforts in this new discipline are heralding results, but mostly in the area of improving properties simply by making existing additives smaller. The carbon nanotubes show real promise: they offer advances into entirely new microstructures. It should be noted here, however, that we also need effective regulation of these new entities. No one is yet sure what the long-term effects are likely to be, especially if dispersed into the atmosphere. Small amounts could pollute huge areas, simply because of their tiny size. Along with innovation should come effective regulation.

CNTs, as well as the preceding innovations discussed above, still do not offer the advantages that would be possible if Feynman's predictions were realized. For that we are still some fifteen to twenty years off; it has taken nature billions of years to develop to this degree of molecular control, we should allow ourselves at least another decade or so.

FABRICATION INNOVATION

No matter how good a material is, if it can't be formed into the right shape, or stuck to another material, or if even a small amount of it is too heavy to lift, it will not be a successful product. The material is only half the story. A major part of product innovation is how it is produced, how the polymer or ceramic or metal is formed, cast or heat-treated. This processing will have as much effect on the final properties of aluminum or alumina as its chemical composition.

The explosion in the use of plastics over the last ten years has less to do with new compositions (there have been few completely new plastics introduced to the market)

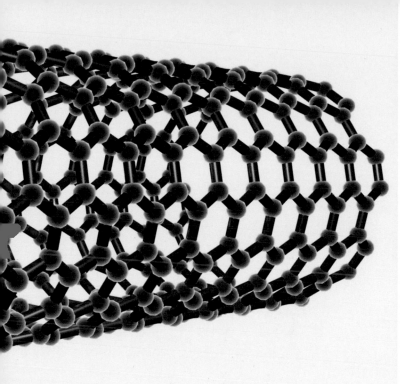

3

than improvements in moulding and shaping, additives and surface effects. In some ways, this could be classed as a minor materials revolution, allowing us much greater design freedom simply because we can now form and roto-mould certain polymers that could not previously be worked with in this way. Polymers are not the only examples of this unnoticed revolution; concrete, light metals and plastics have experienced wider application simply because of new processing techniques.

Ductal®, a recently developed form of cement that is used in construction, is a good example of this. Exacting control of the composition, particle size as well as the porosity and curing rate has enabled innovators to develop toughness previously unheard of. Such close control often precludes the need for reinforcing bars or glass fibre meshes to maintain strength. As a result, civil engineering structures, buildings and sculptures can take on thinner, lighter and more convoluted forms than ever before, and Ductal® has already been used for a host of high-profile civil engineering structures all over the world. Similarly, magnesium casting using a new process called TMag, creates exceptionally high-quality non-porous castings allowing them to be used in applications such as engine blocks. It is the processing control that enables this new application for what is in fact a fairly old material.

One cannot conclude a discussion of innovative processing without mention of rapid prototyping. Originally developed as a tool for producing moulds for casting engineering parts, this process offers unlimited creativity of form, from intricate textiles to objects within objects, all built from powder. The basic process for all of the different types of rapid prototyping is as follows: create a three-dimensional CAD (computer aided design) model of the design you wish to produce; convert this CAD model into thinly sliced two-dimensional cross sections (the thinner the slices, the more accurate the final rendition); then physically build up each layer one on top of another in order to construct the model. The layers can be built up in one of two ways: each layer can be laid down like dots of ink from an inkjet printer, or else a laser can be selectively shot into a 1 mm-deep (¹⁄₁₆ in) stratum of a powdered substance (starch,

1

2

1 This is a further example of a metal sheet formed by a process that uses high pressure fluid. Aluminum or steel sheet may be drawn to create patterns, either as a 'positive' or 'negative' surface. The pattern is created by the nature of the object over which the metal is drawn (ball bearings, rods or geometric objects), but the edges of the sheet around the pattern remain flat and undeformed.

2 This lightweight clear plastic film incorporates LED lights for inclusion in glass or polymer sheeting. White LEDs are embedded into PVB and connected using invisible conductors, enabling the lights to be laminated into glass with the illusion of wireless connectivity. The LEDs do not emit heat and may be embedded in a regular array or any custom pattern required by the client.

OPPOSITE This form has been created using glass-filled fine polyamide powder for synthetic laser sinter systems for the direct production of objects like replacement parts, functional prototypes and models for investment and vacuum casting. Objects made with this material have good mechanical properties, smooth surfaces and tight tolerances, a great improvement over previous materials. It is highly abrasion and chemical resistant as well as biocompatible.

plastic, metal or ceramic), fusing the powder where it hits. Subsequent layers are built up on top of the existing ones in response to each cross-sectional data slice until the whole three-dimensional object is formed.

Currently, objects may be made from materials such as polymers, nylon, some metals and ceramics, with a maximum volume of 6500 cubic cm (approximately that of a cathode ray tube computer monitor). Extrapolation of this idea suggests that in the not-too-distant future, anything and everything may be able to be produced on demand – simply download the CAD file for that day's clothing and the rapid prototyping machine will build it while you drink your morning coffee. Of course, in order to create more complex working parts (something as simple as a retractable pen requires a plastic housing and retracting mechanism, a metal ballpoint and liquid ink), two or more different materials are required in the same manufacturing process; something which has not yet been fully realized. It is likely, however, to be only a matter of time.

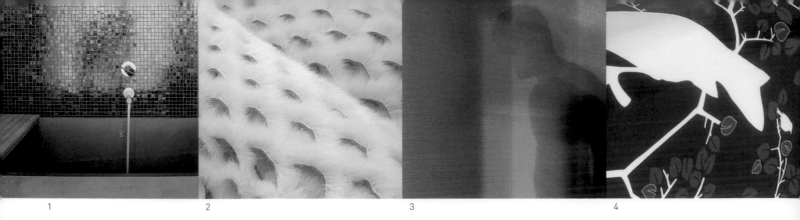

MATERIAL INTELLIGENCE

BRADLEY QUINN

PREVIOUS PAGE The extruded aluminum modular sections of Mathias Bengtsson's award-winning Modular Aluminium Bench were originally coated in chrome. This new version, produced in 2006, is coated to create a white finish. The coating is formed by giving the powder a negative charge and spraying it onto the positive-charged surface. The entire chair is then heated, causing the powder to sinter into a strong, protective surface.
1–8 Architecture and design utilize virtually all known materials. As high-tech metals meet today's technology, new hybrid materials emerge that work as well in cutting-edge fashion as they do in body-conscious buildings. Light has been redefined as an aesthetic technique to give materials expressive subtleties, yet also creates lasers and new cutting processes.
OPPOSITE Just like yarns and filaments, separate strands of carbon fibres can be woven, bundled or braided into ropes and cords. This detail from Mathias Bengtsson's Spun chair reveals that when woven in a continuous pattern, carbon fibres can also create a seamless mesh.

The worlds of materials and design are merging. At the dawn of the 21st century, materials advanced to become more adaptable, tactile and empathic, and the demand for objects with sculptural, aesthetic and multi-functional qualities rocketed. As high-performance materials were reconceived as immersive webs, structural networks and technological interfaces, their ability to engage with the built environment resulted in a whole new paradigm of design. Today, the carbon-fibre matrices, woven wooden panels and metallic meshes of contemporary architecture have more in common with the high-tech filaments of techno fashion than they do with modernist monoliths. Membrane skins and pneumatic structures are as common in furniture design as they are in interior design and textiles, while tactile fibres and triaxial weaves are aligning vehicle design with public artworks. From the traditional to the intangible, from the technical to the tectonic, the exchanges taking place between materials and design are forging a uniquely multi-disciplinary arena.

Many advanced materials have fluid properties that engineers can synchronize in order to suit a product or environment. Interactive materials, such as photochromatic pigments that change colour when subjected to daylight, light-emitting electroluminescent films, shape-changing polymeric gels and shape-memory alloys eliminate the need for technological triggers. The discovery of polymers, the invention of nanotechnology and recent developments in biomimicry have created the most technologically advanced materials imaginable. Yet, few new materials have proved their worth, because relatively few practitioners have been able to put them to the test.

By investigating the works of key practitioners in architecture, interior design, fashion, textiles, furniture design, vehicle design and the arts, this chapter reveals many of the breakthroughs, obstacles, victories and challenges these practitioners experience. As today's generation of materials change how the human body is experienced and how the urban environment is built, they reveal their capacity to transform our world today more dramatically than any other time in history.

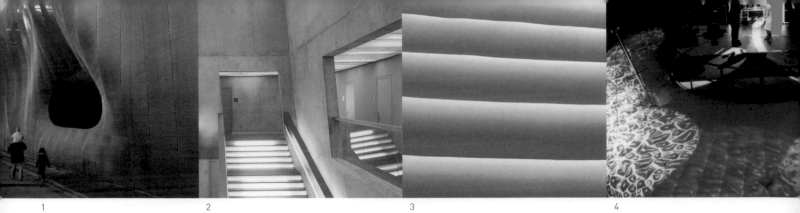

ARCHITECTURE

1 Dutch architect Lars Spuybroek's 'Maison Folie' project, a cultural centre in Lille, France, exemplifies Spuybroek's technique of merging structure and texture, using 'soft' materials that rigidify during construction to become hard surfaces.
2 Light and transparency contrast with the dense concrete in Jürgen Mayer's Stuttgart Stadthaus municipal building, Germany.
3 Inflatable membranes have emerged as a popular architectural material. Lightweight, flexible and easily portable, they imbue structures with unprecedented elasticity.
4 Veech Media Architecture's 'Radionight' installation showcases both the brilliance and the durability of inflatable materials.
5 + OPPOSITE The inflatable Sprach pavilion by Veech Media Architecture outlines a new niche for tensile architectonic materials. Quick to install, easy to disassemble and pack flat, the pavilion is a prime example of pneumatic architecture. A close-up reveals the tailoring techniques used to stitch and to bond heavy-duty seams that can expand as well as withstand pressure.
6 The translucent glass and silicon fabric used in the pavilion also diffuses light.
7 Chimney-like vents in the pavilion's structure promote air circulation and minimize the risk of wind damage.
8 From above, the pavilion's steel lintel frame is visible under the illuminated fabric.

Visionaries know that the cutting edge in architecture is not sharp, but sensuous and soft instead. These days, carbon-fibre matrices, woven wood panels, coated textiles, metallic skins and triaxial meshes are popular alternatives to simple bricks and mortar. As a result, tensile buildings, membrane exteriors and pneumatic structures forge a new direction for outdoor pavilions and mobile environments. Likewise, the pliability of textiles has revolutionized earthquake construction where they act as shock absorbers, and landscape architects have literally taken fabric underground to sculpt and reshape the natural terrain. As soft materials change how architecture is built, their ability to interface with the built environment has resulted in a new paradigm of lightweight, elastic architecture.

Dutch architect Lars Spuybroek advocates a merger of structure and texture in his work, starting with 'soft' materials that rigidify during the construction stages to become hard surfaces later on. This process is exemplified in his 'Maison Folie' project, a cultural centre located in the heart of the French city of Lille. The whole façade was conceived as an undulating expression of labile form and constructed from Escale, a stainless mesh produced by GKD Metal Fabrics in Germany. This pliable mesh becomes rigid as it locks to the steel structures that support it. So although the building looks wavy and curvaceous, its façade is actually rock hard.

Pneumatic structures are one of the most elastic expressions of architecture today. Practices such as Veech Media Architecture, Inflate and Architects of Air are able to create outdoor pavilions and tensile buildings as well as membrane exteriors by using a variety of woven and non-woven fabrics. These structures quickly gain mass as the air-filled membranes stitched into the fabric inflate and then expand. Moreover, these inflatables can be recreated in different locations instantly; they take only minutes to erect and later shrink to one-tenth of their expanded size when deflated. As they are supported by steel lintels, they can be used as portable outdoor architecture as well as indoor pavilions, in order to provide a uniform backdrop for exhibitions or events.

5   6   7   8

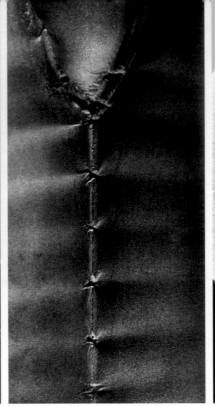

1

2

3

1 Canadian architect Mark West moulds concrete using pliable membranes rather than traditional wooden casing. Imitating cushions, the membrane's elasticity makes the creation of 'soft' shapes possible.

2+3 West's use of textile technology enables him to mould concrete into fashionable shapes. These columns echo the musculature of the male torso and the contours of the female form, creating a uniquely 'gendered' architecture.

BELOW Testa & Weiser's vision for carbon construction is created using complex computer modelling tools. New buildings like this one require materials and techniques that just might transform the building industry.

Just as a corset moulds the body's contours into an hourglass shape, reinforced textile sheaths fabricated with eyelets and laces sculpt wet concrete into curvaceous silhouettes. The Fabric Formwork project, an initiative developed by Mark West at the Centre for Architectural Structure and Technology at the University of Manitoba in Canada, claim that tube-like textile structures are far more effective than conventional moulds. West uses the 5½-metre-wide (18-ft) woven polypropylene textile known by the trade name 'Propex #2006'. After the concrete is poured, the laces are drawn in and tightened, creating a mould that compresses the concrete exactly as a corset would cinch a waistline.

When flexible fibres and supple strands are braided and bundled, the structures that result can create tension and compression more efficiently than masonry. Braiding and weaving are systems in which all fibres are continuously mechanically interlocked at regular intervals; applied architecturally, they create a mechanism that distributes the load evenly throughout the structure. This makes buildings much lighter and yet more resistant to impact, introducing an unprecedented degree of elasticity that can act as a shock absorber during an earthquake. Forward-thinking architect Peter Testa has a vision for constructing vertiginous skyscrapers through weaving and braiding techniques, by using carbon fibres and composite materials. Together with his partner, Devyn Weiser, Los Angeles-based Testa & Weiser have designed a carbon-fibre high-rise, a complex building largely designed through computer modelling tools. Testa & Weiser are developing the project with industrial partners from the manufacturing industry. Companies that fabricate composite materials stand to profit from investing in the project, in order to make large-scale carbon-fibre construction possible. According to Testa, 'the construction industry isn't completely fixed. If one finds applications for materials that are provocative and at a big enough scale, it is possible to engender new divisions of industry.'

Testa has designed a forty-storey office building that is woven together from bundled fibres rather than assembled from conventional construction materials.

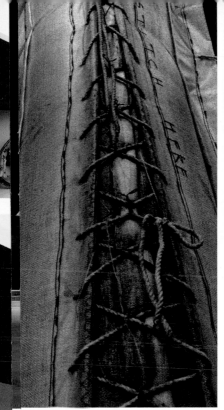
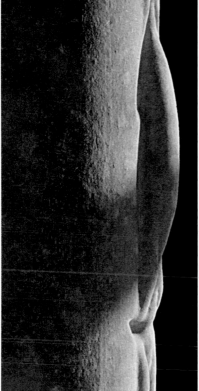

4   5   6

The structure's shell comprises forty helical bands that coil in two directions to create a cylindrical volume. The structure doesn't rely on a network of columns or an internal framework for support; it uses bands of carbon fibres drawn from the base of the building to the top to support the entire vertical compressive load. The helix encircles woven composite floor plates anchored to the external structure on each storey. Just as they are supported by the helix, the tension the floor plates create prevents the helix from collapsing.

The retractable external walls of Shigeru Ban's 'Curtain Wall House' create a novel dynamic in architecture. Constructed from fabric, the supple surfaces and pleated folds of the textile walls evoke the fluid construction of a garment more than they do an architectural structure. Just as some garments are worn open or closed to reveal or conceal parts of the body, the retractable walls open to expose the structure or close to hide them from public view. As wind and weather conditions also cause the textiles to move, the house becomes a kinetic structure that challenges the notion that architecture should be a fixed entity.

Sheila Kennedy, one of the principal founders of Kennedy & Violich Architecture (KVA) in Boston, also established MATx, a materials research unit that engages with the fields of electronics, architecture and material design. By drawing upon MATx's research and digital facilities, KVA work collaboratively with business leaders, manufacturers, cultural institutions and public agencies to advance the integration of energy efficient digital technologies and architecture. Kennedy believes that architects should play a prominent role in the development of design strategies that respond to complex global problems such as energy and water. She believes that contemporary architecture needs to move beyond the modernism inheritance of what she describes as 'bundled services within chase walls and hung ceilings'. 'Design today provides the opportunity to imagine new models for living and working,' Kennedy explains, 'whereas a diaspora of distributed materials can work together to provide light and electrical power.'

4 From fashion, Mark West borrowed traditional corsetry and reclaimed it as an architectural technique. As the laces are drawn in, the wet concrete is squeezed into a contoured shape, which resembles an hourglass silhouette when it drys.
5 The moulded membranes create contours and curves that would be almost impossible to achieve with a wooden form.
6 West is introducing new types of concrete surfaces that can't be created with conventional moulds.

ABOVE The Wellcome Trust commissioned Thomas Heatherwick to design a sculpture for an eight-storey-high interior space and suspend it above a pool of water. Heatherwick decided to emulate the extruded shapes of molten metal being poured into a reflective pool. The resulting sculpture consists of 142,000 glass spheres suspended by 27,000 high-tensile steel wires, comprising fifteen tonnes of glass and just under one million metres of wire. The glass spheres were made in collaboration with Flux Glass, who fused each glass sphere with a layer of dichroic film to create a colourful prism effect.

The high-strength and malleability of the steel enables the interior to express a body-consciousness that mirrors the message of the Marni brand. As the streamlined arcs strike a balance between form and functionality, they yield to the items they display like a hand sliding into a glove.

Marni's new boutiques are designed in the same style today but now under the direction of the London-based practice Sybarite, who find new ways of working with the materials originally chosen for the project. 'Because the metal display rails are long and slender, supports were initially placed every 1.2 metres (4 ft),' Sybarite explained. 'Today, after several years of working with the steel, we can span distances of over 12 metres (39½ ft) and allow the metal to bend and flex with its own weight.'

When French fashion house Longchamp commissioned British architect Thomas Heatherwick to design an expandable shopping bag, few people would have guessed that the spiralling bands of its leather and canvas construction would later echo in the brand's flagship interior. Heatherwick's design for Longchamp's biggest boutique – a project the brand's owners christened 'La Maison Unique' – was a one-off flagship shop that signalled a new direction for Longchamp's retail profile. The site, located in New York's SoHo neighbourhood, comprises a two-storey retail space situated on the first and second floors of a commercial building.

'This project broke all the rules of retail,' Heatherwick explained. 'Our problem was how to draw people upstairs into the main shopping space.' Heatherwick's solution was to carve a shaft right through the building's core, creating a 20 metre-deep (65½ ft) atrium which is crowned by a gleaming skylight. Heatherwick then wound a sinuous staircase through the space, made it so eye-catching that shoppers feel almost compelled to climb its ribbon-like treads to the retail showrooms situated on the floors above.

The design is created with thirty strips of material that alternately divide and converge to form a topography of walkways, landings and steps. The strips are actually cut from heat-rolled steel and then coated in a special rubberized flooring material that gives them a lightweight, textile-like appearance. However, the combined load of the entire staircase weighs in at 55 tonnes. The sheer density of the staircase was cleverly foiled by using transparent balustrades, which Heatherwick specially designed using aerospace technology so that they drape with the apparent fluidity of fabric. By projecting the natural light drawn through the skylight towards the entrance, passers-by are also drawn into the building's luminous core and enticed to climb up the vertical strips that lead to the top.

ABOVE Heatherwick used aerospace technology to design the balustrades at the Longchamp flagship boutique, which he fabricated as a series of contouring panels that drape with the fluidity of fabric. Their wavy configurations echo the ribbon-like contours of the staircase and display units.

1

THE APARTMENT

The Apartment is a New York-based creative agency that merges interior design, architecture and graphic design with space planning, branding and art direction.

Established by Stefan Boublil and Gina Alvarez in 1999, The Apartment was initially an experimental retail venture aimed at promoting forward-thinking designers and brands. Over time, however, the agency became known for its quirky style, unique design and witty delivery, expanding its reach through its events, editorial, online shopping platforms and branding initiatives.

1 The Apartment was commissioned to design, brand and market a new sandwich shop chain in Manhattan. The brief was to bring an old-fashioned neighbourhood café quality to a wide consumer audience, and at the same time create a trademark minimal interior. The project balances the practical need for signage and display with sleek, untainted surfaces. The bar surface divides the work area from the public space, yet facilitates easy communication between the two. This picture is actually a work-in-progress image, made while the project was still under construction.
2-6 The Condesa Hotel in Mexico, where Mahdavi recreated her signature style using materials sourced from the Mexican landscape.

How do you choose materials for your projects?

We make a meticulous search for the right, complementary elements for each project. From dark walnut to stainless steel, from subway tiles to mirrors, we look at many different ways of achieving the right effect

What materials inspire you?

Brick: the New Yorker's material of choice.
Concrete: when used in broad strokes, not just as an accent.
Cork: the feeling of nature with none of the inconvenience.
Walnut: rich and long lasting.
Birch: the best wood for modern furniture.
White carrara marble: with as little veining as possible and put on all six sides of a room: absolute luxury.
Travertine: when used on the 'wrong' side, the holes in the surface make you feel like the stone is breathing.
Felt: especially remnants, what most people don't use.
Grass: the unity in a patch of green lawn is amazing.
Dirt: chaotic nature waiting to be domesticated.

You listed traditional materials. Are there any new materials that you use?

We prefer to recontextualize basic materials. We treat the material as installation art, which transcends any banality that could be associated with it. It would be easy to use the latest material from Dupont, but there's a need for poetry in design today, not just material innovation.

2   3 5   4 6

INDIA MAHDAVI

India Mahdavi is an interior architect and furniture designer based in Paris. Her studio, IMH, was established in 1999 and quickly became known internationally. Mahdavi has a vast repertoire of styles and materials, including exotic interiors in Mexico and Egypt, slick interiors in Paris and New York, and gentrified country interiors in England. Among her most important projects are the Condesa Hotel in Mexico City, the Rivington Hotel and APT lounge bar in New York, Miami's Townhouse hotel, the Dragon-i restaurant in Hong Kong, Givenchy's boutiques in Paris, Trussardi in Milan and private residences in Sydney, London, New York, Paris and Siwa.

When Mahdavi was commissioned to design the interior of the Condesa Hotel she scoured the Mexican landscape for fragrant woods, smooth stones and hand-forged hardware to transform a crumbling colonial-style landmark into a lush oasis of contemporary chic. Elements of the natural world loom large throughout the Condesa; the grainy textures of the shimmering white walls mimic the crystalline sands of Mexico's Caribbean coastline, and the Condesa's signature turquoise accents are true to the desert gemstone after which the colour was named. Nature comes indoors in the patio restaurant's tropical garden, where a vast swathe of sunlight is channelled into the Condesa's inner core. Come nightfall, the hotel is a candlelit dreamscape where stargazers can marvel at the night sky from the rooftop cocktail lounge, or slip into the secluded mosaic pool and splash under the waterfall.

For her furniture designs, Mahdavi sourced Mexican hardwoods which she crafted into tiered side tables, colossal dining tables, ottomans, robust wing chairs and sleek rockers. Some were upholstered in leather panels, cowhide and suede, but most were covered in natural fibres dyed in vibrant pigments. Mexican linens and richly textured woollen textiles covered the beds, while lampshades and upholstery fabrics featured Mahdavi's signature turquoise motif.

Where does craftsmanship meet natural materials in your work?

The Condesa Hotel is a good example. I wanted to oppose cold and warm materials, so I paired ceramics with cowhide, wood with resin, cement tiles with wool carpets, white cotton sheets with roughly-textured wool blankets. This association of materials gave the project texture and richness, an elegant mix for a very urban environment with a tropical feel. I wanted to introduce a European feel yet make foreigners feel very much in Mexico.

What limits your choice of materials?

Mostly production constraints. I design and produce my own furniture by working with local craftsmen. Because my pieces are not mass-produced, it limits the materials I can use.

What materials do you work with the most?

Mostly classic materials. I like opposing materials and shapes. If I create a defined structured sofa, I will soften it with a feminine fabric such as velvet. There is nothing more beautiful than wood. It has life, authenticity, it ages beautifully, and is full of sensuality. There are feminine woods and masculine woods. I like using their sexuality.

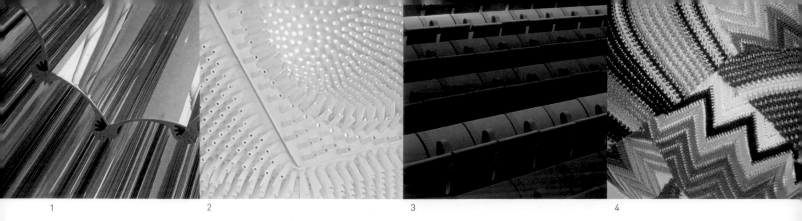

1   2   3   4

PRODUCT DESIGN

1 Mathias Bengtsson's modular M.A.C. bench pioneers a new direction for the design of extruded metal components.
2 The photoelectric cells in Mathieu Lehanneur's 'K' light source trigger high-luminosity LEDs and sheathed optical fibres in order to project ambient light.
3 The Flow seating system by Monica Förster for Poltrona Frau is fabricated from memory materials that retract to their original shape after those seated have risen.
4 Stephen Burks' glassware for Missoni incorporates fabric into glass without scorching the material during the intense heat involved in glass production.
5 Lehanneur's 'C' apparatus senses drops in temperature and emits heat. The design encloses heat sensors, infra-red heat emitters, a thermic camera and memory-shape alloys inside an inverted cone.
6 Lehanneur's sketch for his 'O' apparatus.
7 Also by Lehanneur, the 'dB' device propels itself in the direction of high-decibel noises and counters them by emitting white noise.
8 Lehanneur's sketch for the 'K' light source, which uses optical fibres, photoelectric cells, high-luminosity LEDS and sensors to receive light, recharge and project it back.
OPPOSITE Lehanneur's interest in eco-design inspired his 'O' device: a vessel filled with spirulina platensis suspended in purified water. Incorporating an oxymetric probe and LEDs, 'O' facilitates a photosynthetic process, enabling it to produce oxygen when it detects a rise in pollution levels.

Whether regarded as indulgent, edgy, challenging or just downright funny, the material-centric products created by today's designers are not design as we once knew it. These days, a new generation is fighting against the backlash of bent shapes, rectilinear forms and mundane materials in order to explore strident sources of innovation. As they investigate the shifting relationship between object and user, designers challenge the premise that a fixed structure should constitute the basis of formation. As a result, interactive designs, retractable surfaces, technological interfaces and labile textile components are transforming everyday functional objects into dynamic tools for contemporary life.

The Paris-based industrial designer Mathieu Lehanneur invents cerebral designs that appear to think for themselves. By mimicking the functions of biological reflexes, Lehanneur has created empathetic interactive objects that react and adapt to changes in temperature, light intensity, ambient noise and levels of oxygen. Heat sensors, infra-red heat emitters and memory-shape alloys enclosed inside an inverted cone of tiered elastomer bands enables his 'C' (Celsius) device to sense drops in temperature and emit heat. The device automatically moves towards areas where it detects chills, and remains until the temperature rises. The 'K' (Kelvin) device is a dodecahedron covered with optical fibres that monitor light levels and respond by emitting an illuminating charge when light levels drop. K is equipped with capillary tubes that react to reconstituted sunlight, providing an extra light source for those suffering from light deprivation. 'O' (Oxygen) is a transparent vessel filled with spirulina platensis that triggers a photosynthetic process in order to produce oxygen when it detects a rise in pollution levels. Last in the series is the 'dB' (Decibel) device, a ball that propels itself in the direction of high-decibel noises and counters them by emitting white noise.

The Swedish design group Front have also combined technological interfaces with design. They sketch furniture designs freehand in thin air and use the Motion Capture technology developed for movie animations and computer games, they capture the pen strokes and record them on three-dimensional digital files. Once transferred into

5

6

7

8

REMPLIR UNIQUEMENT AVEC DE L'EAU DE SOURCE

1   2

1 Research into memory alloy textiles enabled Monica Förster to simplify the design of her Flow seating system. Elastic properties in the fabric enable the seats to stretch downwards rather than cantilever outwards. When the seat is released, the fabric retracts back to its original shape.
2 By recycling selvedge fibres and suspending them in a glass body, designer Stephen Burks created a unique pattern on a range of glassware for Missoni.
3+4 Naoto Fukasawa's Cosmos 1 & 2 lamp incorporates two lights in one. Fukasawa used a line of Swarovski crystals to map an imaginary after-image, tracing them along a line of electroluminescent film to recreate this otherworldly glow.
BELOW The feather-light, semi-transparent structure of Mathias Bengtsson's spun carbon fibre chaise longue belies the extraordinary strength of the carbon material.

in a resin coating. The patchwork vases that resulted were striking and unique, not least because they introduced a recycling method that could showcase the beauty of the Missoni fabrics in a new form. The series of vases was also the inspiration behind the bottle and packaging of the Missoni Profumi collection; the first Missoni fragrance launched in seventeen years.

Although fabric skins and high-tech furniture may seem irreconcilably diverse, there are threads that bind. Mathias Bengtsson's feather-light, semi-transparent spun carbon-fibre furniture belie the extraordinary strength of carbon fibre. Bengtsson spins a single carbon thread into a slender, mesh-like layer that weaves a cylindrical shape. The flexibility of the mesh moulds to the body as it cradles the sitter in the same comfort that would be afforded by a sprung base. In his quest for new forms, Bengtsson appears to have invented a direction so promising that it could portend the furniture of the future.

Finding inspiration in memory materials and the elasticity of textile structures encouraged Monica Förster to design the wave-like 'Flow' auditorium chair for Poltrona Frau. Förster created a curvaceous metal shell and coated it with varying densities of injection-moulded polyurethane foam before upholstering it. Förster fitted the chairs with specially-developed hinges made from steel and reinforced rubber that would strengthen and support the armrests when folded out, yet collapse completely and tuck behind the seat when folded in, making the chair exceptionally compact. Förster anticipates a time when the chairs will unfold automatically and even repair themselves if the materials start to fail. 'There is a lot of potential for new technology to completely transform materials and design. However, the industry doesn't seem to be ready for the investments that are necessary to create these kinds of materials.'

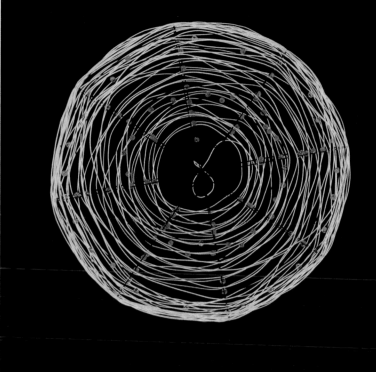

3

4

NAOTO FUKASAWA

The stylized objects Naoto Fukasawa designs are beautiful tools for modern life, crafted in forward-thinking designs that bridge the gulf between everyday functionality and ideals of luxury and beauty.

Fukasawa is known for his minimalist approach and his poetic sensibilities. Whether designing complex electronic objects or efficient household accessories, each product is characterized by a unique balance of art and design.

Fukasawa was born in Japan in 1956. He attended Tama Art University's product design department and studied both art and 3-D design before graduating in 1980. He left Japan for San Francisco in 1989 where he worked for a small office studio formerly known as 'ID2' – predecessor to the acclaimed IDEO design studio which currently employs some 450 staff members around the world.

When Fukasawa returned to Japan in 1996 he helped establish a branch of IDEO in Tokyo to work within the Japanese market. In 2003 he established Naoto Fukasawa Design and subsequently joined the advisory board of Japanese retail brand MUJI.

Since then, Fukasawa has set up a new product brand named ±0 in collaboration with the Japanese toy manufacturer Takara, to create a range of home appliances branded Plusminuszero. The brand ranges from umbrellas to electronics, including a humidifier, an LCD screen, a mini-disc player, a torch, an electric coffeemaker, telephones and even a toaster.

Is your poetic approach to design reflected in your choice of materials?

I think that many materials can give you inspirations that can be translated as a poetic aesthetic or phenomena like magic. However, whether this poetic factor can be realized and understood by others comes down to a basic question: does what we create actually have meaning or not? If there is no real sense of meaning in the finished project, what we produce will never result in a product that has poetic content.

Can a material be interactive enough to enable a product to reflect the owner's identity?

The handle of a hand tool such as a hammer does this, because wood changes through use to reflect the way that it is used. If an adaptive, modern material that evolves over time could be created, it would reflect the owner's habits and become personalized by its use.

Which materials would you use to create the mobile phones of the future?

I would like to have a material for the outer shell that produces all the functional elements. Then only one single material would house the circuits, provide a screen function, respond to interactive touch and act as a sensor.

Your Cosmos 1 & 2 lighting is widely acclaimed. How were they created?

Their shapes are inspired by the afterimage that appears when you hold a light in your hand and draw circles in the air. The form has a metal wire frame structure inside it, to which 125 metres (410 ft) of EL wire is randomly applied by rolling it around like a ball of yarn.

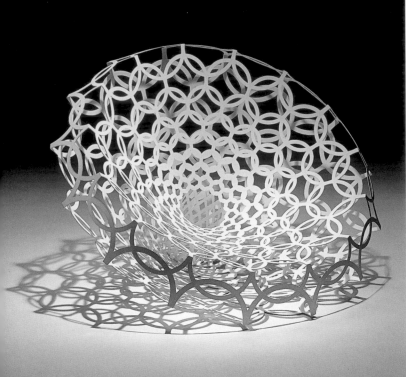

LOUISE CAMPBELL

Danish designer Louise Campbell's work is based on three simple rules: always start from scratch, find the core of the issue and dare to be different. Based in Copenhagen, she set up her studio in an old workshop in the heart of the city. Campbell whimsically describes how, shortly after moving in, she discovered that the studio floor drops nearly 30 cm from one end to the other. This means that all of the studio's rubbish and coffee-spills eventually roll down towards her workstation, surrounding her with an abundance of unexpected materials.

1 Laser-cut steel becomes a malleable material in Campbell's hands, whose Very Round Chair for Zanotta blurs the boundaries between craft and design.
2 Designed for the Crown Prince of Denmark, Campbell's 'Between Two Chairs' design is crafted in water-cut rubber fitted to a laser-cut metal frame, and manufactured by Hay in Denmark.

What is your starting point: materials or ideas?

I often find completely new directions to work in by toying with materials without a specific purpose. This sandpit approach always provides inspiration, and the ideas seem to follow.

Do you try to create unique materials?

I wanted to fold a chair from a single piece of perfectly square felt, and I wanted to harden it with an equally natural material. I tested various solutions before I opted for gelatine. After dipping the felt in a huge basin of water and 750 sheets of dissolved domestic gelatine (an exercise which required timely precision, as the gelatine goes lumpy within about ten minutes) the wet material was suspended within a large wooden frame by hundreds of meticulously positioned strings. The felt

was left to dry for two weeks before being dismantled. In all, a low-tech way of achieving a complex and surprisingly strong construction. Why do all this? To see what would happen. Was it a waste of time? Certainly not. This chair has inspired many later works.

Have you used any materials that have had unexpected results?

A colleague and I designed a lamp that combined dyed latex with fibreglass, and the result was beautiful. The lamp was soft and bouncy to the touch, and the colouring possibilities were endless. The structure was unusual, and filtered the light very well. The really fascinating part of this combination of materials, which were layered by hand over a mould, was the fact that no two lamps were the same due to the nature of fibreglass.

By coincidence, we created an industrial process that allowed for uniqueness in each piece, thereby turning a dream that all designers have into reality.

What material inspires you the most?

The one material that inspires me more than all the rest put together is plain paper. If an idea, particularly with regard to furniture design, works in paper, it is bound to work in other materials as well. The ease with which one can sit down with a pile of white paper, a pair of scissors and a roll of tape and just let loose is incredible. Every time I do this, something useful appears between my fingers.

3

4

ED ANNINK

Ed Annink is a partner in Ontwerpwerk, a design study known for its interdisciplinary approach, and designs for manufacturers such as Driade, Authentics, Designum and Droog Design. His work is suffused with wit, irreverence and poetry – Annink's designs bring art into everyday life. Parallel to his design practice, Annink has also published books and curated exhibitions.

3 Annink's striking coathooks for Droog Design are crafted in polyurethane.
4 Annink broke away from homeware conventions when he designed these bowls for Driade. Rather than craft all three pieces in a uniform style and fabricate them in a single material, he used pewter, glass and ceramic.
BELOW + OPPOSITE Birdlife was the inspiration behind these polished stainless steel mirrors for Driade.

What material do you think is the best of all?

Skin is a wonderfully sensible material. It's unique and impossible to manufacture. A jewelry designer once designed a bracelet for the upper arm, crafted from an exquisite piece of gold wire. He tightened the wire around a woman's upper arm until she said, 'Ouch, that hurts, you bastard!' He then took away the wire and a mark was left on the skin. That mark was in fact the piece he had wanted to create from the start. And what about a necklace made out of love bites? It lasts for two days, quite simply a temporary love affair. Both of these examples are proof of what a remarkable material skin really is, both environmentally and emotionally, but also irrationally.

Which materials inspire you the most?

Ones that are soft, hard, rough, smooth, smelly, stinky, shiny, matt, warmth, cold, heavy, light, transparent and all other combinations imaginable. I'm describing them like this because it's the physical or psychological trigger that attracts me to a material. I've used heat-resistant silicone for a disposable ashtray, harvested environment-friendly hard wood for a fruitbowl, polished industrial stainless steel for a bird-shaped mirror, melted pewter into a nutbowl and bent polyurethane into a hanger.

What is the most innovative material you use today?

Spray paint with silicon particles. Aerosol material is shaped by the object that it's sprayed on. Silicon creates a skin that isn't slippery, which is good for certain products.

I designed a computer for Nexus Technology made from extruded aluminum and moulded plastic covered with a heat-resistant glossy white spray paint. The interior is lined with a material used in aircraft to reduce the noise of the engines.

Why do you claim it is possible to design without materials?

It seems that the design industry is hyping the roles of materials in design. Materials should be a catalyst to trigger an experience. I like the idea of breaking away from material conventions. As Einstein said, 'Logic gets you from A to B, but fantasy will take you everywhere'.

1   2   3   4

TEXTILES

Contemporary textiles seem to polarize at technological extremes: the high-tech fabrics synthesized from unexpected materials, and the ultra-organics that are as sustainable as they are chic.

1 From Germany, Veredelte textiles are screen-printed with copper alloys, bronze and brass in several printing sequences. The coatings react to environmental influences and form a living patina over time.

2+4 Anne Kyyrö Quinn identified acoustic properties and insulation capabilities in felt. The fabric has emerged as a material of choice for many of today's designers.

3 Ranging from hemp fibres to horsehair, there are many innovative organic materials.

5 Durable and pliable, geotextiles are friction-resistant, have low creep properties and withstand constant freezing and thawing.

6 Wovenit fibre optic fabric comprises self-luminous fibres created by a 3-D knitting/weaving technique.

7 Contimetalflex® is coated with metallic pigments. A fluoropolymer base coats the textile and vulcanizes to bond to the textile.

8 This non-woven upholstery textile is abrasion-resistant, yet has a soft texture and a silky sheen. The textile is embroidered to create a 3-D decorative pattern and ruched to give it a structured texture.

OPPOSITE As textiles emerge as a mega-material, they are becoming stronger than ever before. By the same token, they are also getting softer, even soft enough to mimic fur.

Textiles connect a variety of practices and traditions, ranging from the refined couture garments of Parisian fashion to the high-tech gossamer filaments strong enough to hoist a satellite into space. High-performance fabrics are being reconceived as immersive webs, structural networks and information exchanges, and their ability to interface with technology is changing how the human body is experienced and how the urban environment is built. Today, textiles reveal their capacity to transform our world more than any other material.

Textiles can contribute to our well being in a number of ways: colourways and surface motifs are believed to stimulate the body's innate healing ability, while textiles constructed from encapsulated fibres medicate the wearer through the skin. Sensors in undergarments could register secretions that signal changes in cervical cells and fertility. Healthcare textiles are used in seating and bedding to reduce discomfort and promote improved circulation, while wicking away perspiration and maintaining pressure against the patient's skin to accelerate the healing of wounds. Fashioned into cushions, mattresses, blankets or wheelchair seats, sensors can record the temperature and movements of the patient and diagnose changes in their medical condition.

Ionized fibres have anti-microbial properties that protect the body from deadly bacteria and simultaneously resist odour-causing bacteria, while sterile 'contaminate-aware' textiles change colour if their surfaces are breached by germs. The discovery of a deadly single-cell bacteria, Strain 121, that survives autoclave temperatures, has lead scientists to conclude that there are other bacteria, viruses, fungi and spores that are not destroyed by autoclaving. This has made contaminate-aware and anti-microbial textiles a huge growth area for scientific researchers, healthcare specialists and textile practitioners.

New types of hybrid textiles are combining biological and engineering parts, bringing cybernetic organisms to mind. Heart valves, cardiac support devices, bone tissue, arterial filters and bioimplants are knitted and embroidered from a range of

1

1 This colourful textile sleeve is created
by braiding nylon fibres. Waterproof and
unable to conduct an electrical charge,
the sleeve makes the ideal casing for
electric cables used in wet environments.
2 This waterproof nanosphere fabric from
Schoeler is made with a Teflon®-like coating,
so that water and dirt rolls off the surface.
3 The tufted textures of this laser-cut
fabric mimics fur fibres. Fabrics like this
have outstanding acoustic properties.
OPPOSITE Andrea Valentini's moulded textile
is designed for use as a decorative surface.
Valentini fuses polyurethane foam to
a PVC-coated knit fleece and moulds
into flexible forms. The textile may be
cut, stitched, heat-welded or bonded onto
other materials, is lightweight, durable
and also washable. The fabric has sound-
proofing characteristics that make it
a good alternative to acoustic panels, and
can also be fabricated into soft furnishings.

textile fibres and electrospun fibres can be used in cosmetic and reconstructive
surgery. The growing symbiosis between body and textile now extends beyond the
heroes of science fiction, bringing with it a new body awareness. As designers explore
new construction processes and new thoughts about the body's capabilities, textiles
are slowly beginning to define body ideals rather than be shaped by them.

The new generation of textiles made for use in interior design transcend the
decorative and functional attributes traditionally attributed to soft furnishings.
Interior textiles are being reconceived as technological interfaces, acoustic exchanges,
light sources and portable environments. Fibreglass has been moulded into sliding
doors, sinks, partition walls and whole staircases. This signals a shift in the functions
of interior textiles as they move away from use as an architectural 'lining' to a new role
as structural components.

Fabrics interwoven with digital impulses can be programmed to change colours
and patterns, or to pulsate and illuminate. Tectonic fabrics reveal new colours,
textures and motifs through wear and tear, redefining wear as a factor that
completes the design process rather than destroys the fabric. These textiles give
the user a new role in consuming fabric as they engage with the design process.
As a design innovation, a transformable textile highlights new multi-functional
purposes; as a wearable textile, they imbue garments with a whole new range of
possibilities.

The 'soft circuits' woven into fabric furnishings range from sensors, switches
and LEDs to mini computers and micro processors. As they engage with other
systems, they interface with audio-visual technology. For example, a tap on one area
of an upholstery motif could change the television channel, while a tap on another
area could switch the television off. When woven into wall hangings, upholstery,
wall coverings and curtains, plastic LEDs can be connected by soft circuitry that
programmes their colourways and patterns according to the wishes of the owner.
Conventional lighting could be completely replaced by LED textiles and woven fibre

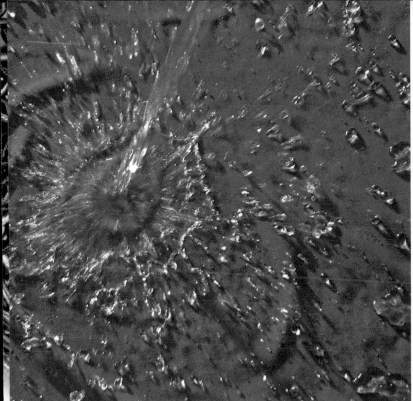

1   2   3   4

FASHION

1–4 New materials are redefining fashion.
Super-strong fabrics that conduct digital
signals are creating a technical exoskeleton
around the body. Liquid fibres that can fuse
together into membranes or interlinking
components present new possibilities for
fashion and accessories. The growing
movement in sustainable fashion introduces
new materials and new processes that
help to minimize environmental waste.
5–8 With their luminescent surfaces,
technological interfaces and interactive
capacities, Pia Myrvold's garments
integrate fashion with a range of high-tech
materials. Myrvold used graphics by Karim
Rashid in prêt-a-porter collections titled
Hypermix, Slow Tech and Cyberware, and
transferred reflective pixels onto lightweight
fabrics in her Fast Forward collection.
OPPOSITE Myrvold is pioneering an
information-based approach to fashion,
embedding communication sensors in
her garments and accessorizing them
with wireless transmitters.

Radical exchanges are taking place between fashion and technology. As fashion
designers embrace techno fabrics and new technologies, a new dynamic between
the body and non-fashion materials is beginning to evolve. This crossover marks an
exciting moment in fashion, where the possibilities of new materials and high-tech
processes are enhancing the performance of clothing. New technologies now free
fashion designers from many of the physical demands of production, allowing them
to focus more on the creative aspects that translate ideas into material form. Now
that three-dimensional garments can be produced by a printer, sprayed from aerosol
cans or fabricated in cyberspace, exciting new forms of fashion are remerging.

Pia Myrvold transforms modern technology into wearable couture. Originally from
Norway but now based in Paris, Myrvold gives a technological twist to contemporary
clothing by bringing cyberspace into the fashion arena. Working within cyberspace
allows her to pioneer new relationships between fashion, technologies and materials,
as well as offering her a platform from which to challenge traditional ideas about the
construction of clothing.

Myrvold creates her innovative range of couture-inspired clothing via her website,
www.cybercouture.com. Myrvold's fascination with multimedia and information
technologies led her to the interactive potential of the Internet. Web interactivity,
though still dependent on photo-based media, makes this new information-based
approach to fashion possible. Myrvold has established an internet forum in which her
clients can participate through her website. Her interactive fashion collections are
published online, and with a click and a drag of the mouse, visitors can decide how
they'd like their choices put together. Each garment is initially displayed in white; once
selected, the image rotates three-dimensionally to display the garment's construction
and detail. Visitors can browse among Myrvold's range of prints, or drag them onto the
garment to get a scaled view of how the pattern will once its made. Each order must
include the concise measurements of the client, as each piece is made to a custom fit.
The clients then email their orders to Myrvold's workshop, where the garments are cut

5 6 7 8

1 At first glance this halter-neck dress
from Freedom of Creation appears to be
made from a woven fabric, but it is actually
fabricated from liquid plastic hardened
into a flexible garment that resembles
chain mail more than a conventional textile.
2 Freedom of Creation can fabricate a range
of products through the rapid manufacturing
process they use. All parts of this handbag
were produced simultaneously as individual
layers of liquid plastic hardened one by one.

according to specification, printing the selected patterns via a heat process. The
garment is then sewn together and shipped to the client more or less immediately.

When describing her choice materials, Myrvold names a substantial range of
synthetic fabrics, then goes on to add wires, connectors, sensors, switches and
batteries to the list. 'I have a vision for the seamless integration of fashion textiles
and technology,' she explained. 'But right now, there aren't fabrics durable enough
to be interwoven with cables and circuitry and still be worn comfortably on the body.
In the meantime, my "Female Interfaces" collection provides me with a means of
experimenting with how hardware can be integrated into fashion, so hopefully,
phasing in software will be the next step.'

Before she began engaging with technology, Myrvold looked for fashion materials
in unlikely outlets such as yachting supply wholesalers and interior textile shops. The
fabrics were customized by dye and paint, or subjected to specialist processes such
as printing, laser-cutting, stitching or embroidery. 'When it comes to hand-finishing,
these days I like to melt PVC into tulle, or cut up plastic bags and sew them onto toile.
I'm also developing a silkscreen technique using concrete or metallic paint.' Myrvold
often incorporates light effects into her garments by including reflective materials
and shining surfaces. 'Reflective PVC has a dynamic surface that reacts to light and
movement,' Myrvold said. 'By combining it with tulle and denim, or using it as trim,
it transforms matt materials into lustruous surfaces.'

For Myrvold's Cybercouture collections, her choice of fabric is limited to materials
that can be printed on. 'The material has to absorb ink and create a high-resolution
image, and be durable enough to withstand normal wear and tear and laundering,'
Myrvold explained. 'I often like inexpensive materials, like toile and ordinary silk,
but my concept relies on the use of interactive technology that can produce original
garments exactly like the client wants them. Although there is never a shortage
of fashion materials that can be cut, printed and sewn, there is a limit to the
technological processes that can be used. Manufacturing real garments designed

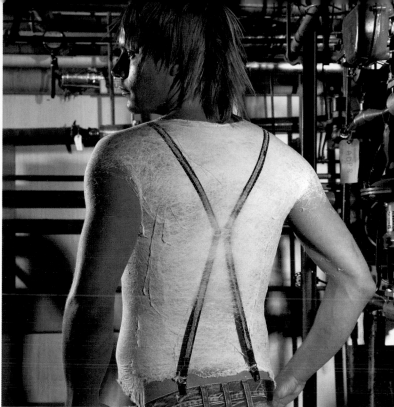

3

4

in cyberspace requires a lot of technical expertise. Even though there is some new technology available, the programming logistics still present a lot of limitations.'

A vision for integrating technology, materials and design methodology is driving Freedom of Creation, an Amsterdam-based design lab who believe that rapid manufacturing processes portend how garments and accessories will be made in the future. Also known as rapid prototyping and stereolithography, the process reads files created in three-dimensional modelling software applications such as Solidworks or 3-D Studio Max and fabricates the object by firing a laser into a chamber of liquid material such as plastic or metal. The laser solidifies a tiny layer of material at a time, slowly building up a three-dimensional object.

When Jiri Evenhuis and Janne Kyttanen, founders of Freedom of Creation, started to use the process, they realized it could create forms that would be impossible to produce by traditional manufacturing processes such as moulding or pressing. Because the process creates forms by building up thin 'printed' layers, it can create objects inside other objects, objects with deep recesses or undercuts, or objects comprised of numerous interlocking forms. Producing a non-woven textile made up of interlocking parts led to a breakthrough when they realized that chain mail-like garments made up of thousands of tiny, interlocking pieces could be created. Handbags, purses, watch straps and jewelry were created in the same style, and the potential to produce sportswear and shoes was also revealed.

The capacity to produce clothing on demand could mean that the fashion industry no longer runs the risk of over-producing garments or conversely, manufacturing too few. Garments could be produced as consumers order them, and even customized to suit the need of individual customers. Exploiting rapid manufacturing's ability to create objects within objects makes it possible to produce the packaging at the same time as the garment. If this process could be combined with Myrvold's vision for a web-based fashion system, garments could be ordered online and dispatched to the wearer without any human intervention whatsoever.

3+4 Fabrican by Manel Torres makes fashion choices easy and fun. Tiny fibres suspended in an aerosol solution can be sprayed directly onto the skin to create instant garments. A similar material was first introduced in pharmaceuticals as a bandage preparation, which Torres appropriated for fashion.

1

2

While Freedom of Creation's model eradicates the need for machinists, the 'spray-on chic' invented by Manel Torres radically eliminates the need for a fashion designer. Fabrican, an aerosol preparation that suspends fibres in a chemical solution, is a liquid fabric that becomes a non-woven textile when sprayed onto the body. The dry fibres have the appearance of felt and the performance of knitwear, making it possible for the wearer to create their own clothing just by spraying it on.

Giving the wearer control of the finished design is at the very core of Danish designer Tine Jensen's system of modular clothing. By using conventional fabrics, such as cotton, silk chiffon, silk taffeta, wool and jersey, Jensen provides an alternative to the fixed construction of mainstream garments, and enables the wearer to continually reconfigure the components into expressions of individual style. In collaboration with chemists and engineers, Jensen is pioneering an elastic garment whose necklines and armholes can be interchanged. The garment's deliberate ambiguity enables it to be worn in a variety of styles.

1, 2 + OPPOSITE Tine Jensen designed a basic wardrobe of layered separates that can be combined and reconfigured to create new styles. Jensen's modular system moves away from the fashion cycle, encouraging wearers to invent new garments from existing pieces rather than invest in a new wardrobe each season.

1

2

3

YEOHLEE

Born in Malaysia but based in Manhattan, Yeohlee Teng is a visionary designer who uses fashion to generate a critical discourse on the body, architecture and design. Her experiments with new forms and fabrics result in clothing imbued with utility and elegance.

1 Designed for her autumn/winter 2007 collection, Yeohlee used velvet and silk organdy for the Ellipse dress and Möbius scarf to give a subtle sheen.
2 For the same collection, the dark grey silk lurex Bellows dress was chosen for its mercurial colour and metallic sheen.
3 This silk, linen and polyester fabric has a soft texture yet an unusually firm structure that enables it to hold its shape.

How would you describe your approach to fashion materials?

I would describe my approach to material as frugal. I like to maintain precise conservation of energy and material to avoid wasting fabric. Some of my designs were made from a single length of fabric, crafting the garment, belt, ties, collars, cuffs, waistband and lapels without leaving a single scrap of fabric behind. I like to cut out my patterns by hand, and to find unconventional shortcuts. One of my favourites is combining the bust dart and side seam by contouring them into one.

Are materials your starting point?

I'm probably different to most fashion designers. I don't often use traditional approaches, like sketching pictorial references on paper or draping muslin on a mannequin. I tend to use

geometry to plot something two dimensionally and make a flat pattern that will have three-dimensional proportions. Knowing these measurements is like making a witch's brew: you throw numbers into the pot and come up with a formula. To determine the sweep of the garment you have to calculate the stride. Once you attribute that to the scale of people the whole equation is demystified.

How do concepts and materials come together in your work?

As far as my design process goes, materials and ideas exist in a symbiotic relationship. Sometimes the colour and construction of a material can spark an idea; at other times the idea of a form leads me to search out a material of a particular weight and texture that will support the shape.

What types of fabrics are you using?

Because my spring 2007 collection was themed reduction, I wanted to reduce the number of fabrics used and cuts made. I found a coarsely woven, yarn-dyed silk, linen and polyester produced by Bartolini Sestilio. It has a stiff waxy finish that doesn't fray excessively, so less seaming and sewing is necessary. The fabric is mercurial in both colour and performance. It's translucent when one sheet is layered over another. The stiff 'body' of the fabric creates structure and shape rather like the wings of a dragonfly. In some garments I combined it with a textured cotton woven in differing waves, a fabric I call vintage iron embro which is an all-over floral embroidery done in silk and viscose yarn on a cotton and metal weave.

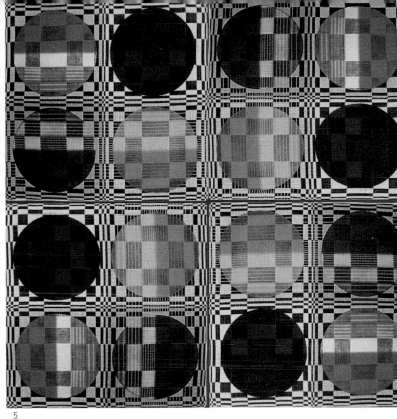

4

5

INTERNATIONAL FASHION MACHINES

IFM is led by Maggie Orth, an artist and technologist who designs and invents interactive textiles for fashion. IFM's vision of interactive fashion is driven by the combination of interactive technology, electronic textiles, wearable computer interfaces and creative expression.

4 The animated module on this prototype can be incorporated into fabric, leather or almost any fashion material. It can also be used as a decorative accessory, like a buckle for a belt or a shoe, or combined with jewelry. Each module is powered by a low-voltage battery that keeps the animation constantly in motion.
5 IFM's Electric Plaid textile is woven with electronic circuits that enable it to change colour. The circuitry connects modules that control eight colour change areas, also known as woven pixels. Each woven pixel contains four to eight woven electronic yarns that create a pattern.

Is techno fashion focused more on materials or technology?

I see electronic textiles as an enabling physical material, a new medium, and highly symbolic material. They allow me to explore the relationship of physical form, material-making and computation in a formal manner. They allow me to transform technology objects, from hard to soft. They allow me to bring together traditional and extremely satisfying arts and crafts practices with computation and interaction. We're breaking new ground in developing techno textiles as part of what we do, but they have to be advanced further if the clothes are to be durable enough to support the technology.

Where does your interest in materials come from?

Although I work within a technologized industry, natural materials have a strong appeal. There seems to be a common human desire to transform nature into something else. One of the major influences in my work was Herman Melville's novel, *Moby Dick*. For me, the main premise of that book was that the whale was a material for making everything.

What materials do you like the most?

I find that I am not drawn to intrinsically beautiful materials. I like materials that are used in the wrong way, or that defy their engineering boundaries. I like transparent, gooey materials. I like materials that I can touch and experience sensually. I like silicon caulk. I like rubbers. I like plastics. I like organic materials that decay. I like materials that elicit the feeling of entropy. I recently saw a piece in the Seattle airport that combined repeated pod-like ceramic elements with sugar. The sugar acted as amorphous cement that held the ceramic elements together. I particularly like the use of sugar, a crystalline material in this entropic manner, and in contrast with the highly organized, yet organic pod-like ceramic elements.

Is there any potential to use carbon fibres in techno fashion?

We recently discovered a black cardboard with hidden conductive properties. We were using it to mount a fabric sensor and it was causing all kinds of electrical problems. The cardboard was conductive because it was made with carbon (which makes it black). The cardboard had hidden material powers, beyond what we imagined when we first encountered it.

1

2

3

4

to the lasers that projected the images almost 5 kilometres (3 miles) across Bamiyan's plain. The lasers are 100-watts strong, and are powered by a network of solar panels that generate enough electricity for 20,000 local households that would not have had a power source otherwise.

London-based, Usman Haque creates responsive environments, interactive installations, digital interface devices and choreographed performances. Since his tenure as artist-in-residence at the International Academy of Media Arts and Sciences in Japan, Haque has used a wide range of unexpected materials in his art. Haque creates architectural environments, then deploys sensory stimuli to bring them to life. Haque has used a range of analogue and digital equipment to produce electromagnetic waves, subsonic frequencies, anechoic and acoustic cancellation systems, and ephemeral forms are his materials of choice. By using intangibles such as scent, humidity, ambient light, temperature and air circulation to generate a response among his audience, Haque triggers reactions by using materials that the individuals were not immediately conscious of.

These ingredients came together spectacularly in Haque's 'Haunt' installation, a project that recreated some of the sensations that parapsychologists have recorded in haunted spaces. Inside a specially-built chamber, Haque used coils and audio equipment to create an environment where electromagnetic fields, temperature fluctuations and infrasonic frequencies combined to induce the perception of invisible forces, like movement, taste and sound, and the sensation of the presence of others. The installation elicited responses described as a 'sense of presence', 'chills on the spine', 'uneasiness' in some parts of the chamber, 'dizziness' and visual and auditory hallucinations, including seeing flies in the chamber and hearing the sound of someone coughing. As expected, it showed how ephemeral materials and conditions could elicit spooky sensations.

Sound is an invisible and intangible material that can completely transform energy, mood and perception. Sound often features in installation art; unlike visual materials

1, 2 + OPPOSITE Rather than work with conventional materials, Usman Haque instead chooses to work within existing environments to present new interpretations of them. Describing technological interfaces as his materials of choice, Haque creates interactive installations or transforms architectural settings in order to introduce new spatial conditions.
3 + 4 Haque turned fear into an art form when he used a range of media to recreate the sensations commonly identified in a 'haunted' house. Visitors reported being terrified, even though the paranormal experiences were human-made.

1   2

that closed eyes can shut out, its presence is almost unavoidable. Sound works
at a sensorial level and its vibrations can be powerful and evocative. Yet, its effects
are not always consciously noticed. Even when devoid of musical or communicative
associations, sound carries an abstract language that we respond to at a primal level.

Sound was an important medium for those in the Fluxus network, and more
recently for artists such as Bruce Nauman. *Raw Materials*, Nauman's installation at
London's Tate Modern, broadcasts an indistinct hum of human voices, which draws
the public nearer to the artwork as they attempt to distinguish what's being said.
The sound creates a point of orientation that the public engage with, manipulating
them physically as it draws them closer, or drives them away.

Paris-based sound artist Valerie Vivancos uses what she describes as 'the most
basic materials known to man': resonance, vibrations and the audible word. She
regards sound as an uncharted territory within the arts, underpinned by many of the
same theoretical constructs applied to visual arts, performance or writing. During the
last decade, Vivancos has exhibited sound installations in museums, galleries and off-
site spaces, and published her work in the French sound art journal, *Vibrö*. Her artwork
has contributed to the field of vibro-acoustics, and she has conducted interactive
sound programmes with the hearing impaired. Her 'Towards Silence' project at the
Parque Das Ruinas Art Centre in Rio de Janeiro resulted from one of her sound
workshops, including a participatory performance that explored the absence of sound.

Despite its ephemeral nature, Vivancos' work revealed that sound has palpable
impact. Sensations that could not be heard through the ears could be experienced
corporeally through tissues and bones. Deaf people called each other's attention
by hitting the wooden floor, creating a resonance that others could sense. At 'Deaf
Discos,' deep bass music was played, very similar to the Rastafarian Aba Shanti sound
system. Soundboxes, soundbeds and soundchairs play low frequency music to rouse
different parts of the body, enabling the hearing impaired to enjoy the music with the
whole body rather instead of the ears.

3

4   6

5   7

JANET ECHELMAN

Janet Echelman is an American artist whose sculptural installations interact with natural forces such as wind and water. Recent works include the extraordinary wind sculpture titled 'She Changes' built on the waterfront in Porto, Portugal in 2005. Commissioned the following year to create a '9/11' memorial, Echelman conceived of a man-made island in New York's Hudson River accessed by bridge from Hoboken, New Jersey.

2–7 Although she works within a vast repertoire of materials, many of Janet Echelman's works are fibre-based. The scope and scale of this artwork has inspired both textile practitioners and architects to reevaluate the structural potentials that textiles have.

Measuring 46 metres in diameter and 14 floors high, 'She Changes' is one of the biggest public sculptures in existence. How did you achieve it?

Through collaboration with a textile manufacturer, an architect and a software developer. The artwork is actually a complex, multi-layered form created by twisting, braiding and knotting nearly one ton of Tenara® fibres produced by WL Gore and Associates. I got help from Phillip Speranza, a New York-based architect, who translated my drawings into 3-D computer models, then asked Peter Heppel & Associates in Paris develop a software programme for the piece. The software showed me how the sculpture would move in the wind and revealed the engineering considerations there would be.

The textile structure was fabricated in Washington State by hand and machine, then shipped to Portugal in pieces where it was hung from a massive ring of hollow steel suspended between three steel poles of varying heights.

You mean the sculpture is a giant textile?

It's similar to a net. It was created using a fibre that could withstand a windy environment with long periods of UV exposure. Tenara® is light enough to respond to the wind and durable enough to retain its red pigment despite long periods of UV exposure. I had looked at plant fibres, silk and nylon, but none of them have the durability of Tenara®.

Why is Tenara® so durable?

It's made by expanding Polytetrafluoroethylene (PTFE), a chemical found in Teflon®, into a yarn coated with an expandable fluoro-polymer. PTFE is the most inert polymer known. It is difficult to manipulate but can be coaxed into rod shapes that form fibres. Tenara® has high tensile strength, doesn't creep and has flex resistance.

Would you also use the same materials for an indoor space?

The public sculpture I created for a multi storey car park in Tampa, Florida, is made from multi-filament polypropylene. There's little natural light, so I included 36-degree ellipsoidal spotlights and dichroic glass filters in the work. There are two parts: a 3-D line drawing suspended from the ceiling, and another with no physical presence: it is a projection of the other, creating a long shadow drawing. I saw this as a modern interpretation of Plato's *Allegory of the Cave*, using urban infrastructure as a modern-day cave wall.

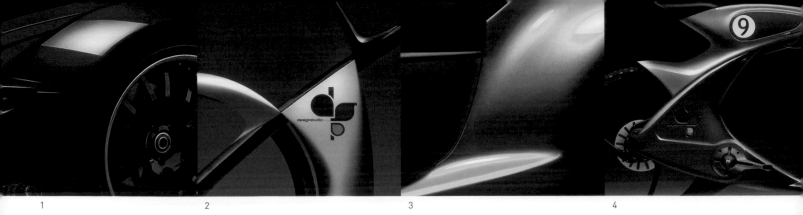

1   2   3   4

VEHICLE DESIGN

1–8 From his studio in Los Angeles, Scott Robertson designs the vehicles of the future. His cars and bikes have been featured in sci-fi films and futuristic set designs. Robertson's work has been influential among automotive designers.
OPPOSITE The Veyron is an impressive feat of materials technology and automotive expertise. It features a 7-speed sequential DSG double-clutch gearbox and a unique 6-cylinder 8.0 litre engine. The Veyron's lightweight aluminum body and carbon fibre monocoque chassis results in a low power-to-weight ratio. Fitted with a carbon-ceramic braking system and retracted wing/spoiler angle suspension heights, the Veyron merges racetrack technology with everyday traffic.
BELOW This bicycle design was drawn for Robertson's book, *Start Your Engines*, and has not yet been rendered in built form.

Vehicle design is a fast-moving field. Small cars are shaped by big issues, such as the drive to find emissions-free fuel sources, the quest for greater sustainability in automotive design, and greater concern for passenger safety. Lightweight materials provide a solution for most of these concerns; as they reduce the load they lessen energy consumption, and the new manufacturing processes developed to fabricate them offer environmentally friendly alternatives to the industry's high-pollution processes. Composite materials are often lighter and stronger than fabricated sheet steel and armour-like metal casing, and materials research reveals that a high absorption of crush energy per kilogram can be achieved.

As the debate on global warming heats up, the development of eco-friendly automobiles is on the rise. Some of the best fuel economy options are mini-diesel vehicles, or hybrid options. Large model vehicles usually have enough space for batteries or an electric engine alongside the motor. Hybrid versions of the S-Class Mercedes, the 7 series BMW and Audi's proposed Q7 SUV herald a viable alternative to fossil fuel. As Lexus proposes to seamlessly integrate hybrid power across its entire range, it sets a new standard of sustainability in the motor trade. The Lexus RX400h already packs intermediate car economy into a performance SUV package, and their forthcoming RX Hybrid and 2007 GS Hybrid promises to deliver even more. SAAB, on the other hand, eschews both batteries and fossil fuels. Instead, it advocates the advantages of bioethanol, which is made from eighty-five per cent renewable fuels, such as recycled wood pulp. Prototype vehicles co-developed by Shell and Audi are powered by a natural gas-based, CO_2-neutral fuel. Together with Volvo's multi-fuel prototype, which can operate on four different alternative fuels as well as petrol, all are pioneering realistic antidotes to the fuel-consumption dilemma.

The sustainable energy debate fuelled Ross Lovegrove's decision to embark on a quest for a solar energy source. As a result, the surface of Lovegrove's futuristic concept 'Aerospace' car is covered in 969 custom-engineered crystals that harness energy from the sun.

1

1 Scott Robertson designed bikes like these for the feature film, *Minority Report*.
BELOW Also featured on page 110, Ross Lovegrove's aerodynamic concept car is powered by solar radiation rather than conventional fuel.

By working in collaboration with Sharp Solar Europe, Swarovski Optical Laboratories and the automobile manufacturer Coggiola, Lovegrove revealed that crystals could enhance the energy potential of photovoltaics, and therefore power a lightweight vehicle. The car body is engineered to sit at a precise height in order to maximize the solar-absorbing properties of the crystals. Although the car is still at concept stage, it provides a benchmark of innovation and sustainability.

High-performance vehicles are rarely renowned for their ecological outlook, but their commitment to materials research often leads to cutting-edge developments. The Bugatti Veyron 16.4 broke new ground when it was acclaimed for having 'the most powerful car engine ever made'. The Veyron's W16 engine is comprised of two V8 engine's joined together, and features four valves per cylinder. Capable of 1001 BHP, the Veyron accelerates at an incredible speed. Its engine includes electronic control systems that enable the chassis and powertrain to function together in seamless harmony. Following in the footsteps of the all-carbon McLaren FI and the Resin Transfer Moulding carbon Mercedes-Benz SLR, the Veyron's chassis includes lightweight carbon-fibre panels in the vehicle's primary structure and an aluminum alloy for the body and front crash structure. As with the Porsche GT and the SLR, the Veyron is fitted with carbon-ceramic brakes developed by the aerospace technology and used in Formula One racing. They are lighter than conventional brakes, absorb more heat and prevent brake fade. The vehicle's tyres were fabricated by Michelin, where they were engineered to hold the road at speeds of 400 kph (250 mph). Measuring 36.6 cm (14⅜ in) across, they are reportedly the widest car tyres ever made. Carefully composed and constructed from lightweight, durable materials, the Veyron's high-speed materials signal a fresh direction for the cars of the future.

SCOTT ROBERTSON

Scott Robertson is a vehicle designer and illustrator who also works as a consultant to the entertainment and transportation industries. Robertson designs both real and imaginary vehicles; his designs have been produced by sports companies and toy manufacturers, made for film, such as *Minority Report*, and created for gaming software. Scott's clients include BMW, Fiat, Universal Studios, Raleigh Bicycles, Mattel Toys, Patagonia, Nike, Rockstar Games, Sony Online Entertainment and Buena Vista Games.

2 + RIGHT Robertson explains that 'These cars are really nothing special in regards to material usage. They simply exist as a figment of my imagination and provide me with the subject matter for attempting to render vehicles overly shiny and colourful in an indoor studio environment.'

What do you imagine the car of the future to look like?

The cars of the future probably won't look much different than they do now. Motor manufacturers lack the risk taking, innovative attitude needed to truly provide the marketplace with something that looks different than what we have today. New materials might help the situation, but given the consumer's conservative nature, combined with a lack of daring by the marketing teams, the high cost of vehicle development and the associated risk of a failure, the automotive world will remain 'visually boring' for the foreseeable future.

How does knowledge of materials inform the designs you produce?

I design both real and imaginary objects. Understanding what can be done with materials, makes the imagery more believable. In the case of designing real vehicles and props for the entertainment industry, making the right material choices will give the designs more credibility.

How do you gain in-depth knowledge of the materials you use?

When designing something such as a carbon-fibre bicycle or an expanded polystyrene helmet, I work closely with the engineers to learn as much as I can about the limitations and the flexibility the materials will provide. It never hurts to ask the dumb questions either, because the answers can lead to innovative new material choices.

What new roles will materials play in vehicle design?

I think the materials of the future will continue to become lighter, stronger and more sophisticated in being able to accomplish multiple functions with only one material.

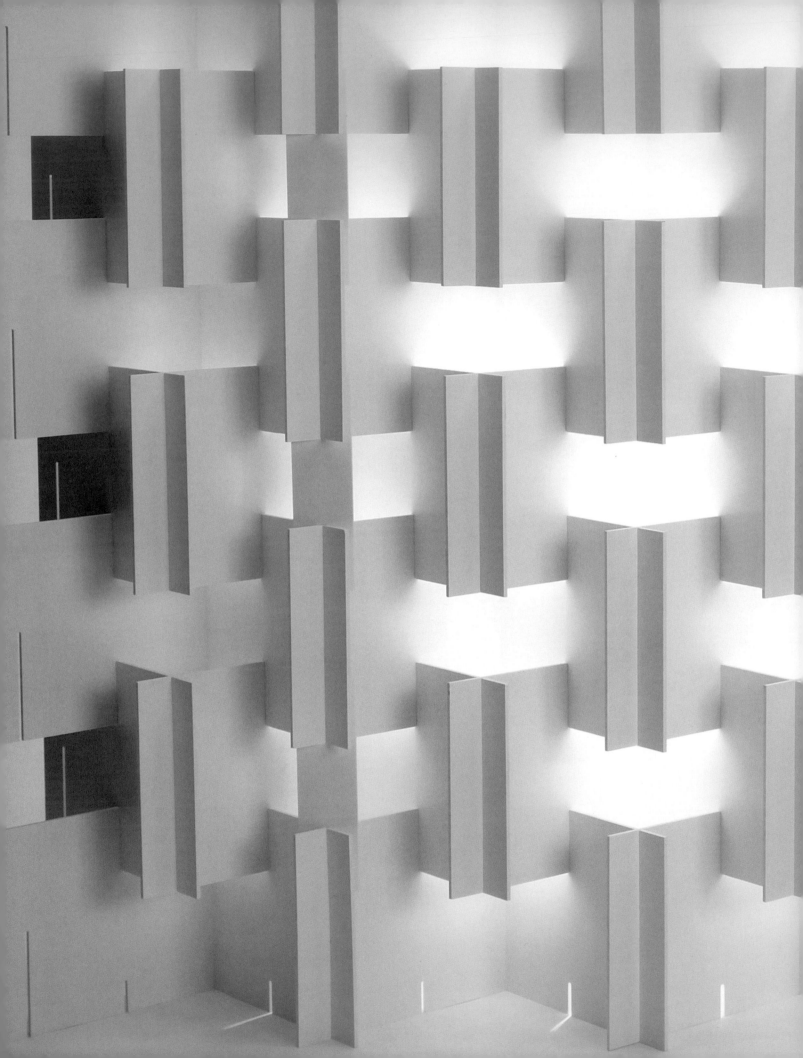

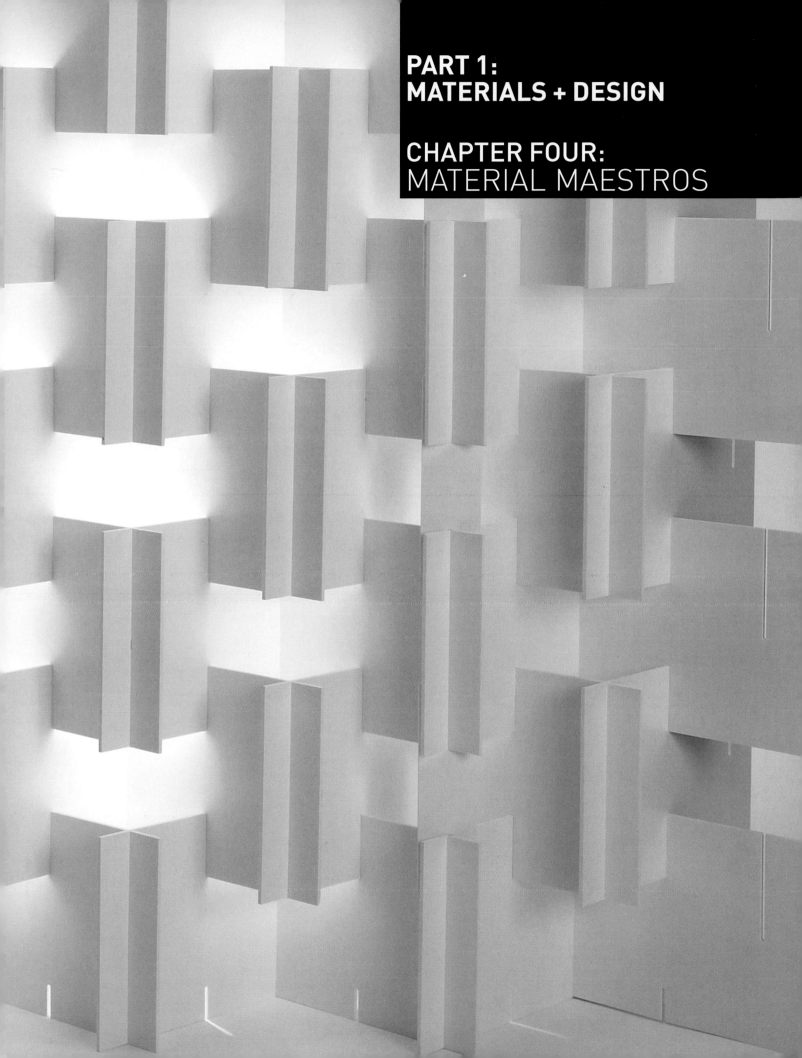

1 2 3 4

MATERIAL MAESTROS

BRADLEY QUINN + MICHELE CANIATO

PREVIOUS PAGE Achyut Kantawala and Edward Ng's screen is easy to assemble, and can be expanded vertically and horizontally.
1 Patricia Urquiola designed the Antibodi chair with an economy of materials that seems to belie its multi-faceted abilities.
2 Paola Lenti creates delicate but durable products (such as this 'Grass' rug) from synthetic materials of her own design.
3 David Adjaye considers light to be a versatile material, which he deployed to create dramatic effects in the galleries of the Nobel Peace Centre in Oslo.
4 Natural forms and synthetic materials blend with beautiful results in Patricia Urquiola's T-Table, designed for Kartell.
5 Toyo Ito used conventional concrete to create an unconventional rooftop for this crematorium, in Kagamigahara, Japan.
6 In his polyethylene Bubble chair for Kartell, Philippe Starck took the classic Club out of the living room into the garden.
7 Marcel Wanders' Sponge Vase begins with a real sponge, so each piece is unique.
8 The subtle pattern on the polymer shade of Philippe Starck's Miss K lamp glows when the lamp is illuminated.
OPPOSITE Ross Lovegrove's experiment with fossil forms, organic shapes and geometric repeats inspired this dramatic spiral staircase.

For architects and designers, the challenge of using a new material is both exciting and terrifying. With a new material comes risks and uncertainties; it could fail to perform, discolour, create a chemical reaction or even disintegrate over time. Introducing a new material means evaluating its impact on the environment and the likelihood of developing an alternative construction process. Even though new materials require investment and experimentation, the possibilities that they present make it well worth the effort.

When new materials prove their merits, they reveal fresh potentials for the creative disciplines today, but also determine how architecture and design will take shape in the future. Twenty-first-century materials are becoming aligned with technological processes, and these new interfaces are slowly beginning to define materials rather than be shaped by them. As the applications for high-tech materials escalate, designs that reflect their power and efficiency result, often creating a product that can be viewed from multiple perspectives. Not only does the new breed of materials provide fresh inspiration for architects and product designers, they also present fresh possibilities for fashion experts and textile technologists.

This chapter features interviews with some of today's leading practitioners in the creative industries. Individually they represent cultures in Africa, Asia, Europe, the Middle East and North America, but collectively their works are pulling together some of the most predictive strands of material expertise in circulation today. As they describe the dynamic exchanges taking place between materials and design, they reveal the groundbreaking forms that new materials promise to create in this century and beyond.

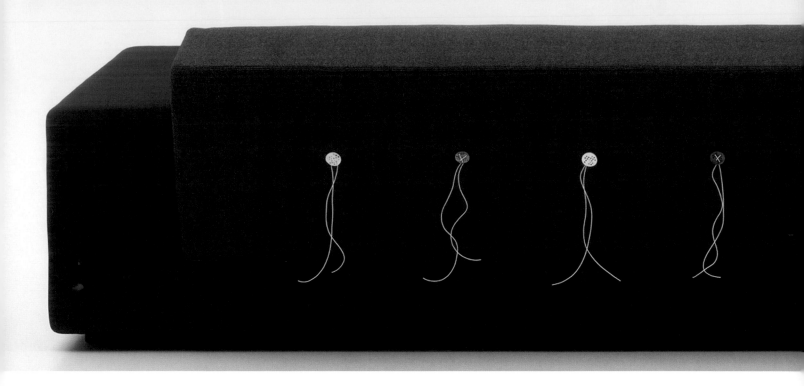

HELLA JONGERIUS
BRADLEY QUINN

ABOVE The Worker armchair was designed by Jongerius for the Vitra Home Collection and derives its unusual appeal from the intriguing combination of obviously hand-crafted elements and technologically sophisticated features.

Funny, flawed or forward-thinking? Words like these often attach to the products created by Dutch designer Hella Jongerius. Finding expressions that describe her approach is sometimes difficult, because many of her works straddle the divide between tradition and innovation, or move between playful irony and heavyweight ideas. Jongerius' designs have been made from a vast repertoire of materials, ranging from polyurethane, latex, foam and plastics, to steel, felt, porcelain, glass, bronze and gold. But irrespective of her choices of media and sources of inspiration, the stylized objects that result from Jongerius' designs are beautiful tools for modern life, crafted in forward-thinking designs that help to bridge the gulf between everyday functionality and ideals of comfort, efficiency and beauty.

For almost fifteen years, Jongerius' work has been strongly rooted in concepts, ranging from subtle poetic statements to self-assured declarations that boldly outline a new rationale for design. 'I'm certainly not unique in making designs that realize ideas,' Jongerius says. 'In fact, one of the things I noticed when I first became a designer was how everything seemed to rotate around the concepts already underpinning design. That made me want to pare every product down to the bone, so I did, asking myself what they were for, what history clung to them, and what ideas lurked beneath our understanding of them. As a result, I completely undressed the products. It may not have led me to discover any real meanings in them, but it meant that I could see what the materials were really about.'

Jongerius' interest in materials differentiates her designs and her work from most other designers precisely because she considers materials to be much more important than form. 'My work doesn't make a big deal of form in itself. I work with archetypal forms because I don't believe that we actually need any new forms today,' she explains. 'Why should I design anything new if certain forms have long proved their usefulness? To me, the ideal vase has already been invented. It's round-bellied and has a narrow neck. Vases have been made that way for hundreds of years, and for a good reason.'

Rather than respect traditional divisions between design, materials and creative inspiration, Jongerius folds each one into the others. 'The basis of my work is often materials rather than ideas,' she explains. 'Once I have the materials in hand I start bending, gluing, sewing or experimenting with other techniques. Sometimes I'll decide to bring other materials into the process as well, and that can mean that the product moves in an unexpected direction. Responding and reacting to what a material can do gives the whole thing an element of spontaneity that I really like.'

Observing and experimenting with materials is an important part of Jongerius' process, and her approach is unequivocally 'hands on': 'I believe in getting my hands dirty, and I practically abuse the materials until I stumble upon new ideas, new ways of seeing things. There is an incredible amount of innovation involved in the process of making itself.' Jongerius prefers sketching by hand to designing with computer software, but uses CAD to transpose her designs into final renderings for clients and manufacturers. 'Even before I handle the materials, my starting point is making drawings.' Sketching and making small prototypes keeps me closer to the materials. My big clients are only set up to handle computer files, so by the time the final version of the design is ready, you could say that the product is a combination of craft and technology.'

Jongerius describes craft techniques as an obvious choice for her work. 'A craft-based approach is one that you can apply to industrial products and new, high-tech materials as well, and still produce unique objects. People are fed up with all the throwaway rubbish that is manufactured and labelled "contemporary design", and they long for things that have some significance to them,' she says. Even though the majority of Jongerius' products are made in multiples, she maintains a vision for producing each individual piece as a 'one-off'. 'I'm trying to balance the individuality that unique objects have with the reality of serial outputs,' she notes. 'This means creating a higher level of quality that treats every production run as a limited edition. It may sound contradictory, but finding a way to incorporate flaws into each piece can actually create a higher standard.'

ABOVE, THIS PAGE + OPPOSITE The elongated shape of the Polder sofa is created from a wooden frame cushioned with foam and upholstered with a technical textile. The sofa is upholstered in different fabrics in five coordinating colours. Jongerius played with colours and textures to underscore the asymmetry of the piece. The buttons are made of natural materials and sewn to the cushions with bold cross stitches. **BELOW** This 'Delft in Detail' B-set jug by Jongerius was manufactured by Makkum.

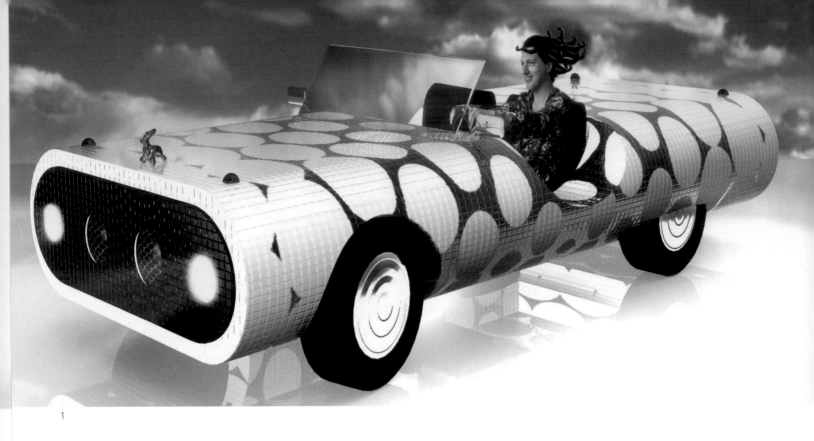

1

MARCEL WANDERS
MICHELE CANIATO

Marcel Wanders is a walking contradiction: at any moment, he might be completely silly, deathly serious, adamant about his ability to be the best designer in the world, or equally adamant that he is a complete amateur. Reviewers have labelled his work 'ironic', but Wanders' response to this is swift and sure: 'I'm not ironic at all. I'm very serious.' Yet by being both ironic and serious, his work is well received and critically acclaimed.

Wanders' work is constantly evolving as he experiments and learns. Since graduating from the Hogeschool voor de Kunsten in Arnhem, The Netherlands, he has been at the centre of the Dutch design movement – one of the most highly regarded design movements in recent years. Beginning with the Droog design cooperative in the 1990s, and proceeding right up to his involvement with Moooi today, Wanders found the leading design edge and seems content to stay there. 'I believe that my profession is creative and experimental. This means that I have to commit to go in unknown places, to blind my eyes and dare to run, to follow my belief that I cannot fail because I will always stand up after falling.'

In daring to run with his eyes covered, Wanders has succeeded in creating designs that constantly challenge us: 'I call design "the unexpected welcome". Something is happening. You didn't expect it and it's very welcome. This is what I do. And the sequence of what happens to you when you enter the product resembles the moment that you are in when I tell you a joke. When that is all there is for a product I would never make it because a joke is funny perhaps for one time. A product needs to live a long life and needs to be valuable. But the secret of that moment really resembles that.'

In his iconic 'Knotted Chair', which resides in the permanent collection of the Museum of Modern Art (MoMA), New York, Wanders has created a visual surprise that is followed by a physical one. The chair is fabricated from carbon and epoxy-

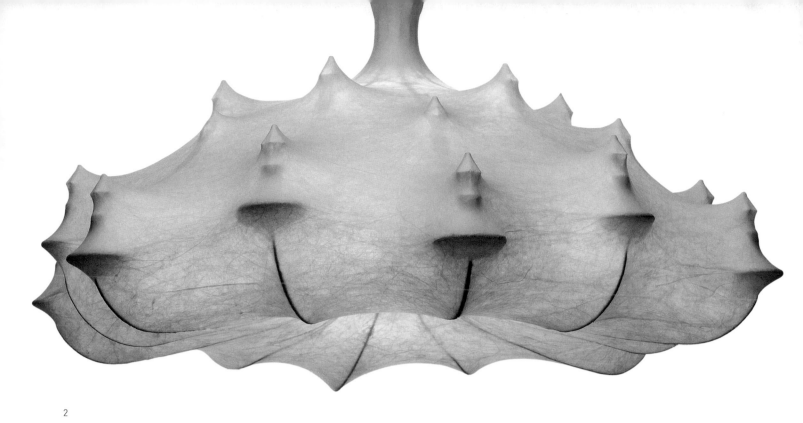

2

coated Aramid fibres and resembles a beautifully woven piece of macramé that has been frozen in space. The lacy structure looks like it has no business standing up on its own, but it does, and it is virtually weightless. The fibres used to create the chair are extremely light but also extremely strong, allowing Wanders to achieve his 'unexpected welcome'.

Another Wanders product that owes its enduring appeal to novel materials and processes is his 'Sponge Vase', created for Moooi in 2002. Upon first encountering the piece, one has the immediate sense that the vase is quite literally a sea sponge, bleached to achieve its pure white colour. This first impression is completely shattered once the vase is in hand; quite heavy and brutally hard, the piece is completely made of ceramic. Created through an innovative process by which an actual sponge is soaked in liquid ceramic and then fired, the vase is an exact replica of the original sponge that has been burned off in the kiln.

From these two pieces alone, one gets the impression that Wanders is a designer with a love of new materials and techniques. But that is not the whole story. 'Materials are not inspiring, they are dead,' he says. Wanders has been let down by the promise of new materials, most notably carbon fibre, and is wary of relying on them. Having come up with a beautiful design for a carbon chair a few years ago, and possessing significant interest in producing it, he was unable to source the material following a worldwide shortage of production. As if to counter this situation, Wanders praises a recent project with a much less advanced material: 'I love my private holiday-car made with Bisazza Mosaic, I guess in the (at least) 1,000 years of the history of mosaics, it is probably the first time it covered a car. Innovation is not always very smart, sometimes it can even be a bit silly. But it can touch the heart and make straight lips curl up a little. Perhaps that is a new, and ultimately a beautiful functionality for mosaic?'

Combining the spirit of that whim with a touch of the 'smart' is his Wave-TV for Holland Electro. 'My Wave-TV combines a microwave oven and a flatscreen television. We use a very special and innovative and secret material to stop the microwaves and

1 This mosaic car created for Bisazza shows how Marcel Wanders takes materials and processes from one discipline to another, and from one millennium to another.
2 Paying homage to Archille Castiglioni – who created his own series of 'cocoon' lamps in the 1960s – Wanders created his own lamp, featuring lamps within the lamp. In an interesting twist, the lamps protruding from the skin don't light up, but become silhouetted by the single light in the centre.
OPPOSITE A wonderful combination of artistry, engineering and materials, the Knotted Chair was destined to become a museum piece.
BELOW Wanders is always looking for an 'unexpected welcome' in his work, but one that doesn't get old over time. This vase, made from a real sea sponge that was soaked in ceramic liquid and fired to become rock hard, provides an enduring surprise to all who see it – and then touch it.

1

1 Perhaps the first to see furniture as truly capable of wearing 'clothes', Wanders sees the base upholstery of this sofa as its 'underwear', or the base from which to dress it up according to location, mood or taste. **BELOW** Combining two of the things that seem to occupy a sizeable portion of our lives – food and entertainment – in one package, this Wave-TV can cook your dinner and entertain you at the same time.

heat from the oven from affecting the screen, so we do not 'fry your favorite soapstars'. Integrating a DVD player as well, the Wave-TV promises to redefine 'TV dinners', and is a perfect example of Wanders' customer-focused philosophy.

'Designers are the advocates of the consumer: they have to fight for the quality of life of their public. If we help fulfill these needs for our customers we will contribute to their lives and be successful. The whole idea behind design is to create more value! Customization is the respect for the individual, the significance of variety, the connection to your clan, the security of perfection, to be part of a greater source.'

Though perhaps not as iconic as the 'Knotted Chair', or as striking as his 'Snotty Vases' (just what they sound like, rendered in ceramic), his new couch for Moooi is exuberant, serious, customer-focused, clever and surprising. The basic form of the object is covered in what Wanders calls 'underwear', and customers can choose from a wide range of slipcovers, skirts and cushions to create their personal look. With styles and finishes ranging from classic and clean (named 'Daddy' and 'Narcissus') to vivid and wild ('Deer' and 'Jester'), the possible combinations are infinite.

Slipcovers are not a new concept, but this system of tailored covers offer consumers a way to keep a single piece of furniture and easily update it over time. Despite changes in location, changes in taste or messy guests (or hosts), this could be the last couch you ever need. 'We want to make sofas as something fun. You have a great time, then after three, four, five years perhaps, you move houses and you want to change the slipcover. You can do it because we keep the same sofa in production. We will inform you every now and then about the new slipcovers because we have your email address, and we'll send you inspirational new slipcovers. For a third of the price of a new couch, you buy a new slipcover.'

As always, Wanders has the customer in mind, his eyes blinded, and his vision clear: 'I always begin with a dream and I always hope I can create the miracle without any material, sometimes miracles occur, most of the time I have to carry the weight of the material world, I do this with love and respect.'

2

A quick look at LOT-EK's mission statement reveals that the partners are not typical architects. In their own words, LOT-EK is an 'ongoing investigation into the artificial nature, or the unmappable outgrowth of familiar, unexplored, man-made and technological elements woven into the urban/suburban environment. LOT-EK is extracting from this artificial nature prefabricated objects, systems and technologies to be used as raw materials. LOT-EK is blurring the boundaries between art, architecture, entertainment and information.'

Ada Tolla and her partner, Giuseppe Lignano – two architects from Naples who have since moved to New York – have a very different vision of the built environment and its application in the next generation of buildings for the human race. To them, the 'building blocks' of architecture would mean everything: water tanks, shipping containers, airplane fuselages. LOT-EK remarked that 'we were fascinated with all these objects. We were fascinated also with the way that they come into play with everything else. So the modality, the ways in which they stack – they protrude – is very different from the typical way you actually think of them. There is something very genuine in the way that these things come into play – so for us it's looking at the objects themselves.'

LOT-EK constructs a dialogue between the histories of their materials and their functional and spatial transformations. Shipping containers, the epitome of transience, become objects of static residence while at the same time retaining their mobile sensibilities. Aircraft fuselages become both structural devices and a framework for conceptual transport. LOT-EK's work is not only an innovative use of materials, but it is also an investigation of the histories of materials within cultural systems, and the systems' consequential reactions to our own evolution. It is all about giving a 'new' life to industrial products that had already delivered on their original 'mission.'

'We work very much with three-dimensional objects that already exist and most of the time are already used, so most of the time they have a lot of history: and they take with them all their history,' Tolla and Lignano explain. 'Our work is about reusing these objects, cutting them, doing things to them, and then retro-fitting them. But we do

LOT-EK

MICHELE CANIATO

2 + ABOVE Giving new meaning to the words 'mobile home', this Mobile Dwelling Unit (MDU) by LOT-EK is constructed from a standard shipping container and has expandable compartments for all of the necessary components of a home. These compartments – for living, working or storage space – can be retracted back into the unit such that it can be transported to whatever new location is desired. The architects envisioned an enormous rack system that would house multiple MDUs in a community that would constantly evolve as people – and their homes – moved in and out.

1

2

1 + 2 Here are two more examples of LOT-EK's Container Home Kit (CHK). This modular system uses the worldwide surplus of shipping containers to create sustainable housing, exploiting their inherent structural properties to create affordable – and exciting – living quarters. **BELOW** A digital rendering of the 'harbour' housing multiple Mobile Dwelling Units. A crane would be used to raise and lower units as needed, and all services – water, power, etc – would run through the framework to supply the individual units.

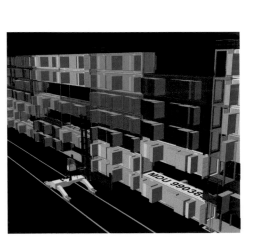

need a lot of materials to complement [them] and to make them do what we need to do. So the types of materials that we look for are materials that contrast. Our work is all based on contrast, you know. Like our name LOT-EK: we don't mean by that "low technology", we mean low-end technology, meaning the contrast between the two.'

This interest in fabricated materials has led to a dynamic practice that is internationally recognized. Winning competitions, and constructing architecture that reinvigorates our sense of space, LOT-EK uses industrial production artifacts as a natural resource from which to build upon. They recall that 'the observation of [these industrial objects] made us very interested in not being ashamed of them, as we generally are, and actually seeing [them] with a positive attitude – acknowledging this is who we are.' They explain that, 'recycling objects and systems is not just about recycling the material. It's recycling space that is contained by the thing, and all the intelligence that has gone behind the thing.'

Intelligence in the recycled resources they have used has led to striking developments, like their Container Home Kit (CHK). Utilizing the mobility and standardization principles of its material, the CHK takes recycled shipping containers and transforms them into modular elements that are sent to a location and assembled on site. 'It's based on the idea that it's a moveable home, not a shippable home,' said LOT-EK. This modular and moveable principle of the shipping container resonates throughout the work of LOT-EK, and is also apparent in projects like the exhibition space for the Bohen Foundation in New York. Inside the space, eight shipping containers ride along tracks embedded in the cement floor and can be moved, along with moveable gypsum walls suspended from the ceilings, to suit the varying exhibition or administrative purposes of the foundation. Each container houses a different functional aspect of the foundation, and many feature windows and other openings cut through the brightly painted sides of the boxes.

LOT-EK has recently taken a keen interest in the discarded aluminum fuselages of airplanes. For a proposed building at the University of Washington in Seattle – the home of the Boeing aircraft company – the pair planned to use the main portion of a Boeing 747 fuselage. They discovered that the fuselages of planes were often discarded once

3

4

the plane was stripped of its components. They explain that, 'the incredible thing about the fuselage is that it is the strongest structure, lightest structure, and most durable structure ever invented because of what it needs to do.' While a new fuselage could cost tens of millions of dollars, a salvaged fuselage costs only a few thousand – and is therefore a cost-effective solution.

LOT-EK explains that 'we learned that the people that deal with the airplanes call the fuselage the "beer can" because there's nothing they can do with it. They sell everything [else]. They strip down the airplanes, really like a whale. They take everything apart, sell it and make a lot of money; but the fuselage is impossible because it's a very, very strong construction.'

Connected conceptually to the shipping containers through the framework of transport, the fuselages also maintain their 'object memory' of speed and flight: the gleaming raw aluminum evokes motion and speed. This character is also evident in the LOT-EK proposal for a library in Guadalajara, Mexico, that would have used some 250 fuselages from Boeing 727s and Boeing 737s. Structurally strong, and aesthetically innovative, this plan capitalized on both the conceptual and technical advantages of the fuselage material. Acting as a metaphor for transport – much like the library – and resembling a neatly assembled set of scrolls, the fuselages are effective at every level.

LOT-EK is currently working on two projects in Beijing, incorporating their aesthetic and conceptual ideologies with the fast-paced building boom of the city. LOT-EK explains that 'in Beijing they're building a lot – buildings the size of Rockefeller Center. They are building mainly office space – offices and retail – which they didn't have, as the city was mainly residence and government buildings.' One of the buildings they intend to build will incorporate a number of shipping containers, 'but the shipping containers will be newly manufactured,' says LOT-EK.

The structural rhythm of this building – based on the regular dimensions of the shipping containers – is created by the random insertion of actual containers into the façade of the building. Functioning on the ground level as canopies for the retail space

3+4 These examples show a proposal for a student pavilion for the University of Washington, Seattle, created from a section of a Boeing 747. Inside of the section, everything is stripped away to reveal the intricate structure of the fuselage and a clear floor is installed to provide the occupants with the perception of greater space. The seating is reconfigurable to accommodate a variety of functions and activities.

1

2

1 Yet another LOT-EK project utilizing aircraft fuselages. In this proposal for a library in Guadalajara, Mexico, hundreds of 727/737 sections would form both the structure and the interior spaces of the library.

2 A rendering of the soon-to-be-realized Sanlitun North, a mixed-use development in Beijing, China, shows the architect's vision of a building that embodies the constant change being experienced in that country. Blue mesh surrounds most of the structure, referencing construction and diffusing light and sound to the apartments behind it. Parts of the structure pierce the mesh for shop fronts and office windows. **BELOW** At the other end of the development, Sanlitun North, the architects have created a retail complex using their favourite material – the shipping container. Here, they create a rhythm of shapes and spaces and form billboards and canopies for the various stores.

entrances, they also house display or other small functions of the interior. Plastered with logos and signage – the containers speak to their commercial and industrial origins. Thus, by the incorporation of newly fabricated containers into the structure, the commercial aspects of culture become an aesthetic in itself – recycling is no longer the focus, production is.

This approach to the sourcing of their containers is not the only new investigation for them. At the other end of the massive Beijing development, they are working on a concrete building that incorporates a new duct-like motif as a way of creating large-scale windows. The structure is built off of an existing concrete structure, and is wrapped with a woven steel mesh coated with blue epoxy that references the idea of a construction site and reduces passive solar gain, while also providing privacy to the apartments within. A building under constant visual construction, this project reflects a pervasive atmosphere that speaks to the rising cultural, commercial and industrial potential of China.

LOT-EK is also working on a large project in New Jersey for the largest metal recycler in America. Creating a dialogue directly with the function of the company, their plan is exclusively constructed of shipping containers. The building is three containers high, and elevated off of the ground to provide parking. Containers jutting out of the sides of the structure are influenced by the organization of the company itself. LOT-EK explains, '[the company] became the largest metal recycler in America by merging, merging, merging all these kind of mom and pop companies.' Recycling becomes both the topic of the architecture, and the topic of the company, establishing both a synergy and a contrast that is emblematic of LOT-EK.

After fifteen years of collaboration, Tolla and Lignano have developed an architectural sensibility that is unique in its approach to reusing industrial objects as materials. LOT-EK dreams, 'to discover more and more objects – more quality with objects – possibly big municipal water tanks, or big gas tanks.' Though the aqueducts and columns of our childhood might be as permanent in their ruins as we imagined them, it would seem that the structures that followed them might live to see another use in a new day.

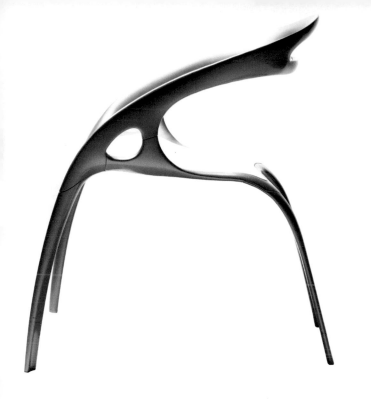

3

4

It's a typical day in Ross Lovegrove's studio. He flew back from Los Angeles this morning and is struggling to finish designing a furniture series before jetting off to China tomorrow. The latest version of the milled aluminum table he's working on – machined and polished this time – has just been delivered to the studio. Lovegrove beams at those around him, while casually proclaiming that the new table has, 'finally confirmed my belief that modern technologies really can create liquid sculptural forms.' Lovegrove was drawn to aluminum because of its malleability, its sheen and its low density, but wanted to find new methods of working with it. As a result, he decided to mill a block of solid aluminum to see if the milling process could yield the fluid form he had in mind. It has.

It's typical of Lovegrove to push the boundaries between form, built structures, materials and technology, and forge unexpected alliances between them. Lovegrove's work refutes the premise that nature, materials and the creative disciplines are separate entities. In fact, much of his output over the past twenty years has brokered significant connections between them. As Lovegrove builds bridges between the visual, the ideological, the superficial and the natural, his use of materials has consistently challenged preconceived notions of what design can mean.

Lovegrove's point of departure from conventional methods was his decision to treat design as a site of exploration. Many of his works have been created as expressions of concepts rather than as objects made with just functionality in mind. 'Henry Moore once said that form is actually very difficult to comprehend, and I agree with that,' Lovegrove said. 'To me, form is about capturing the essence of an object by giving it a sense of equilibrium. You craft it by using only essential materials, bringing the idea behind the design to life. An object is created through the techniques we call design, but an object can also be liberated in the process.'

His cerebral approach is refreshing in an industry characterized by style over content and image over substance. 'When I think about the designs that characterize our era I can tell they're based on constructing an object,' he suggests. 'My own view of design is that it's a reductive process rather than a method of assembling materials.'

ROSS LOVEGROVE
BRADLEY QUINN

3 Its magnesium-coated frame and contoured profile makes Lovegrove's iconic Go chair unique and comfortable. The Go is stackable, and is also made in a polycarbonate version for outdoor use.
4 The legs of this milled aluminum table appear to have been drawn out of its surface.
ABOVE Lovegrove's Biolove bicycle for Biomega pairs the strength of steel with the durability of bamboo to produce a flexible, yet strong, bicycle frame. The bicycle's natural materials make it a strikingly sustainable design.

When Lovegrove was studying industrial design at the Royal College of Art, synthetic materials ruled and the aerodynamic silhouettes of the early 1980s prevailed. Organic, uncontrolled shapes and free-flowing forms had been displaced by new rectilinear standards. 'No one related design to nature then or even talked about the dynamics of natural form,' Lovegrove recalled. 'People thought that using new materials made things look as modern as possible. I always believed that there was a big difference between what looked modern and what really was modern.' One day, Lovegrove stared out the classroom windows and his gaze fell upon the trees growing across the road in Kensington Gardens. 'I thought, "Yes! Trees and everything else in nature grow to the right height and proportions, reach a level of equilibrium and stop" while man only constrains things.' From that moment on, Lovegrove's fascination for natural processes became central to his work.

'Design is just an extension of what nature does,' explained Lovegrove, comparing how we adapt the built environment to suit human needs with how mankind evolved to accommodate significant changes in climate and diet. 'Pretty much all my work has evolutionary links, and my processes, choice of materials, applications of technology and aesthetics come out of that. Look at how the tiger's skull evolved to become lighter in weight so that they could capture prey more quickly. Nature designed holes in its skull to liberate mass, taking away the elements that were extraneous and inefficient.'

The tiger skull's evolution was mirrored in Lovegrove's 'Go' chair, designed for furniture designer Bernhardt in 2001. 'I was determined to make the chair as lightweight as possible,' Lovegrove recalled. 'I kept finding ways to eliminate extraneous parts of the frame, making the structure appear lighter in mass and weigh less.' Finding a material that could withstand Lovegrove's reductive technique and retain structural strength led him to magnesium. As a result, 'Go' weighs only 2.2 kgs (4.84 lbs) and surpasses the strength of most metal chairs. Once the design was complete, Lovegrove started thinking about how the chairs should be packed for

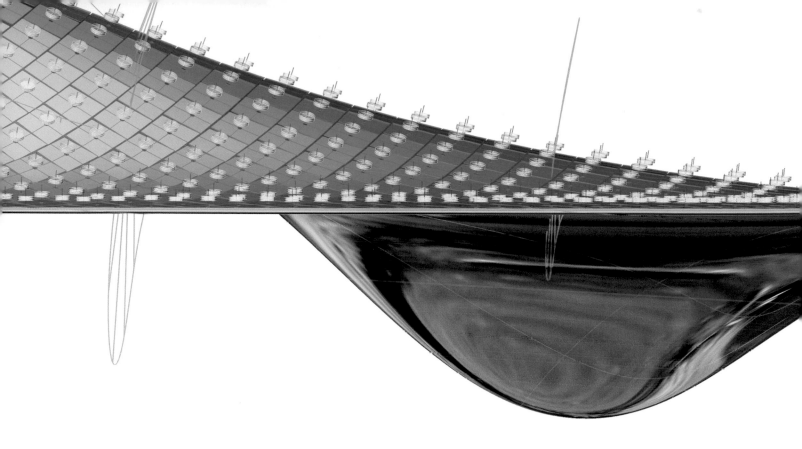

transport. 'When I realized that a skull is only polysaccharines and proteins it got me thinking about what else could be done with a material made from those substances. At one point, I considered creating a packing foam from them. What I had in mind was a water-soluble foam that you could dissolve completely after use rather than send it to the local landfill.'

For his stackable 'Supernatural' chair for the Italian furniture designer Moroso, Lovegrove combined injection-moulded glass fibre with reinforced polyamide to produce one model with a perforated back and another version with a solid back. Lovegrove pioneered a complex process using two layers of polyamide with glass fibres that would make the chair's structure lightweight, yet give it a seamless surface area. 'The Supernatural's structure also resulted from a process that mirrors evolution more than design,' Lovegrove said. 'The liquid, organic nature of its form combines the beauty of the human anatomy with one of the most advanced industrial applications of 21st-century polymers.'

More recently, Lovegrove also designed a line of furniture for New York's Morimoto restaurant, as part of an interior designed by Japanese architect Tadao Ando. Manufactured by the furniture design company Poltrona Frau, Lovegrove's dining chairs feature an exoskeleton-like exterior foiled by a soft, sinuous interior volume that references the orthogonal structures in Ando's design. 'I evolved the chairs from within a cube in order to interrelate them to Ando's architectonics. If you think about how water erodes soil and stones you'll see that the cube is eroded internally to make space for the body,' Lovegrove explained. 'In some respects, the chair represents a negative relief of the seated human form.' The restaurant also features tables and armchairs crafted in injected polyurethane foam, and the bar is flanked with acrylic and steel stools. 'Acrylic and injected polyurethane foam are not new materials by any means, but they have a certain integrity,' he said. 'I'm starting to work more with compression-moulded polycarbonate in other projects – now, that material is very much an expression of our times.'

BELOW Lovegrove believes that good design is evolutionary. One of his inspirations is the tiger's skull, which evolved to become lighter in weight so that the animal could capture prey more quickly. The body lightened the skull by 'designing' holes in it to eliminate material that nature considered to be extraneous.

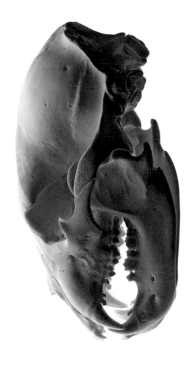

PATRICIA URQUIOLA

MICHELE CANIATO

While Patricia Urquiola seems always to be mentioned along with powerful forces of nature – words such as 'volcano' and 'hurricane' have been used to describe her in the past – this Spanish-born designer's work is more about the calm, rather than the storm. Born in Oviedo in Asturias, on the northern Atlantic coast of Spain, Urquiola was educated in Madrid and later in Milan, and now calls Italy home. Despite this progression toward the Mediterranean, and even her admission that she was professionally 'born' in Italy, Urquiola remains anchored to her Asturian heritage.

Her career took shape after her graduation from the Milan Polytechnic: Achille Castiglioni supervised her thesis, and she went on to assist him at the school after graduating. It was he who convinced the talented architecture graduate to concentrate on design. And it was from him that she took the notion of focusing on the relationship between the individual and the object: 'We should try to build an ethic that focuses on the pleasure of using a product rather than on a possession,' Urquiola explains.

Urquiola has worked for, and with, the likes of Castiglioni, Vico Magistretti and Piero Lissoni, but she also formed her own studio in recent years. Her work focuses on creating useful, comfortable and personal products – design for the individual, not for the sake of design – primarily in the area of home products. Her chairs, lounges, lamps and other furnishings are produced by a number of different firms but all reflect her practical and intimate ideals. In an oft-repeated quote, Urquiola famously said: 'If my product is very contemporary, very trendy, very communicative, but not useful, I will be an idiot.'

In keeping with that sense of comfort, her designs incorporate materials for a tactile and visual appeal that goes far beyond their clean and dramatic shapes. Particularly fond of textiles, she incorporates interesting juxtapositions in her choice of applications. 'I like to use an old material in a new contemporaneous way or a new technology for a classical execution.'

For her FLO chairs, Urquiola exploited design company Driade's ability to fabricate with straw. Taking a wholly contemporary shape, she stretched woven wicker seats

and backs in contrasting patterns reminiscent of kitschy cafés and bistros. 'I always look for the best use of a material depending on the challenges of each project. Getting help from the internal research done in my studio, or together with my clients, is essential.' This somewhat tongue-in-cheek line ('It was a nice amusement' said Urquiola) has been hugely popular with her clients and underscores her ability to connect to the end user.

In her installation at the 2005 International Furniture Fair (IMM) in Cologne (executed with Hella Jongerius), textiles and other tactile materials took centre stage. Assembling multiple floors of tables, seating and other home products in what looked like macramé scaffolding, Urquiola created a landscape of textures and patterns. In this 'Ideal House' installation, she constructed huge chandeliers from her 'Bague' lamp for Italian lighting designer, Foscarini.

A perfect expression of Urquiola's use of materials, these mesh lamps are made of a stainless steel mesh that is dipped in silicon, allowing them to have a tactile presence as well as a visual one. This silicon coating actually changes the visual appeal of the material by adding a level of jewel-like iridescence to the mesh, and also changes the tactility of the material: while dramatically aesthetic, the industrial steel mesh would be too rough to touch, whereas the silicon is smooth and pleasant to the hand.

Another one of her award-winning designs, her Antibodi chair for Moroso, brings this tactile aesthetic to new levels. 'The goal in the Antibodi collection was to reduce to the limit the relationship of structure-padding-cover: to it's essence,' Urquiola says. 'Transforming the cover into a structural element.' Using either leather or felt backed with a wool fabric, she has created an origami-like, reversible cover/pad that is laid upon a steel frame. The cover has two distinct sides and two distinct design personalities. On one side, the 'finished' side, the mood is tailored and geometric. On the other side, the edges of the sections are allowed to protrude creating 'petals' that also reveal a more frenetic two-toned effect. These petals provide cushioning without requiring

ABOVE Named 'Lazy' but looking anything but, this line of furniture for B+B Italia embodies Urquiola's emphasis on practical and useful design. The chrome metal frames can be covered in a wide range of materials, from mesh fabrics to textured leather.
OPPOSITE Urquiola's wicker FLO chair for Driade is both modern and traditional.
BELOW The Antibodi chair, created for Moroso, looks almost alive: its textile petals ready to burst into bloom at any moment.

ABOVE Blending earthy design with high-tech plastic, Urquiola's T-Table for Kartell features a pierced top and legs made from durable PMMA (Polymethyl methacrylate).
BELOW These 'Bague' lamps are created from steel mesh dipped in silicon, giving them a luminous appearance and a soft touch, as well as incredible strength.

foam or other conventional padding. 'Utilizing a decorative pattern as functional solution, we have transformed the modular pattern as a whole,' she says. 'Using the lightest connection system,' and the least materials necessary, 'we have still made it strong and resistant.'

Despite her interest in the personal and intimate relationship that exists between a product and an individual, Urquiola is committed to a very democratic idea of design. 'I'm interested in industrial production, rather than limited editions, that's one of my main challenges,' she says. In creating each of her individual pieces, Urquiola seeks out those materials that are well suited to reproducibility, and enjoys the challenge of working within the traditional parameters of the manufacturing process. Her 'Fjord chair', also for Moroso, was made feasible mainly because of an innovative process for moulding a new polyurethane foam to the steel frames.

To Urquiola, materials are 'absolutely fundamental' and her explorations of the variety of options are fuelled by her endless and enduring curiosity. She searches for materials used in industries outside the furniture business in order to find new ideas, and believes in bringing all available tools to the job at hand. 'We have to mix different types of knowledge,' Urquiola explains, 'we need to see the potential of virtual reality computer creations alongside the touch of reality and curiosity for materials.'

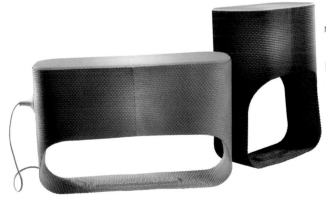

Known for this curiosity in materials and production techniques and for pushing both to their limits, Urquiola is quick to caution against newness and innovation as ends rather than means. 'I would never use a material just because it's new, or looks technological or futuristic.' Moreover, Urquiola is very aware of the development time for her products – measured in years – and of the hazards of appealing solely to contemporary trends and the latest craze. Rather, she continues to pursue her focus on those elements that create a real relationship between a product and an individual: an intimate and equal respect for the needs of the user and the technical requirements to make her vision into reality.

1

2

Zaha Hadid has become a powerful presence in architecture. A visionary who explores the boundaries of construction and the possibilities of space, she engineers new environments that map changes in society and new directions for industry. As Hadid revolutionizes the urban landscape, so too is she transforming how we think about materials and how we will use them in the future.

From the end of the 1990s onwards, Hadid's architecture rapidly evolved to meet the needs of individuals just like herself: people who are constantly short of time, and under pressure to produce. So when BMW commissioned Hadid to build the Central Building at their new premises in Leipzig, the pair-off seemed like a match made in heaven. 'I started thinking about the car as an architectural concept,' Hadid explained. 'How it lets us live, how it moves us through space, and what parts of the landscape it allows us to see.' Translating the car's momentum into built form eventually led Hadid to view Central Building as a vehicle for egress rather than a static object. As she explains: 'From the beginning, the building would plug into the two existing ones, so understanding how the flow would work between them was paramount. The entrance to Central Building channels energy and materials into one space and then throws them out into all the different facilities on the other side. When you're inside you have to move horizontally because it's a very long site that runs almost the whole length of the factory. All these lines of movement had an impact on the structure.'

Hadid's contribution to the Leipzig site acknowledged the architecture of the two existing buildings but remained true to her own distinctive style at the same time. 'A narrative in my work of the past five years or so has been about topography and landscape, drawing on the idea of terracing to make an interior landscape,' she said. 'I landed Central Building on the ground very lightly and rooted it in tropes such as transparency and porosity.' The building's design presents a radical new interpretation of open-plan office space, using transparency as a means of facilitating the experience of connectivity within it and beyond its walls. 'Over time, we made a thesis of the

ZAHA HADID

BRADLEY QUINN

1 BMW's Central Building is the epicentre of the entire factory complex, where all aspects of the BMW's production and administration gather together and branch out again. Hadid's design echoes this dynamic programme by charging the structure with a sense of movement.
2 Hadid transformed the assembly line into an arena that showcases the slick aesthetics of mechanical construction.
ADOVE The architecture blurs the boundaries between production areas, offices and amenities by overlapping them on different levels. Hadid intended to avoid the traditional divide between production and administration by interconnecting as many parts of the factory as she could.

1 Although most of the building's façade is transparent, special glazing techniques minimize the amount of sun it absorbs in summer and the heat that escapes in winter. 'Active shading' in the form of deciduous trees and shadows cast by other parts of the site modulate the amount of solar radiation that travels across the façade.

transparency–porosity trajectory, but ultimately it was about creating a special experience and a new dynamic. Anti-fortification, you could say. The building also creates different adjacencies that anyone could move through.'

Central Building is the epicentre of the whole factory complex where all the building's activities gather in and branch out again. The building connects the three main manufacturing areas and the administrative offices while also serving as the entrance to the site. All movements converging in the site are funnelled through what Hadid describes as a 'compression chamber' squeezed in between these main areas. Hadid's strategy applies not only to the cycles and routines of the workers but also to the production line, which traverses this central point and is made visible in the space. As a transition zone between manufacturing halls and public space, Central Building acts as what Hadid describes as a 'mediator' intended to enhance communication by providing the staff with an area that facilitates social exchanges and practical needs. 'My idea of different adjacencies reconciled the differences between the production facility and administrative offices, creating a space where blue-collar and white-collar employees come together. The space had to channel energy and materials into a single space and filter them out into other spaces,' she noted. As a result, administrative offices are located on both the ground and the first floors, as are areas designated for manual workers' use.

The building's primary organization is the scissor-section that interconnects the ground and first floors. Two sequences of terraced plates, which resemble giant staircases, step up from north to south and from south to north respectively. One of them rises from the public lobby, overlooking the forum below as it climbs up to the first floor. The other ascends from an area near the cafeteria at the south end, moving up to meet the first staircase as it continues to rise over the entrance. The two cascading sequences revolve around a long open void between them. At the bottom of this void lies the auditing area, while above it, the assembly of the cars is open to view as they move along their tracks through the various production units surrounding them.

2   3   4
   5   6   7

Hadid's choice of materials amplifies the feeling of transparency with the space. Self-compacting concrete created sleek vertical slopes, rising to meet a roof structure assembled with a series of H-steel beams. The underlying ground conditions on the site facilitated use of traditional spread footings. Given the concentration of loads born by isolated columns, reinforced concrete pad footings were necessary. When designing the superstructure, Hadid took both sustainability and ease of construction into account, selecting materials that are widely available and opted to use the same construction technology commonly used in Germany.

The main superstructure elements consist of pre-cast, pre-stressed cement slabs supported on pre-cast concrete beams and columns, while the ground floor slab comprises load-bearing fabric-reinforced concrete built directly on the ground. 'Soft spots' in the terrain were excavated and backfilled with graded material and compacted in layers to provide a firm substrate from which to support the slab construction. Movement joints were then placed within the structure in order to minimize the effects of any possible movement that could be caused by shrinkage, temperature variations, creep and settlement. These movement joints are located adjacent to column locations, serving to divide the structure into a number of individual sections.

The structure is framed on both sides of the joints by means of nibs or corbels provided off the walls and columns, complete with a slideable bearing to support the slabs or beams to one side. The concrete walls surrounding the stair and lift cores were reinforced in situ in order to act as main bracing elements that would ensure lateral stability loadings from the structures at each level of the building. In addition to providing lateral stability to the structure, these walls also provide vertical support to the first floor and the roof slabs. This lightweight roof consists of elongated hexagonal cells constructed from hollow section steelwork and was clad with a standing seam system of Kalzip (a standing seam roofing system) fitted with random roof light inserts.

2-7 Hadid describes the BMW project as 'heavyweight construction' due to the mass and strength of the materials chosen for the project. One of her goals was to create a low-energy building that would maximize thermal mass, solar shading and natural ventilation. The details highlighted here reveal how Hadid's design juxtaposes shaded areas with light-filled sections, contrasting opacity and transparency as the solid concrete structure is foiled by fragile glass.

1

DAVID ADJAYE

BRADLEY QUINN

David Adjaye is a romantic at heart. When describing the passions that drive him, he cites ideals such as beauty and classicism, or tropes like tragedy and decay. Adjaye believes in the transcendence of architecture, and the need to break away from classical notions of form to achieve it. 'Naturally I believe that architecture has to be able to set up heroic things,' Adjaye explained, 'but ultimately I think architecture almost always fails to do so. When I see the soulless glass towers and vacuous aluminum structures that attempted to be iconic but didn't succeed, I think they represent a kind of fantastic tragedy. I think of a hero who has killed himself because of unrequited love.'

Fortunately, Adjaye is much less fatalistic when it comes to his own projects. As the first years of the 21st century unfolded, his work seemed to enter a new phase. By his mid-thirties, Adjaye, whose parents come from Ghana, was already one of Britain's most prolific young architects. Best known for the private houses and slick interiors he'd designed, he got the chance to enact his ideas on a larger scale when he was commissioned to design five public buildings over a three-year period. Some, like the Stephen Lawrence Centre and the Whitechapel Idea Store in London, came with a pre-existing media profile that escalated when Adjaye's design received critical acclaim. Others, such as the group of rehearsal and performance buildings known as the Bernie Grant Centre for Performing Arts, also in London, are said to have introduced new ideas about urban design. Perhaps most iconic to date is the Nobel Peace Centre in Oslo and the Museum of Contemporary Art in Denver. The Nobel building is intended to be the permanent museum of the Nobel Peace Prize and imbibes, architecturally, the process of making peace in the world. The Museum of Contemporary Art in Denver is a 7620-square-metre (25,000 ft^2) space in the city's urban centre that creates a sharp contrast to Daniel Libeskind's much-publicized addition to the Denver Art Museum.

Adjaye's romantic principles slightly conflict with the modernist contexts that he finds himself working in. 'I make a serious effort to try to deliver something that has

2

meaning,' he explains 'But if I try to live up to my own ideals I will never succeed, so I figure there's something very beautiful and heroic here. There's a kind of failure but also a kind of fantastic heroism.'

Adjaye's work is characterized by his own brand of heroism, and often punctuated with poetic reflections and subtle symbolism. Take the Nobel project, for instance. Entrance to the museum is gained through a freestanding entrance portal that is essentially a perforated rectangular box cast in aluminum. Its floor is steep and curvaceous, leading visitors to gauge that the path to peace may be difficult to negotiate. The perforations appear in random clusters, as if the building had been exposed to gunfire. But the holes are far from random; they form a map of the world, whose coordinates identify centres of conflict. Just inside the museum, visitors pass through another version of the idea, where the holes, if you listen carefully, whisper about the struggle for peace in a chaotic and volatile world.

Today, Adjaye doesn't really want to talk about romanticism, and he's even more reluctant to talk about specific projects. But when it comes to his use of intense colours, shimmering textures and spectacular light effects, he has a lot to say: 'It's not so much the materials themselves' he suggests, 'its our ability to perceive them in different ways. What may look like stone to you could actually represent sand or earth, and surfaces that look like aluminum may well be glass. Materials are about creating transformations. Some transformations take place in the built structure, some occur in the mind of the onlooker. I don't just look at materials in terms of what they can do. I look at the effect that a material can create.'

Shifting perceptions appear to be the key to much of Adjaye's output. He avoids making a house look like a house, aiming instead to design buildings that make an individual statement based on how they are experienced rather than by what they are supposed to be. 'Architecture is obsessed with typologies,' Adjaye believes. 'For architects, materials are a way of working through a process and a means of colonizing space, just like the way scientists use formulas to do it and writers use words.

1 Adjaye was not permitted to make major changes to this listed landmark, originally built as Oslo's main railway hub. In order to amplify the building's new programme, he took advantage of the urban space outside it and built a pavilion in the path of approaching visitors. The freestanding pavilion echoes the cutting-edge design of the modern interior within the main building.
2 The pavilion is a rectangular sleeve of sandblasted aluminum, with a sloping floor and curved ceiling. The structure remains open along its two longer sides, and a walk through evokes the experience of traversing a small covered footbridge. Ironically, the pavilion, which is a monument to peace, is made in aluminum panels that had previously been purchased for a Greek warship, but never used.

1

An example from my own work would be the Idea Store in Whitechapel. I started off by checking out the physical and social quality of life in the area, how one could transform and re-picture it. As I scanned the neighbourhood for references, the street markets emerged as a common theme. They have plastic canopies in a range of bright colours. Thinking about a transformed version of the market stall led me on to glasses tinted in the same colours as the plastics. So you see, I didn't go to a trade fair and select materials, I went to the site and decided what types of references I'd use. These references were reflected in the recycled timber, plywood laminates, tinted glass and rubber I chose later.'

Adjaye's starting point is rarely materials or typography; his practice evolves through pursuing his ideas. 'When I studied, theory was the big thing, not materials. I was fascinated by the materials and processes used in industrial design at the time, but I was hanging out with artists more than I was designers. Just like the art students were carving out their own styles, I was looking for my own niche within architecture. My way of working starts with understanding what the project is about and what it has the potential to be. Then the ideas about materials become aligned with the project. Those ideas and inspirations can come from anywhere, because I often think about what's going on in other areas of design.'

Famously stepping into the world of fashion design, Adjaye co-designed a dress with British fashion label Boudicca for a *Vogue* feature. Realizing that Boudicca envisioned a starburst shape that would project outwards from the body, Adjaye designed a stationary structure that used rays to preserve the modesty of the wearer. The entire structure was built from wooden poles, transformed into a structure that provided some of the functions a garment would. 'That project relied on linearity and recycled timber as a means of configuring a fresh form. The material had to support the weight of the model and at the same time mimic the rays of a starburst. Wood served those purposes perfectly, but the intention was not just about performance, it was about creating an effect.'

2

As an architect who works mostly in urban centres, Adjaye is forced to work with shifting parameters as planning regulations and local requirements impact on the project. 'By the time the Bernie Grant Centre was built, it had had three evolutions, which meant that the roles that the materials played changed considerably. In the end I realized that we had actually created an anthropology of materials, because the roles, values and significance of the materials we were working with had evolved along with the project.'

But as his work continues to premise experience as much as function, Adjaye gives materials a uniquely sensorial role within architecture. 'Our relationship to materials relies on a wide range of cultural factors that we don't always understand,' Adjaye explains. 'What we do know is that the human needs to produce inhabited spaces, and that it will always require materials to do it. Not everyone in architecture values materials for their sensuous qualities, because for many architects they only play a functional role. But whatever view you take there is always one thing that holds true: if you want to make forms that are beautiful, materials hold the key to creating them.'

2 Adjaye's design for the Museum of Contemporary Art in Denver, Colorado, is characterized by a translucent façade that breaks down the structure's mass. By day, the passing light breaks down the barrier between interior and exterior spaces, while, at night, it becomes a luminous landmark.

1   2   3
          4   5

TOYO ITO

BRADLEY QUINN

With their iconic silhouettes, spatial extremes, technological interfaces and interactive surfaces, the structures created by Toyo Ito are some of the most dynamic expressions of architecture today. Ito's designs often defy typical architectural terminology as they evoke descriptions of fluid spaces, seamless constitutions and cloudy translucence; terms that seem to dematerialize architecture rather than validate it. Many of his buildings are characterized by sculptural, sensual contours sculpted in poured concrete, whose cloudy exteriors give way to lustrous glass surfaces. Others boldly encircle a skeletal core with a translucent shield, suggesting an ambivalent border condition rather than a fixed façade. But irrespective of their hi-tech expressions and their vibrant optimism, each of Ito's designs still captures the understated elegance of the Japanese tradition.

Along with light, transparency and nature, transcendence and poetry have long been important inspirations for Japanese architects. Although these factors remain central to Ito's work, he is one of the few pioneering a fresh vision of what this legacy can mean. Ito does not describe his inspirations in terms of physical elements like materials, or even ephemeral constructs such as ideas, but identifies semantics as the basis of his approach. 'Even though I have thoughts about what I would like to design, the starting point for each project begins with a word. You utter one word, then another. After three or four words you can identify a structure of some kind, be it grammar, syntax, or something else. The words take form in empty space, and that space gradually fills with ideas. Eventually, much further down the road, they take form as materials. Materials, in turn, come together to create the built structure.' Ito believes that good architecture is spoken into being, just as much as it is constructed through materials.

Ito has never intended to align architecture with what he described as, 'Japan's increasingly electronic, image-oriented culture,' but seeks to use constructed forms to melt our physical and virtual existences. 'My work lies between two worlds,' Ito said. 'I believe that every structure has a virtual equivalent and I reflect that in my

6

7

8

architecture. I strive to create equilibrium between the virtual world and the real one. Just as a building has elements of transparency and opacity, individuals have a public life and a private one. These tensions can be resolved by architecture, because it can soothe the pressures of modern life.'

One of Ito's signature projects is the monolithic Tod's building that opened in Tokyo in 2004, characterized by its large-scale pattern of overlapping tree branches. Ito set out to create an absolute surface by eliminating the need for frames or rims between the glass and the concrete. 'Traditionally, a building's structure and surface are dual elements, but in this one I melted them into one and unified them. I achieved that by using minimalist tactics and respecting the purism of materials. Because I could combine the concrete and glass in the right way, I was able to create synergy that gives them more power than if they had remained separate.'

Looking at some of Ito's other visionary edifices such as the Tower of the Wind, the Sendai Mediatheque, the Serpentine Pavilion, the Kagamigahara Crematorium and the new Mikimoto building, few architects would guess that Ito considers himself to have a low-tech approach. 'I use computer technology and find inspiration in the forms it can create, like wave shapes, for example,' he says. 'But I use easily accessible industrial materials to build them. Kagamigahara's roof is actually constructed from wood and concrete, and the Serpentine Pavilion was made from wood, glass and particleboard.'

When they collaborated on the Serpentine Pavilion in London, Cecil Balmond, the acclaimed structural engineer and architectural innovator, introduced Ito to new ways of thinking about geometry and form. 'Neither geometry nor geometric shapes are pure forms. The points are never fixed, so cubes are flexible, circles can expand and contract, and a grid can be rotated by algorithms. The temporary floor I built at the New National Gallery in Berlin is a 120 x 120 grid rotated into a wave form and covered with wood. That floor changes the impression of the entire space, and it was achieved with just wood and a layer of paint.'

1–5 The Kagamigahara Crematorium is covered by an organic, undulating roof that covers a sleek linear interior. The roof's profile mirrors the hills in the surrounding countryside, yet it's white concrete surface differentiates it from natural landscape.
6 When Ito was commissioned to design Mikimoto's flagship shop, his work contributed to the trend of pairing renowned architects with luxury brands. The pink building that resulted features irregularly shaped windows spontaneously interspersed throughout the structure.
7 + 8 Ito merged surface ornamentation with structural integrity as he perforated the façade with unusual shapes. When critics compared the structure to a piece of cheese, Ito pointed out that the holes in cheese are actually small compartments. 'It's the opposite in this building,' Ito explained. 'The holes go all the way through, opening up in a single space.'

1

3

PAOLA LENTI

MICHELE CANIATO

How does one go from designing for two dimensions to designing for three? For Paola Lenti, the answer lies in the materials. Formerly a graphic designer, Lenti created her eponymous company in 1994, and it is now one of Italy's leading producers of high-end textiles and home furnishings.

As Lenti puts it herself, 'I have always dedicated time and attention to materials, even when I was a graphic designer. Working with paper, for example, I always preferred structured papers to plain, coated paper. I always liked more the three-dimensional side of my practice, such as display or innovative and original packaging design. Actually, the transition from the image to the object was done well before, and the transition from a two-dimensional to a physical dimension represents the natural evolution of my work.'

That evolution – from concept to final product – begins with research on materials. Lenti seeks out materials that will satisfy what she perceives as a need in the market, and identifies those specific materials that embody the necessary characteristics such as solidity, aesthetics and functionality. Once a material or group of materials has been identified, then a fabric is created and the three-dimensional object follows. According to Lenti, 'it is the subsequent phase to the creation of the fabric. The form is the natural consequence of the material.'

Although she pushes the limits of a wide variety of modern-day contemporary materials, Lenti is perhaps best known for her sleek, elegant shapes created in wool felt that take a material common to nomadic tribal chiefs from the 5th century and transform it into designs of great beauty and versatility that are never more than they absolutely need to be.

In many respects, her current work speaks volumes about her past experiences and work. 'It is natural that past experiences influence my present activity,' Lenti says. 'I think this is more than natural: what a person is today is the result and the evolution of the past personal experience. I agree anyway, my fabrics have a strong graphic component, which derives from my search for the essential; I always try to get to the

3

4

very core of the material, leaving behind redundancies and concentrating on the structure more than on the decoration.'

Today, however, Lenti remains squarely focused on the future. '[My] brand is distinctive for the innovative materials, the research of which is the starting point of each collection creation. With an innovative material, processed in different ways, we then produce fabrics, rugs, or furniture, to offer the possibility to create a coordinated environment.'

Her deceptively simple designs are the result of both experimentation and functionality. Her Mat Rugs and Twist Seating Units are made from Rope, a textile created from just that – rope. High-tenacity rope, made from a stranded nylon core with a rubber and nylon protective sheath, is woven to produce a textile that is non-toxic, anti-bacterial, resistant to dirt and easy to wash. This makes the furniture perfectly suited for modern interiors with fluid indoor/outdoor spaces, including environments that come into contact with water. The material has a subtle chromatic effect that gives her undulating forms richness and complexity.

Prior to her development of Rope, outdoor rugs were mostly produced using natural fibres, and this meant that they had limited resistance to environmental factors. Outdoor furniture, by extension, generally consisted of a steel, wood or plastic structure covered with cushions, or – more rarely – with other materials that could not be considered real fabric, predominantly vinyl strapping.

The introduction of Rope, even though a synthetic material, has allowed for the weave of a real fabric to upholster outdoor furniture much like normal home sofas or armchairs. What's more, Rope allows for the production of long-lasting, easy-to-clean rugs that are resistant to possible damage from ultra-violet rays, chlorine or salt water, but so unique that they are often used in contemporary interior design. 'Basically Rope has introduced the textural richness and warmth into exterior design and has filled a void satisfying the need for a valid alternative to the traditional outdoor furniture,' explains Lenti.

1 Creating a variety of textiles for a wide range of applications, Lenti's work begins with the appropriate materials. These Bliss textiles are created for interior applications.
2 For outdoor applications, Lenti has created specific textiles that are resistant to UV radiation, chlorine, salt and water. When stretched over these frames, the material is both strong and supportive.
3 Lenti uses both colour and texture to create bold and exciting textiles that can be used indoors and our, such as this Grass rug.
4 Unlike traditional outdoor furniture, these lounges made using Lenti's textiles offer the comfort and appearance of upholstered indoor furniture. Designed by Francesca Rota, the pieces give the textiles a structural quality by wrapping them around aluminum extrusions.

1

2

The combination of modern and traditional, and of natural and human-made, pervade Lenti's work and the work featured in her collections. One of her more recent materials, Aquatech, has the appearance of natural straw, both in its form and in the colours that were chosen for it. Unlike straw, however, Aquatech is made from a polyamide – the family of polymers that includes nylon and Aramids, the material which is used to make bulletproof vests. Extremely durable, weather-resistant, and washable, much like the Rope product, Aquatech also dries very quickly. Lenti uses this material to produce fabrics for furniture and rugs: 'With Aquatech, we produce the Twiga fabric, the braids that upholster the pieces of the Frame Collection,' Lenti says, 'and the rugs Cocos and Sahara. [These are] very similar to straw mats but almost indestructible.'

Lenti designs herself, but also invites other renowned designers, such as the Italian deisgner Francesco Rota, to create pieces for the collections. An interpretation of colours and shapes, refined design solutions and a distinctive timeless style are the core elements of Paola Lenti's corporate philosophy. 'I think that the best example [of a successful collaboration] is the Frame Collection, designed by Francesco Rota. It is a seating collection for indoor and outdoor use, where the structure has been conceived to give three-dimensionality to the upholstery fabric. Each piece of furniture is composed of several extruded aluminum profiles, which are upholstered one by one and then assembled to create platforms, lounge chairs, and side tables. This thin, essential structure has really been designed to fill, give body and support the upholstery fabric.'

'Generally, the approach starts from the material that I propose to the designer, asking them to design something that would fit that particular material. From there, the cooperation starts. I think that fresh ideas and teamwork produce the best result. I'd like to point out that all our pieces are the result of an intense teamwork, which each member actively contributes to, coordinated and supervised by myself. The designer proposes the project based on a determined material, we start producing

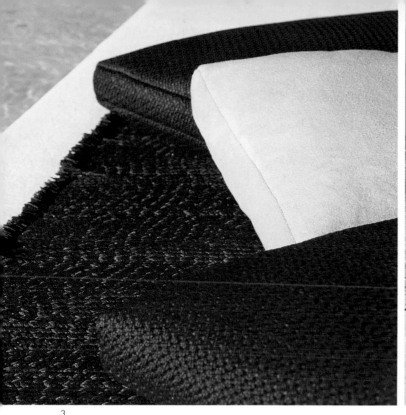

3

4

the prototype and also together with the other team members we introduce the modifications necessary to improve the product, until we, and the designer, reach full satisfaction. I'd like to make clear that the final product must be 100 per cent coherent with our brand; it is not enough to be aesthetically nice, but it also must guarantee functionality and, as I mentioned before, it must respect the correct relation object/human being.'

Lenti's work has evolved from felt to durable but synthetic materials, and she continues to consider where her designs and materials will take her. 'We certainly will have to dedicate more attention to the sustainability of the adopted materials and this might somehow limit the possible choices. On the other end I think that above all the base research activity, more than the applied one, should massively invest in this direction: to find new ecologically friendly material with high performances that, when processed differently, can be used in several sectors. Certainly the increased sensibility towards this matter has already influenced our sector and will do so more and more in the future. At present, I think that this problem is more pressing for the consumer goods sector. We produce objects aimed to last over time and I'd like to think that who ever buys a Paola Lenti product will keep it for many, many years to come.'

1 Rope, as one of Lenti's textiles is named, is created from its namesake – a rope comprised of a nylon core and a rubber and nylon sheath. Beautiful and durable, it will stand up to the toughest conditions.
2 Rope is also used in Lenti's outdoor Sand chair, in her Sahara rugs (3) and in this outdoor Frame lounger (4).

1   2   3

ISAAC MIZRAHI

MICHELE CANIATO

When Isaac Mizrahi speaks about music, you can tell he is hearing it in his head. When he speaks about colour, he uses his entire being in order to convey his vision of the perfect pink in his mind. Yet he is equally passionate about baseball, television and mayonnaise.

Mizrahi is perhaps best known for being himself: campy, brazen, open, everywhere. He sings, he dances, he plays the piano, he hosts eponymous television shows; but he is also a fashion designer who has followed in the footsteps of Pierre Cardin, Calvin Klein and Ralph Lauren by extending his talents to the realm of home furnishings and turning his creative hand to homeware.

When designing, Mizrahi surveys a wide array of materials, and spends time imagining the things that could be made from particular textiles and polymer films. But materials are never his first inspiration. 'I usually start with an idea. But materials and ideas are so closely interlinked that you can hardly think a thought without needing some kind of reference or visual picture. As well as designing fashion and homeware, I also design for the theatre, and I work in different mediums.' Those media show up in fashion, linens, furniture, appliances and footwear.

Inspiration – in the forms of popular culture such as books, movies and television – all serve to provide Mizrahi with ideas. 'Some movies I've seen a million times: when I see them in revival, I see them rendered smaller on television and it's always something different. It's always a different kind of inspiration that fills you. It's like the dresses, the clothes, the hair – it all becomes very precious and jewel-like. They have a visual texture.'

Mizrahi also seems adept at pulling material inspiration from nowhere. On a cab ride home one night, he saw a billboard for a recycling programme called 'We Can' and it led him on an interesting adventure that took aluminum cans – and his idea – around the world, and put a signature Mizrahi-twist on the idea of sustainability. 'We collected Coke cans, 7-Up cans and Budweiser cans – for however long we collected – with the homeless people from the programme: we split them open, washed them, and sent them to Paris, where they were cut into paiettes. And then we sent the paiettes to India to be sewn onto dresses just like sequins. Of course the dresses were mostly

4

5

aluminum, which meant that they were practically weightless. That was so exciting to me because in fashion, most things weigh certain amounts, and I'm always thinking, "Oh, that's too heavy, too heavy – lighter, lighter, lighter, lighter." So without expecting it, I discovered that the material had produced the lightweight dress I wanted.'

Not content with collecting rubbish, Mizrahi calls on a wide range of resources to realize his visions. Paradoxically, his material options increase when designing a $29.99 piece for the US retail chain Target versus a $2,999 piece for his own couture line. 'A lot of times,' Mizrahi explains, 'there are things I can't do in couture because I don't have the resources; and there are a lot of things I can design for Target that I wish I could do for my couture line, but I just can't. It's even beyond democracy. Because you're making something in large quantities, because you're buying so many yards of material, you can afford to use materials that you can't have when you're only making three pieces. If you have to make a mould for a plastic part, you know that's very, very costly; so usually you have to make jillions of them to make it cost effective.'

Whether made as a single piece or in multiples of jillions, Mizrahi is always trying to create something that reaches the next 'level of perfection'. As he tells the story, 'there was a great dress in the last collection that was very material-centric, though it was all about the colour. I kept referring to it as "the pink dress". And it's got like pink and pink and pink and pink: I did get it down to about six or seven colours. I kept trying to add more, or take away colours, but it needed to be those exact colours in those exact materials.'

Mizrahi believes that as with any material, the surface treatment is integral to the way the colour is perceived. 'Every single material, you compare and you correct: if it's a fabric that's dyed, you get the fabric swatch and compare it. The thing is that everything takes on, because every matter has more or less pores, and it takes the light in different ways.

You never know what will materialize out of Mizrahi's mind, but he will never be short of ideas nor the energy to see them through. And with a vast repertoire that includes the natural, the man-made and the reclaimed, his passion for new materials will most likely surface when we least expect it.

1 + 5 Made from cans collected with the help of a not-for-profit recycling programme, this dress is made up of thousands of small discs stitched over its surface. The aluminum creates a striking visual effect as well as a lightweight garment. **2–4 + OPPOSITE** For his 2005 line at Target, Mizrahi had the freedom to specify a wide range of materials thanks to the enormous volume that had to be ordered in advance. Textured leather for handbags and shoes, tortoise-shell plastics for sunglasses and tear-resistant textiles for the rolling bag are all available in products that cost the consumer between US $20 and $70.

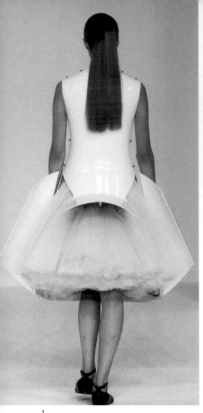

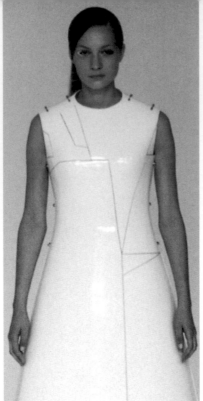

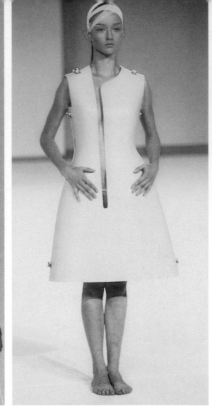

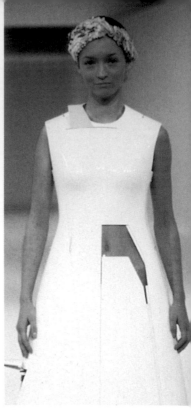

1

2

3

4

HUSSEIN CHALAYAN

BRADLEY QUINN

Hussein Chalayan has strong views about materials, just as he has strong feelings about architecture, technology, the body and design. A self-styled 'ideas person' who forges unexpected alliances between clothing, machinery, built structures and technology, Chalayan is a thinker who refutes the premise that fashion and material intelligence should be separate entities. In fact, much of his output throughout his career has brokered significant connections between them. As Chalayan builds bridges between the visual, the ideological and the tangible, his designs reveal the complex messages that clothing can convey.

Conceptual designers rarely get their moment in the fashion limelight. The industry is characterized by style over content and image over substance, and the vast stranglehold of contemporary fashion caters to mainstream trends and image-making ideals. Chalayan's forward-thinking approach is seldom about the shock of the new, and his vision leads him to explore new materials that most conventional designers would deem to be incompatible with fashion design. 'My approach to materials is probably different to many designers,' he explains. 'They generally serve one of two purposes. They either mirror the shape of the body and amplify its movements, or have the capacity to create an alternative meaning for the body. Materials can imbue fashion with whole new functions, basically creating a character or telling a story.'

Chalayan famously coated a cotton dress with iron filings and buried it in the ground. He later exhumed the dress to see what pattern the process would create, and how the process of burial, exhumation and resurrection could be reflected in the garment. 'All materials have their own persona. I use them as mediums of communication. In many cases, time-honoured materials speak of luxury and comfort, which I may decide to challenge or refute.' In the hands of a conventional designer, 'time-honoured materials' may refer to silk, linen or wool, but to Chalayan, the term also applies to wood, metal, plastic substrates and inflatable fabrics. He has cast hard resins to create moulded dresses, carved wood into corseted silhouettes, crafted accordion-like skirts in wood and used plastic fabrics to support technologically advanced machine-powered dresses.

5

6

7

8

'The messages that new technology and futuristic materials transmit are different to conventional ones,' Chalayan suggests. 'Those that are inorganic and chemically inert have properties that are the direct opposite of the body, so it is fascinating to combine an inert material with living, breathing flesh.' Although much of Chalayan's work connects to a techno-fashion aesthetic, many of his ideas are executed in traditional fabrics. 'I don't always feel it's necessary to process and manipulate materials or try new ones. I remain true to wearable materials. Luxurious fabrics that feel good and perform well can be just as interesting as new materials if you use them in an innovative way.'

Chalayan's drive to innovate has enabled him to find inspiration in a range of unexpected forms and technologies. His fascination with aerodynamic surfaces inspired his synthetic resin Dwell Neck and Aeroplane dresses, which introduced a range of streamlined forms and hard materials that were atypical of fashion. The moulded seams of the Dwell Neck dress were fastened with hardware clasps, and the Aeroplane dress featured sliding panels that operated electronically. 'I realized that the hard shell of the Dwell Neck dress and metal fastenings were new to fashion, but introducing those materials to fashion was not my intention. As it wasn't possible to achieve that aerodynamic shape in conventional fabric, I was forced to find other materials to work with.'

Chalayan cited the Dwell Neck dress as being a typical example of how he encounters new materials in his work. 'The idea usually comes first and then I start looking for materials. The search doesn't always result in being able to use something that would be right for the project. Often the most visionary materials out there aren't ready to be sold commercially or available in a form that can be handled easily, which means you have to look for something more conventional to use.'

Chalayan has also pioneered garments featuring wireless technology, electrical circuitry and automated commands. His Remote Control dress was a high-tech triumph that married fashion to technology, and technology to the body, establishing a dialogue between the body and the environment. 'The dress expressed the body's relationship to a lot of invisible and intangible things – gravity, weather, flight, radio waves, speed, etc.'

1 + 2 Seen from the front and the back, Chalayan's Aeroplane dress is made from glass fibres. A network of panels encased in the dress create a streamlined geometric motif across its surface. Levers in the lower section of the dress open the panels to reveal a tulle crinoline underneath.
3 The Dwell Neck dress was designed by means of the composite technology used to design aircraft, and incorporates principles of aerodynamics into its form and aesthetic. The dress encases the torso in a resin cast, creating a rigid container for the human form
4 The Remote Control dress is a high-tech garment that establishes a dialogue between the wearer and technology. The dress is crafted from glass fibre and resin moulded into smoothly contoured panels.
5 Chalayan often encases the human body in hard materials, almost as if he were constructing an exoskeleton around it.
6 This model wears a wooden corset fastened together by clasps. Chalayan is one of few designers who has successfully appropriated wood as a fashion material.
7 + 8 Chalayan also likes to work in delicate fabrics and fragile materials. The bubbles on model's dress in image 7 make it likely to disintegrate long before it goes out of fashion.
OPPOSITE Chalayan made fashion history with the animatronic designs he premiered in his spring/summer 2007 collection.

 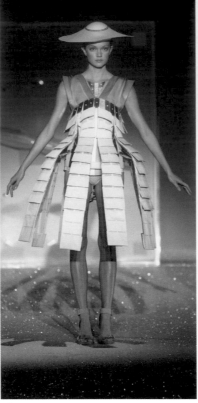 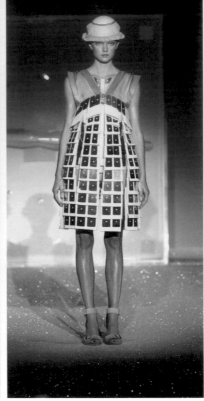 

1   2   3   4

1–3 Chalayan designed dresses powered by machine-driven levers that open and close to reconfigure the shape and silhouette of the garment. Microchips embedded in their fabric panels enable them to move according to programmed sequences. Swarovski crystals embroidered on the surfaces may one day have the capacity to transform solar energy into a power source.
4 The collection featured pieces from cutting-edge jewelry designer Florian, which Chalayan paired with both low- and high-tech garments.

The dress was designed by means of the composite technology used by aircraft engineers, mirroring the systems that enable remote control airplanes to fly. It was made from glass fibre and resin, moulded into two smooth, glossy, pink-coloured front and back panels. Each panel was encased within grooves two millimetres in width that run throughout the length of the dress. These seams create the only textural differences in the dress, revealing interior panels made in translucent white plastic, accentuated by lighting concealed within the solar plexus panel and the left side elevating panel.

The Remote Control dress was not designed specifically to explore the relationship of technology to the body, but to examine how the form of the garment could evolve around the body in a spatial relationship to its environment. 'The dress can also be transformed invisibly by the environment,' explains Chalayan. 'The idea was a technological force between the environment and the person.' The Remote Control dress demonstrates that garments are capable of interaction with other humans and computerized systems distant in time and space.

The structural architecture of the Remote Control dress echoes the attributes of a fashioned rather than an organic body. The structure of the dress forms an exoskeleton around the body, incorporating elements of body consciousness; its contours mimic the curves of the fashioned female body and echo the silhouette of the corset and the crinoline. This gives the dress a defined hourglass shape that incorporates principles of corsetry in its design, emphasizing a conventionally feminine shape, while creating a solid structure that simultaneously masks any undesirable body proportions.

Some of Chalayan's most groundbreaking uses of materials and processes were presented in his spring/summer 2007 collection: dresses powered by machine-driven levers opened and closed to reconfigure the shape and silhouette of the garment, hemlines rose autonomously, a bustier opened of its own accord and a jacket unfastened itself and pulled away from the model's torso. The mechanical dresses were handmade and fitted with electronic machinery and their surfaces embroidered with thousands of Swarovski crystals, giving them the dual appeal of opulent elegance

5   6   7   8

and high-tech savviness. Although the garments were powered by batteries, research into the capacity crystals have for harnessing solar power indicates that they may one day provide a viable power source for techno fashions.

Chalayan's use of shape-shifting fabrics enabled his garments to morph into new designs and radically change shape. Shape-memory fabrics, such as those woven from fibres of the shape-memory alloy Nitinol and interspersed with nylon, make these innovations possible. Nitinol is highly elastic, changes shape when temperatures rise and fall, and then returns to its original shape when temperatures stabilize. It is this property that enables the fabric to shorten and lengthen, which is how the dress will perform when temperatures fluctuate. Nitinol, an acronym for Nickel Titanium Naval Ordinance Laboratory, is a family of intermetallic materials that contain a mixture of nickel and titanium. Because the fabric's weave has five nylon fibres to every Nitinol fibre, the clothing made from it will be high performance, washable and comfortable.

Chalayan was one of the first big-name designers to inject this kind of technology into fashion, and his success seems to anticipate a day when the integration of technology and garment design will be seamless and efficient. This moment marked a radical departure from a world where distinctions between body and technology, body and dress, natural and artificial, once seemed clear and illustrates how social and cultural discourses construct our bodies in a way that makes us as analogous to a machine as possible. The design of the dress is imbued with technologies that make interaction efficient, productive and empowered, akin to the machine-like principles of controlled automation.

As Chalayan continues to pioneer hybrid forms, his work builds bridges between seemingly incompatible materials. 'Duality has always been a part of my work,' he explains. 'I present my sculptures in the same fashion collections as wearable clothes, and I combine scientific ideas with the animal nature of the human body. I think that my choice of materials will always be another manifestation of dual ideas, because I plan to continue combining high-tech materials with handcrafted ones.'

5+6 The dress' hemline rose automatically, the bustier opened by itself and the jacket unfastened and pulled away from the model's torso, all of its own volition.
7+8 Chalayan's use of shape-shifting fabrics enabled the garments to morph into entirely new designs. Shape-memory fabrics containing fibres of the shape-memory alloy Nitinol can make these innovations possible.

1

PHILIPPE STARCK

MICHELE CANIATO

Philippe Starck is based in Paris, but his work transcends virtually all borders. Starck's career spans some three decades of creating countless projects for an almost equally large number of clients in virtually every country on the globe. The scope of his work ranges from basic home accessories and understated underwear to some of the most luxurious establishments in the world. Hip hotels like the Delano in Miami, and the Mondrian in Los Angeles were designed by Starck, as were a line of moulded plastic footwear for Puma, the well-known coloured polycarbonate Miss K lamps for FLOS, and an entire line of children's accessories for Target. Journalist Ed Mae Cooper described him as 'crazy, warm yet terribly lucid,' and depicted him in a photomontage with his head – literally – on backwards for the cover image, so that Starck would seem to live up to his *enfant terrible* reputation.

Starck's life and career have been spent taking things apart and putting them back together – all with an eye to improving the exchange between product and consumer. His expertise in balancing that relationship – through materials, processes, and design – has led to his longstanding prominence in the world of design. 'I start by trying to understand what the human benefit is, what impact the result will have on the lives of the people I love, on the people around me. It's above all choices about human values and then I look for the best materials to express this goal and these ideas.' He continues, 'I am completely open to using any type of material as long as it's coherent with the direction, the cost, and the technology the project requires.'

Starck has no 'signature' style or particular colour palate; rather, he calls upon all of these things to create products that resonate and endure with the consumer. His focus is on the needs of the end user, not on the celebrity of the designer. 'A few years ago, I came upon the concept of democratic design,' he explained, 'which means striving to give the best to the most people, to improve the quality and lower the prices. I think I have almost completed that mission, which could only be done because of progress in plastic injection, monolithic and especially polycarbonates. The democratization of production is essentially done through plastic.'

2

3

Having existed since the mid 19th century, and now an integral part of our daily lives, plastics continue to transform a wide variety of products and industries. Over the past thirty years, plastic has emerged as the single most used material in the world, and for good reason: everything from doll parts to replacement hearts can be made cheaply and effectively from the wide variety of plastics. Plastics are created from polymer binders (the materials that determine the name of the plastic: polycarbonate, polyester, polyurethane, etc.) with added plasticizers, fillers and pigments. Plasticizers influence the physical characteristics of the material, making it bendable or rigid, soft or resilient; fillers are used to change things like optical characteristics or shock resistance; and pigments allow the material to take on virtually every colour – or none at all. By manipulating these various ingredients, an endless variety of materials can be created: fibres, films, gels, foams – and many others – can be created to fit virtually any need.

This has sometimes led to issues of overuse and as a result, to plastic's reputation as a key component of the over abundant waste now evident in many countries. Some types of plastics, however, can be recycled ad infinitum with no loss of performance or quality, other plastics can be recycled and mixed with virgin plastic (plastic that has not been processed before) to reduce cost without sacrificing properties. Recycled plastics can also be used to make a wood-like product that is appropriate for use in toys, decking and outdoor furniture such as picnic tables and chairs.

At the start of his career in 1967, Starck created a prototype for a simple chair as part of what was titled the Crisis Collection. A simple combination of raw wooden boards and hinges, the chair was the essence of a chair, with the added practicality of folding for storage, or, as the name of the collection implied, a hasty move. Nothing frivolous, no extraneous forms or decoration, just a pure expression of function.

In 2000, Starck began to transform an industry through the same combination of concept and materials. His Bubble chair for Kartell was a classic 'club' chair, with a twist. Crafted in the same guise as its upholstered predecessors, it has the classic lines of the style, but was executed using a process borrowed from manufacturing kayaks.

1 Starck's Louis Ghost chairs are fashioned from clear polycarbonate, and appear as apparitions of furniture that almost seem to hover within their environments.
2 For the Moscow location of his restaurant, the Bon, Starck combined his iconic Ghost chairs with his equally well-known chandeliers and sheets of glass in order to create an opulent, crisp presentation.
3 For Baccarat, Starck has used chandeliers of a similar style as those in the Bon, but for this restaurant has placed them in a more traditional and period style. The overall effect is one of longstanding elegance, befitting the Baccarat name.
OPPOSITE Created entirely from PMMA (Polymethyl methacrylate) with a chrome shade, an unlit Miss K lamp appears as a stark, almost harsh lamp. But when lit, the shade becomes almost completely transparent, showing the naked bulb through a subtly diffused pattern.

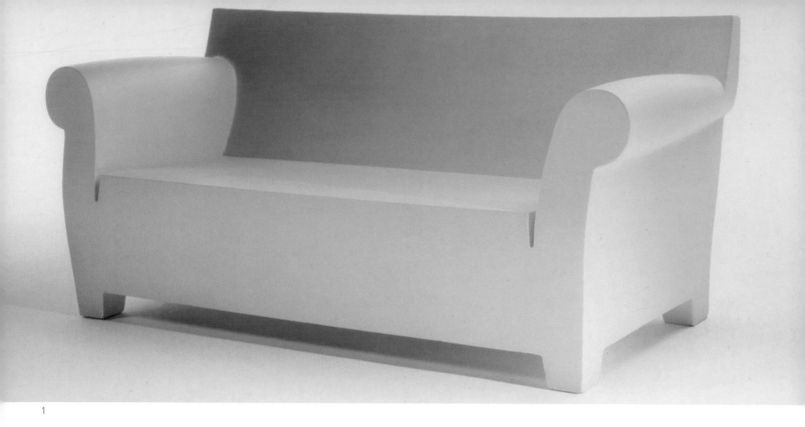

1

'The Kartell Bubble chair was the first piece of furniture done by rotational moulding,' he explained. 'I used it when I was doing a kayak for the School Spirit line. I saw that the kayak was about the same dimensions as a couch, was extremely resistant, light, and very inexpensive. I called the manufacturer of the kayak to see if it was possible to make a couch with rotational moulding. It was done. It was an enormous success and I think that I can say it launched a new material in the furniture industry.' The entire line of Bubble furniture – the chair, a couch, and an end table – is made of durable polyethylene, and is therefore a practical addition to both indoor and outdoor spaces.

A few years later, another essential chair appears; this time, however, the chair is both more and, decidedly, less. For his Louis Ghost chair, Starck took the iconic form of a Rococo armchair and executed it in injection-moulded, clear polycarbonate. The Ghost chair took the form down to a mere outline, treading the dangerous line between the ephemeral and the permanent. As Starck himself explained: 'You might think that clear polycarbonate was used for my Louis Ghost project. In fact, the material used for Louis Ghost is the realization that the goal of our civilization is immaterialism and disappearance. One of the parameters for the Louis Ghost chair is showing the path to disappearance through invisibility.'

Lightweight and incredibly strong (polycarbonate is also found in riot shields and car headlamps), the material allows the wonderful contradiction of materiality and immateriality to exist in a practical, durable and comfortable piece. The effect of invisibility is also enhanced through the material's optical qualities: it has better light transmission characteristics than many kinds of glass.

Proving his ability to work equally comfortably in a wide range of different materials, Starck reinterpreted the very same shape in polished aluminum as his Kong chair for the American manufacturer Emeco. The lustrous surface of the metal could not be further from the traditional wood and fabric used to create the original 18th-century pieces, or the ghostly transparency of the polycarbonate, yet the

2

3

juxtaposition of the style and the material work perfectly. The gentle curvature of the reflections presented in the metal give it life beyond simple patterns, and the metal has been anatomically shaped, making the chair invitingly comfortable despite its lack of cushioning.

As he looks to the future of both design and the use of plastics with that same democratic eye, Starck feels that things will need to change in a variety of ways. 'Today, choosing the materials should mainly be dictated by ecology or by saving energy,' he says. 'The problem is that oil will disappear in about forty years. Everyone thinks it's a crisis for automobiles, but that's not true. In forty years, there will be fuels that replace oil: hydrogen, cold fusion and others. However, the real crisis is when plastic disappears – when oil disappears, quality plastic will disappear. So, the little oil that will be left will be reserved for the elite. We will therefore see a social regression where only the rich will have access to quality plastic products and products that could only exist because of plastic. The poor will have to settle for natural materials, very natural, a lot weaker in their capacities, or recycled materials.'

One of Starck's current projects draws from both efficiency and alternative fuels as core design challenges. 'We are working on a hydrogen-powered vehicle, and we are very interested in a certain moulding process for plastic that can produce almost the entire body of the car in one step that would significantly reduce cost and weight.' Such a vehicle could very well help to stave off the dire future that Starck predicts for us, and he seeks to do it with his time-tested innovative attitude toward the needs of his consumers (his 'tribe' as he refers to them) and his subsequent use of materials and processes.

All of that 'terrible' lucidity gives Starck honest modesty in his assessment of the place of materials and designers in the grand scheme of things: 'Obviously, materials will evolve to accommodate, I hope above all, the needs of ecology and the environment. Then, the social needs of the users, meaning the price. And then, the designer's needs, but that seems totally normal. Voila, done.'

1 The sofa that changed an industry. Classic, fun, comfortable and durable, the whole series of Bubble furniture designed for Kartell has the classic lines of the originals but rendered in a material (polyethylene) that takes them out of the house and into the great outdoors.

2+3 The Kong restaurant in Paris was the venue that gave the name to the popular Emeco aluminum chair that shares its shape with the Louis Ghost chair. At the restaurant, both the polycarbonate and the aluminum chairs make appearances: the aluminum ones are set along with wildly-patterned carpeting, tabletops and décor that is reflected in the sheen of their shapes. Upstairs, in a greenhouse-style structure, the clear polycarbonate chairs mimic the airy walls.

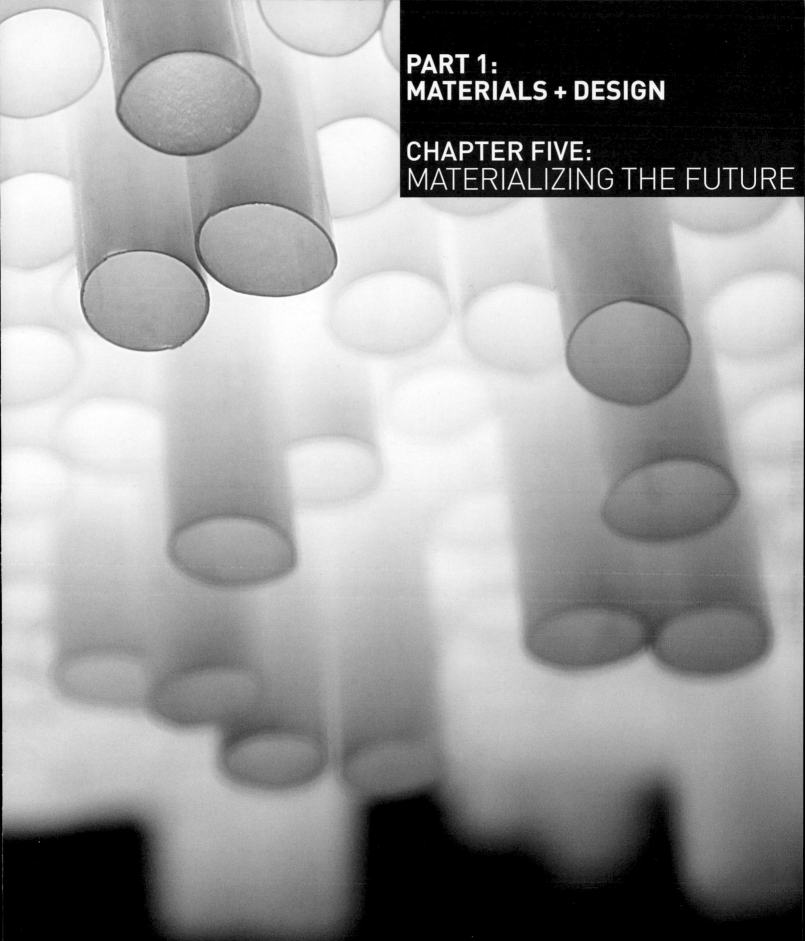

1

2

MATERIALIZING
THE FUTURE

ANDREW DENT + BRADLEY QUINN

1 Through a proprietary moulding and setting process, agricultural waste materials such as reeds, straw, flax, sugar-cane, sisal and jute (or any other high cellulose-based agricultural material) are shaped into rigid, durable, high-quality furniture. This chair, designed by Marc Newson from the material Zelfo, offers a more sustainable alternative to traditional polymer-based moulded seating.
2 Bio-polymers promise to be the material of the future. They provide a sustainable alternative to petro-chemical materials and can be used to produce a wide range of products. Here, DuPont used Bio-PDO™ to create bio-based materials that are both soft and durable.

As the preceding chapters highlighted the developments and applications that are forging fresh directions for the creative industries, they revealed why material research is so essential to design practitioners today. Most of these developments were masterminded by architects, designers and technologists, who revealed how materials' role in product innovation is paralleled by their ability to impact on the fabric of society. Just as these practitioners transform the materials of the past into fresh inspirations for the present, they also lead us to imagine how material innovation will unfold in the future.

This part of the book concludes with the insights of material experts, who tell us, in their own words, what the most important challenges for material science will be in decades to come. Michael Braungart, Kara Johnson, Mihail Rocco, Charles Holliday and Mohsen Mostafavi draw upon their respective expertise and consider what the next stages of material evolution will be. As much as their insights outline a multi-layered, dynamic and fully sustainable urban society, they also reveal the significance that new spatial and tectonic processes will play in the future.

3

4

MICHAEL BRAUNGART

Regarded as one of the world's leading chemists, Michael Braungart also founded the German-based scientific consultancy Environmental Protection Encouragement Agency (EPEA) International, and co-founded McDonough Braungart Design Chemistry (MBDC) in the US. Both EPEA and MBDC embrace intelligent, aesthetic and eco-effective design, and seek to optimize products through the Cradle-to-Cradle framework that MBDC has established. As Braungart explains, recycling biological and synthetic substances promises to outline a new paradigm for future materials.

'At EPEA, we test materials and products to assess their effects on the environment and offer alternatives that are beneficial to nature, rather than damaging. We have distinguished two cycles: a biological cycle, and what we call a technical nutrient cycle. The biological cycle encompasses things that are physically, chemically and biologically consumed, such as brake pads, fabrics, food products and detergents. The technical nutrient cycle charts the use of chemicals. When I analyzed the television set, I identified 4,360 different chemicals. Normal washing machines are even more toxic than televisions, and the off-gassing of a traditional washing machine emits far more benzene than petrol stations. The washing machine is usually situated in the kitchen, so when you are baking a cake, you are basically eating your washing machine.

'We have been testing polymers that can be reused up to 200 times with no loss of performance, which can be used again and again in the same application. In Herman Miller's Mirra chair, the polymers could be reused at least 200 times for similar purposes. Some polymers can last for the next 800 to 1,200 years. They can be used in a chair for five years, then used to make a window frame.

'If our planet is going to survive, we need to pool more materials and reinvent them as nutrients so that they become beneficial to biological systems. Humans have huge potential to support the other species on this planet. If we can be supportive, then the planet can sustain a much greater number of humans than we currently have. We need to think about how we can provide technical and biological nutrients for the future.'

3 + BELOW Taking only five minutes to assemble or disassemble, Herman Miller's Mirra chair is an example of sustainable production. The polymer parts can be recycled endlessly and may be used for another chair or polymer profile such as a window frame, and the metal sections are also repurposed. The additives and colour pigments are benign to humans, animals and micro-organisms and most of the energy used to create the chair was wind-generated.
4 Through the up-cycling of antimony-free polyester from water bottles, this textile may be recycled endlessly. Free of chlorine and any dye or additive that might be harmful to humans or the environment, the resultant upholstery textile, called Eco Intelligence Victor Innovatex, can be classed almost as edible.

1   2   3   4

INTRODUCTION

ANDREW DENT

By the dawn of the 21st century, the inventory of classical materials had reached virtual saturation point. The advantages and limitations of using glass, ceramics and metals in architecture and design had been widely documented, and the chances of forming new alloys or formulations seemed slim. The development of oil-based substances had also levelled out, as had the knowledge of ordinary polymers. A sudden demand for new natural materials sparked a shift from oil-based substances to ones made from organic sources, which generated research into how biopolymers could be synthesized from organic components. The subsequent interest in biological materials heralded a whole new generation of substances created through natural processes. As scientists begin to appreciate the material miracle of creating wood by merely combining seeds, earth, water, sun and oxygen, the value of mimicking nature has generated a fresh direction for research.

Right now, material science may seem paradoxically sophisticated and rudimentary as it reveals an appreciation for organic sources *and* high-tech materials. In many cases, synthetics and naturals can sit harmoniously alongside each other. Almost all materials are derived from a natural source at some point, but most high-tech materials are far removed from nature. Charting these unique syntheses of materials gives this chapter a 21st-century context as it looks at the materials that promise to transform our world.

Organized into seven sections, the categories of materials designated here provide a reference point for how individual materials are produced and applied. This is not a scientific material categorization, but one based on easily recognizable areas of materials rather than their scientific nomenclature. These sections reflect the categorization of materials held in the Material ConneXion libraries. Rather than defining a material solely in terms of its current use, these categories group materials according to chemical composition. In the case of composite materials, each one is categorized by the material that comprises the largest percentage of its total composition.

Each of the following seven sections outlines new research developments and explains how each material has evolved in recent years. This selection of materials is not intended to be exhaustive: thousands of new materials are produced each year but our focus is only on the most innovative. Most of the materials were chosen with their intended consumer audience of artists, fashion designers, architects, interior designers, product developers and industrial designers in mind, but they all promise to inspire and inform everyone with an interest in materials, their application and the future of interior and exterior design.

1   5

2   6

3   7

4   8

CARBON-BASED

1 These semi-rigid thin laminates of woven carbon fibre can be woven into textiles and then laminated with a clear, hard polymer film. Current applications include cabinet inserts, architectural panels, backsplashes, signage, countertops and flooring.

2+6 Using carbon fibre as a reinforcement grid for concrete instead of steel 'rebar' allows fabricators to create thinner, lighter and maintenance-free concrete sections.

3 These pultruded composites use carbon fibre roving for strength that is superior to any other material. Applications include civil construction and racing car profiles.

4 Nanostructured graphite powder acts as a fire retardant. It is typically added to polyurethanes, sealants, rubbers, adhesives, coatings and other polymers.

5+7 This easily formable, 3-D reinforcement is used in order to provide rigidity and high strength in complex composite shapes.

8 Mainly used for food-processing equipment and pipe heating, this non-woven heating textile is made from flexible nickel-coated carbon fibres using a paper-making process and may be laminated.

The sections in this book differentiate between carbon-based and polymer materials, despite the fact that ninety-nine per cent of polymers rely on a carbon backbone as the basis for their long molecules. The reason for this separation is that the two classes of materials, namely plastics and pure carbon (whether in the form of graphite, diamond or some other structure), differ so much in their appearance, properties and uses.

Truly a superlative element, carbon is both the hardest (in the form of diamond), and one of the strongest (in the form of carbon fibre) substance yet known. It is marvellous that the change from diamond, to carbon fibre, to graphite, which is so friable, is simply a rearrangement of the structure of the carbon atoms. It seems that we still have more to learn about this element, even after the discovery of two new forms: C_{60} (Buckminsterfullerene) in 1985 and C_{60} (carbon nanotubes) in 1991. Although only produced in small amounts, the incredible theoretical strengths and electrical properties of these tiny particles suggest amazing future potential. In fact, minuscule amounts added to composite baseball bats have proved *too* good, with manufacturers having to tone *down* the power in order to keep bats within regulation.

Carbon fibre still maintains the cache of a true high performance material, and justly so, with its increasing application in aircraft, such as the Airbus A380 and its continued use in sports equipment and racing car structures. The use of this super-strength material has been such that there has been a general worldwide shortage of the processed fibres, with producers forced to limit supply to new users as a result.

Advances in the processing of carbon fibre composites have enabled the increased mechanization of production, allowing for a wider range of possible applications and more complex parts to be created. In some ways, the limiting factor of these composites will always be the resin that binds the fibres together. This material has been avoided by architects for construction predominantly because of the temperature limitations of the resin, despite its suitability for the production of lightweight rigid forms.

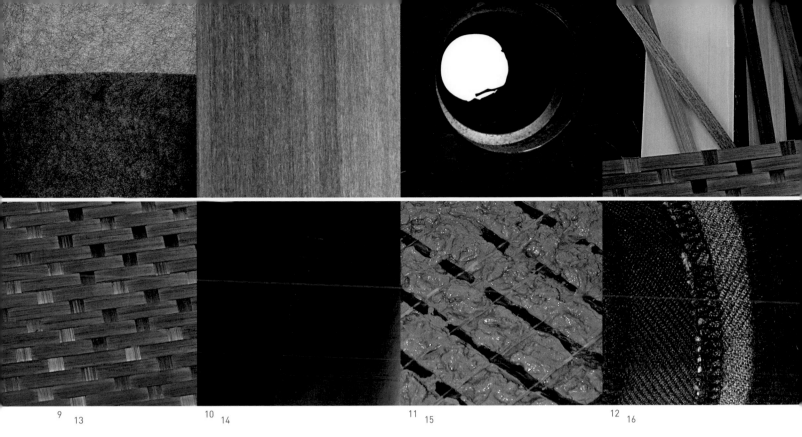

9 13
10 14
11 15
12 16

Though a defining characteristic of woven carbon fibre composites, the deep, light-absorbing black appearance of carbon is often considered a drawback, as it is impossible to change its colour. Indeed, care has to be taken when adding graphite as a heat and electrical conductor to plastic products or textiles because of its tendency to dominate the colour and blacken components. However, if it were possible to colour carbon fibre, would it still hold the same mystique?

The future use of carbon as an elemental form lies firmly in the hands of nanotechnology (see page 38). Carbon nanotubes offer great prospects for physical and electrical properties, and we are only in the initial stages of discovering their potential. However, it will only be through molecular level control that we will be able to fully harness their properties in order to ensure useful application.

9 Applications for this thin, flexible, porous heating pad, which combines electrical and thermal functions with the reinforcement properties of carbon fibre, include heating, swimming pools and consumer products.
10 These unidirectional glass or carbon fibres are incorporated into flat polypropylene tapes for reinforcement, and are used in cars, military gear and consumer appliances.
11 Because of their durability and their heat and chemical resistance, these fibre-reinforced thermoset panels (which are made from sheet-moulding compounds) can be easily moulded into complex shapes and used in cars and consumer products.
12 + 13 These reinforcement fibres for thermoplastic composites offer effective and efficient resin impregnation. These unidirectional fibres, tapes and woven mats are combined with thermoplastic resin. Typical applications are civil engineering and medical and industrial components.
14 Another thin, flexible, lightweight heating pad that combines electrical and thermal functions with the reinforcement properties of carbon fibre. Applications include heating for roads and footpaths to prevent icing.
15 See caption **2 + 6** opposite.
16 Like Nomex, this Carbon X 1st layer apparel for use by fire-fighters will not burn, ignite, char, shrink or decompose at temperatures over 1427°C (2600°F), even for extended periods.

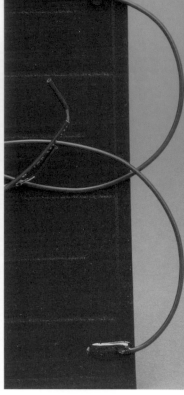

There are few synthetic materials that can withstand elevated heat and flame while still being useable as clothing, especially under-garments. Like Nomex, this Carbon X 1st layer apparel for use by firefighters will not burn, ignite, char, shrink or decompose at temperatures exceeding 1427°C (2600°F), even for extended periods of time. 5149-01

Nanostructured graphite powder that acts as a fire retardant. An intumescent, it expands and extinguishes a flame when exposed to temperatures greater than 200°C (392°F). It is added in volumes up to 20 per cent and has a metallic sheen. It is typically added to polyurethanes, sealants, rubbers, adhesives, coatings and various other polymers. Applications are for addition to materials used in the construction of trains and aeroplanes. 5430-01

These sheet-moulding compounds are fibre-reinforced thermoset panels that can be easily moulded into complex shapes. They are used extensively in the car and consumer products industries due to their durability and their heat and chemical resistance. This version uses super-stiff chopped carbon fibres in order to increase strength. 25–50 mm-long (1–2 in) fibres are added to a vinyester/stryrene resin to create moulded parts that are a low-cost alternative to woven carbon fibre structures. 5540-01

Flexible nickel-coated carbon fibres that are formed together using a paper-making process make up this non-woven textile and offer one of the most efficient ways of producing even heating over a large flat surface. The fabric may be laminated within a range of materials including thermoplastic, thermoset, elastomeric or composites. The textiles are capable of reaching temperatures of over 1000°F (538°C). However, the heaters are typically used in the range 120–350°F (49–177°C). Current applications for these heating pads are for food-processing equipment as well as for heating in industrial situations. 5127-01

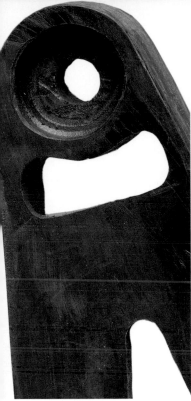

Here we see an example of the first successful, commercially available use of carbon nanotubes (CNT) to strengthen a product. These ultra-fine additives were used to improve the power of aluminum baseball bats. This is likely to be the first of many improvements achievable using these hollow rods as additives to existing materials. Incredible thermal and electrical conductivity are also a hallmark of CNTs.
5253-01

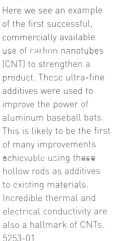

These pultruded composites utilize carbon fibre roving for strength that is superior to any other material. The rigid profiles are produced using unidirectional fibre roving, which provides longitudinal strength. The resin-rich surface of the pultrusion provides resistance to chemicals, corrosive environments, rust, rot and mildew. The composites are formed into shapes by pultrusion, a process in which the fibreglass reinforcements are drawn through a liquid resin (polyester, epoxies, vinylester or phenolics) that coats and mixes them with the carbon fibre, then are pulled through specially designed dies. They are used for aeroplane structural profiles, racing car profiles, bridge construction and also for moulded parts. 5446-01

ABOVE + BELOW

Using carbon fibre as a reinforcement grid for poured concrete instead of traditional steel 'rebar' allows fabricators to create thinner, lighter and more maintenance-free sections. The thin profile of this grid of oriented filaments can also reduce the thickness of pre-cast cladding.
5134-01

It is almost impossible to recreate the distinctive look of woven carbon fibre using other materials. The deep black sheen is unmistakable, and a characteristic of these semi-rigid thin laminates of woven carbon fibre. A range of other high performance fibres including Kevlar® and high-tenacity polyester can also be twill woven into these textiles that are laminated into clear hard polymer films. The type of fibre used determines the colour: carbon fibre is black Kevlar® is yellow, glass fibre is clear or may be aluminized to create a silver colour, and the polyester fibres are blue or red. Current applications include decorative laminates as architectural panels, splashbacks, cabinet inserts, signage, countertops or residential flooring.
5150-01

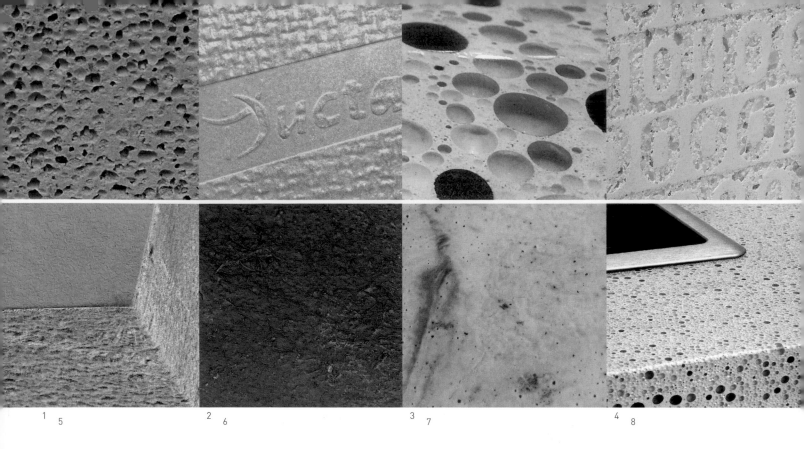

1 5   2 6   3 7   4 8

CEMENT-BASED

1 Made with autoclaved, aerated concrete, these panels are used for construction applications. They are non-combustible, have good sound absorption, high thermal efficiency and a low heat transfer rate.

2 This construction cement has exceptional tensile and compressive strength, ductility, durability and enhanced aesthetics and has been designed to serve contemporary architectural creativity.

3 + 8 A unique surface effect is created in this cement by incorporating glass beads. Once moulded, it is suitable for use in bathroom sinks and work surfaces.

4 Etched utilizing a polymer membrane, these concrete panels are printed with a retarding substance applied to the surface.

5 This wall paint cleans and detoxifies the surrounding air. Activated by minimal amounts of UV radiation, it also breaks down micro-organisms that promote the accumulation of dirt and grease. It is used to paint road tunnels and building exteriors.

6 Glass fibre-reinforced cement (GFRC) such as this may be bent to a tight radius during the curing process. Current uses and applications are for desks, tabletops, shelving, bath vanities and sinks, fireplace surrounds and large format wall tiles.

7 This geopolymer compound is available in a resin form and can withstand extreme heat. Current applications are for fire-resistant coatings for telegraph poles in areas susceptible to brush fires.

Cement-based materials comprise by far the largest volume of any human-made material on earth. The fact that few people notice the amount of concrete materials around them makes this even more surprising. Its plainness perhaps contributes to this, with concretes often used as a base material rather than the cladding (apart from those immense cement edifices that were popular in the 1960s). However, it has demonstrated a surprising durability through the millennia, with many structures created using cement still looking much the same as the day they were created. A good example of this is the immense gravity-defying dome of the Pantheon in Rome, built during the reign of Emperor Hadrian in AD 125 and which had an enormous influence on architecture from the 15th through to the 19th century. The actual composition of cement did not change much until the creation of Portland cement in the early 19th century and this formulation, using quarried minerals, limestone, iron oxide and gypsum, has remained the primary form of cement up to the present day.

Because of this stable material composition, maintained over such a long period, innovation has instead come from either strengthening particulates added to the cement mix, or to exacting process control during manufacture in order to ensure the best possible results from existing materials. From stainless steel reinforcing bars (rebar) that enabled the construction of the first skyscrapers (initially anything higher than five stories) to the use of ultra-thin oriented carbon fibre grids to add strength, concretes have never had sufficient tensile or flexural strength to be used alone. Thus the incorporation of meshes and grids into curing cement or as an external affixed plate or skin is essential, with composites such as carbon fibre, glass fibre or polymer fibre mats and textiles regularly emplyed.

Close control of composition, of water-to-material ratio and of additives, mixing, porosity and moulding has also improved the toughness and versatility of cements, with Ductal® being the most successful of these. In attempts to engineer the addition of certain properties to concretes and cements, polymer additives have

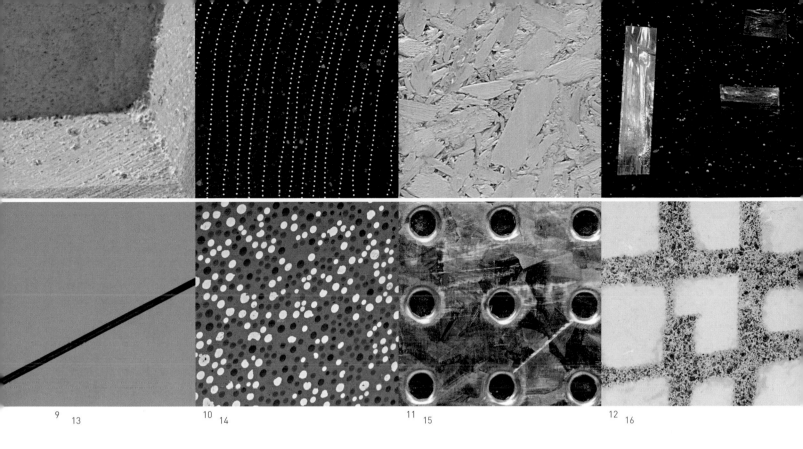

9   13

10   14

11   15

12   16

been used that often push the material closer to the realm of polymer matrix composites rather than traditional cement. Researchers at the University of Michigan's Department of Civil and Environmental Engineering have developed 'bendable concrete' with properties akin to plastics in terms of flexibility but comprising mostly cement. Dubbed 'Engineered Cement Composites' (ECC) they are 500 times more resistant to cracking and forty per cent lighter than standard cements. Yet this highlights the blurring that can develop between materials categories: will the future of materials mean that everything will eventually become a composite?

A review of the innovations in cement-based materials would not be complete without mentioning one of the most intriguing aesthetic properties to be added to concrete: that of translucency. The material Litracon™, invented by Hungarian architect Áron Losonczi, utilizes millions of glass fibres that run through the entire depth of a cured cement tile such that light impinging on one surface is transmitted through to the other side. The fibre size may also be varied from 2 microns (thousandths of a millimetre) to 2 mm, either as glass or plastic, with the proportion of transparent material in the tile also variable up to approximately ten per cent. Though still in the prototypical stage, this development allows architects to completely reimagine structures where the traditional holes used to let light in (windows) may not be necessary. This 'transparent concrete', as it has become known, does actually stop short of being totally transparent, but shadows and movement are recorded accurately on the other side of a cement wall.

9 These eco-cement concretes absorb large amounts of CO_2 from the atmosphere in order to harden and are used for bricks, blocks, pavers, permeable pavements.

10 This translucent concrete is made of fine-grained concrete with an incorporated optical fibre. Applications include interior and exterior panels, counters and lighting.

11 This sheet is a cement-bonded particleboard, which is smooth on both faces and can be worked like wood. It is fire, moisture, decay and vermin resistant and applications include interior and exterior walls, floors and roofing.

12 Transparent and translucent acrylic chips embedded into this concrete tile refract light and create 'shadowing', and may be used as flooring or countertops.

13 This highly durable tile system interlocks without the need for gluing and is suitable for heavy domestic or commercial use with an impact-, abrasion- and burn-resistant surface. Applications include residential flooring, commercial offices and restaurants interiors.

14 This mouldable cement-based material incorporates steel spheres for decorative effect and is suitable for sinks or worktops.

15 These non-combustible, composite panels are made of fibre-reinforced cement, and bonded to punched steel sheets on both sides. The panels can be worked with standard tools, and when used as ductwork, cavity barriers or other interior applications, they greatly reduce thermal and sound transmission.

16 See caption 4 opposite.

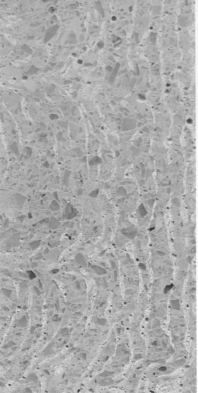

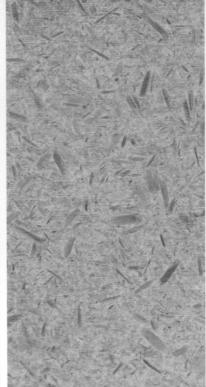

These integrally coloured pre-finished architectural concrete blocks utilize recycled materials. They have had one or more faces ground to expose the aggregate and the surface is then coated with a clear satin gloss acrylic that is easy to clean and has anti-graffiti properties. The blocks are available in five colours, and current applications are for construction walls and flooring. 5222-01

ABOVE + BELOW
Glass fibres run the depth of these cement blocks and tiles, allowing light to pass through the body of the material. The number and design of the fibres is customizable, as well as the size and shape of the blocks. The fibre diameter may also be varied from 2 microns to 2 mm and may be either glass or plastic. 5388-01

Cement-bonded particleboard comprised of mineralized wood particles and Portland cement make up this sheet. It is light grey and smooth on both faces and may be worked like wood. It is fire-resistant, moisture-resistant and resistant to rot, vermin and decay. The sheets may be screwed using steel or wood screws and applications include interior and exterior walls, floors and roofing. 2144-02

It is rare for such a solid material as this to offer interactivity. The effect is created by the use of transparent and translucent acrylic chips embedded into the concrete tile. One hundred per cent polymethyl methacrylate (PMMA) light pipes are incorporated into the tiles in order to refract light and create 'shadowing' from movement near the material. The concrete is available as custom-cast sections and may be used as flooring and countertops. This process is also applicable to large and small sections and is currently available only as a custom production, though waterproofing and scratch-resistance applications to the sheet are possible. 5058-01

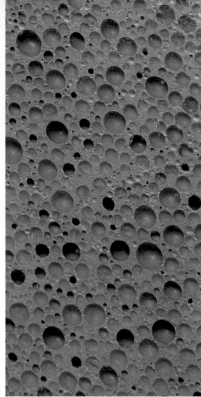
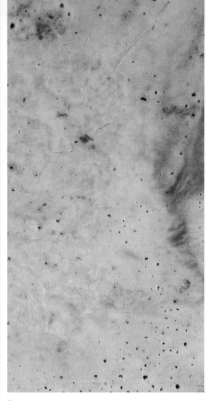

This is a true revolution in construction cement. It possesses a unique combination of properties including good tensile and compressive strength, ductility, durability and enhanced aesthetics. These properties may only be achieved through careful control of composition, porosity and processing. It has been designed to serve contemporary architectural creativity and can be used in a wide range of architectural and engineering applications where high-performance cement is required. 5051-01

ABOVE + BELOW
A unique surface effect is created in this cement by incorporating glass beads. This mouldable material, also available in tiles, is a mixture of cement, sand and glass beads and is available in a wide range of colours. Once moulded, the surface is suitable for bathroom sinks and worktops. 5289-01

Geopolymer compounds have a unique combination of the high temperature resistance of ceramics and the processability of polymers. They are based on phosphates, with different properties of the materials dependent on composition. The material is available in a resin form and is processed like a FRP (fibre reinforced polymer) composite, pouring the geopolymer onto woven layers of ceramic or glass reinforcement. It is then cured at 80°C (176°F). The cured compound withstands heat of up to 1200°C (2192°F), and may be made tougher using inorganic fibre fillers and particulates. Current applications are for fire-resistant coatings for telegraph poles in areas susceptible to brush fires. 478-02

This glass fibre-reinforced cement (GFRC) may be bent to a tight radius during the curing process. Comprised of a mix of Portland cement, fine aggregate, glass fibre and admixes, the thin sheet is similar in weight to an equivalent thickness of ceramic tile or natural stone. The material is fabricated to the client's specifications, with an almost unlimited spectrum of colours; several textures and surface finishes are available. Some current applications are for desks, tabletops, shelving, bath vanities, sinks, fireplace surrounds and large format wall tiles. The curved forms may be used as columns, lighting fixtures and water elements. 5266-02

1   5

2   6

3   7

4   8

CERAMICS

1, 4 + 6 Unique visual effects may be created with these waterproof tiles that are slip, abrasion, ultraviolet radiation, frost, and thermal shock-resistant.
The standard tiles feature designs by the manufacturer but customization is possible. The surface comes in matt or gloss and applications are for kitchen and bathroom floors, fireplaces and pools.
2 These hollow ceramic microspheres are lightweight, inert, non-combustible and uncrushable and are added to pigments, coatings and polymers to reduce density, improve abrasion resistance, reduce gloss and increase hardness. They also improve buoyancy in moulded parts for marine use.
3 + 5 This process converts a digital file of an image into a 3-D surface pattern on either a gypsum-based polymer tile or a ceramic tile. The gypsum tiles may then be coated with a metallic coating.
7 Careful control of surface patterning when firing enables this porcelain stone tile to mimic wood planks. The porcelain is glazed with a textured coating and coloured to give decoration and slip resistance.
8 Liquid lubricants can break down at high temperatures. The most widely used dry lubricant, graphite, tends to turn everything it touches black due to its colour. Boron nitride has similar lubrication properties, is harder (and longer lasting), yet is white.

This group of materials could be classed as both the oldest and most advanced of all. The word ceramic can be traced back to the Greek term *keramos*, meaning 'a potter' or 'pottery', which in turn is related to an older Sanskrit root meaning 'to burn'. Thus the early Greeks used the term to mean 'burned earth' when referring to products obtained through the action of fire upon earthy materials.

Ceramics can be defined as inorganic, non-metallic materials. They are typically crystalline in nature and are compounds formed between metallic and non-metallic elements such as aluminum and oxygen, calcium and oxygen, and silicon and nitrogen. Ceramics can be subdivided into abrasives, cements, refractories (for heat resistance), white wares (dinnerware), glasses (including window glass), structural clay products and advanced ceramics. Material ConneXion categorizes glass (including window glass) in a separate section, mainly because of its uniquely distinct application, and it is this classification that has offered the greatest chances for innovation, though there are still significant hurdles to the use of glass in many applications.

Compared to polymers or metals, the use of ceramics is limited, but if something must perform at high temperatures in a corrosive environment to exceptional accuracy, then nothing else will do. Modern advanced ceramics offer powerful physical, thermal and electrical properties that make them highly resistant to melting, bending, stretching, corrosion, wear, high voltages and currents. This has opened up development opportunities for manufacturers in a wide range of industries such as aerospace, defense, car, medical, electronics, telecommunications, scientific equipment and semiconductor processing. In general, these are the oxides, nitrides and carbides of metals such as aluminum, zirconium, titanium and silicon.

Yet despite their many and varied advantages, ceramics are limited to specialist applications. Current developments in ceramics show that they are used as lubricants, as strengthening additives to other classes of materials and as specialized surfaces and small parts, predominantly in engineering applications. Some are used in consumer products, but mainly in luxury goods and even then, somewhat sparingly.

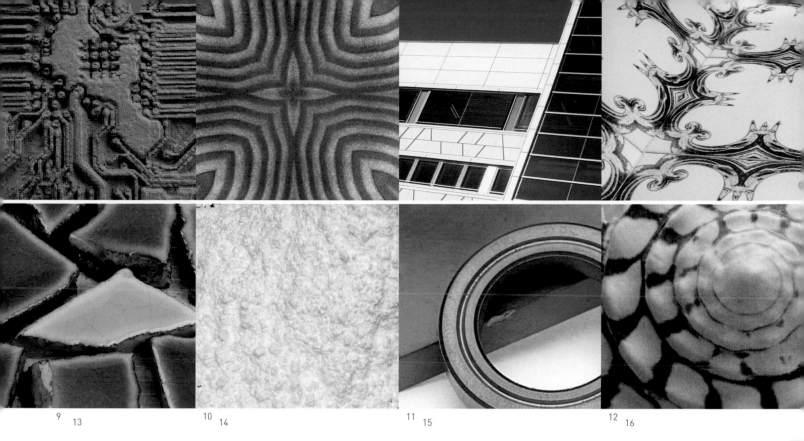

9   13

10   14

11   15

12   16

Continued work into increasing the toughness of ceramics (their resistance to catastrophic failure is a common ailment) has still only achieved minor improvements and we are unlikely to see a ceramic with the malleability of a metal any time soon. However, combinations of ceramics with other materials including metal-matrix composites, multi-laminar materials and thin coatings offer the best of both substances. Metal matrix composites are described in more detail in the section on metals (see page 176), and highlight the synergistic performance of a tough matrix and super-hard particles. The majority of metals can be improved in this way, with better scratch and impact resistance. Multi-laminar materials utilize thin sheets of ceramic with inter-layers of resin. An example of biomimicry (see page 36), these have been developed based on nacre, an ultra-hard shell where each microscopically thin layer is grown by shellfish, alternating elastic biopolymer with calcium carbonate. One human-made version uses thin ceramic sheets with a polyvinyl butyral (PVB) interlayer, enabling large sheets of ceramic to be used in horizontal applications that have spans which are traditionally not achievable without such layering.

Scratch-resistant coatings for clear polymer surfaces including spectacle lenses, ski goggles and electronic equipment have been rendered more durable using tiny transparent flakes of ceramics. Alumina, silica and zirconia have been incorporated as 'nanocomposite' additives to polymer films on screens and lenses. For maximum scratch resistance, a screen made from a single piece of ceramic is preferable. Used in high-end watches and phones, these surfaces are virtually scratch-proof and the only thing likely to cause it damage is diamond – the hardest of all known materials. These parts may be injection-moulded; technical ceramics such as Al_2O_3 (96%), Al_2O_3 (99%), ZrO_2, ZTA and Si_3N_4 powders are compounded with polymers and injection-moulded, followed by debinding (from the polymer) and sintering to achieve full density. They are then manufactured by processes such as Computer Numerical Control (CNC)-milling, grinding, lapping, sandblasting and tumbling. Beautiful and durable, this form of ceramic application is typically used only for small parts.

9   See caption 3 + 5 opposite.

10   See caption 1, 4 + 6 opposite.

11   This ceramic coating forms a dense, hard ceramic surface on aluminum or magnesium alloys. The coating grows into the existing surface, and can coat even the most complex interior diameters. The outer surface is porous and therefore lends itself to painting and lacquering or can form composite coatings for car doors, bicycle frames and eyewear.

12   See caption 1, 4 + 6 opposite.

13   Black and porous, volcanic lava requires additional processing to be used in the home. Applications for this include interior walls, floors and counter surfaces.

14   The production of parts from ceramic materials requires the sintering (baking) of moulded powders. These fine ceramic fibres are used in this process to create hard ceramic products such as knives.

15   Apart from diamond, ceramics are the hardest materials known. These sintered ceramic plates have been designed as the ultimate armour for military vehicles and individual protection. The substance is light and dense, is resistant to heat and can be formed into complex shapes.

16   See caption 1, 4 + 6 opposite.

Concerns over bacteria and microbes have led to the development of 'self-cleaning' surfaces. This version is a quartz composite countertop that incorporates an anti-microbial treatment. The work surface material is made by compressing crystal quartz at molecular level. In the process, the microbe-resistant agent is bonded to the rock so the countertop has a germ-fighting property when cut, shaped or chipped. 5133-01

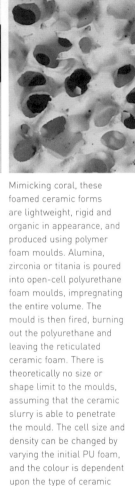

ABOVE + BELOW
Light metals, like aluminum or magnesium, are strong but not scratch-resistant. Anodizing can protect (and decorate) the surface. This forms a dense, hard ceramic coating on the alloy surface by plasma deposition within an alkaline solution bath. The ceramic coating grows into the existing surface and can coat even the most complex interior diameters. The outer surface of the coating is porous and therefore lends itself to painting. The coated surface is typically twice the abrasion resistance (scratch resistance) of anodized surfaces and applications include car doors, bicycle frames and eyewear. 5095-01

Mimicking coral, these foamed ceramic forms are lightweight, rigid and organic in appearance, and produced using polymer foam moulds. Alumina, zirconia or titania is poured into open-cell polyurethane foam moulds, impregnating the entire volume. The mould is then fired, burning out the polyurethane and leaving the reticulated ceramic foam. There is theoretically no size or shape limit to the moulds, assuming that the ceramic slurry is able to penetrate the mould. The cell size and density can be changed by varying the initial PU foam, and the colour is dependent upon the type of ceramic used. The foams find application as catalyst supports, radiant heat shields in furnaces and as decorative shapes. 5147-01

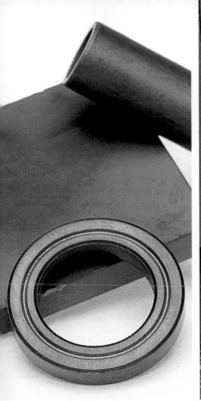

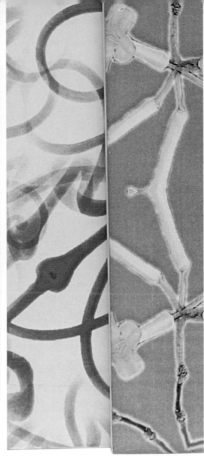

Apart from diamond, ceramics are the hardest materials known. These sintered ceramic plates have been designed as the ultimate armour for military vehicles as well as for individual protection. Alpha silicon carbide is produced by pressureless sintering ultra-pure sub-micron powder mixed with non-oxide sintering aids, then formed into complex shapes by a variety of methods. This is then consolidated by sintering at temperatures above 2000°C (3632°F). The sintering process results in a single-phase, fine-grain silicon carbide product that is pure and uniform, with virtually no porosity. It is relatively light and also dense, is resistant to heat and may be formed into complex shapes. It also resists corrosion. Currently this ceramic is used in tap washers and bearings, and for ballistic armour plate. 5331-01

This is an example of stone that looks like wood but feels like porcelain. Texturing and coating the surface creates this wood-grain look. The surface has a water absorption of less than 0.06 per cent and is 8 on the Mohs hardness scale. Applications are for residential and commercial flooring. 5182-05

ABOVE + BELOW
Unique visual effects may be created with these tiles by digital printing. The tiles are waterproof and resistant to slip, abrasion, ultraviolet radiation, frost and thermal shock. The standard tiles feature designs by the manufacturer but customization is possible (from line art, etchings, pen and ink renderings or drawings, maps, typography, photography, or can be generated on a computer). Applications are for kitchen and bathroom floors, fireplaces and swimming pools. 5393-01

Slate roofing, though beautiful, offers limited thermal insulation and fractures easily. These thick ceramic roofing tiles mimic real slate but are lighter, less brittle and easier to install than conventional slate. The clay-based tile is glazed and fired at 1150°C (2100°F) producing a coloured tile that is available in five styles. 5250-01

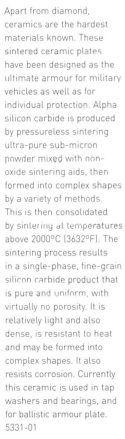

ABOVE + BELOW
Black and very porous, volcanic lava requires additional processing to be used in the home. Glazing of polished lava surfaces creates a unique appearance as well as a durable tile. In this version, volcanic stone from specific sites on the Tyrrhenian Coast was taken from regions where lava cooled quickly without collecting debris such as soil and organic material. There are over forty standard colours including 'metallic', 'glass' and 'natural' tones. Colour customization is also available. Applications include interior wall, floor and countertops.
5314-01

Available in a wide range of pastel colours that may be customized, this mesh-backed, 100 per cent porcelain tile has a matt surface. The mesh-backed sheets are available as individual pieces and come in square, circular and hexagonal shapes. It is recommended for use as flooring, countertops and splashbacks. 4961-03

High concentrations of ceramic particulates make up this exterior building paint. Titanium dioxide ceramic microspheres are incorporated into an acrylic binder at a loading of 61 per cent to create a surface coating paint that has greater longevity, durability and vapour permeability than normal exterior paint. The coatings retains its integrity for up to twenty-five years and is scratch-resistant and fire retardant. Applications are for commercial and residential exterior walls.
5118-01

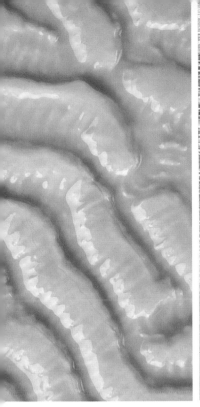

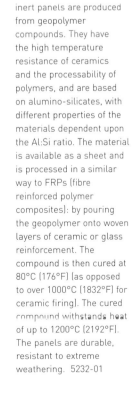

ABOVE + BELOW

This process converts a
digital file of an image into
a surface pattern on either
a gypsum-based polymer
tile or a ceramic tile. There
is no limit to the relief
image. The gypsum tiles
may then be coated with
a metallic coating such as
bronze, brass, nickel/silver
or copper, giving the
appearance of a cast tile.
The ceramic tiles are
available in a wide range
of non-toxic glazes, and
customized sizes are
possible for larger orders.
This process is currently
applied to gypsum and
ceramic tiles but could also
be applied to larger surfaces
of a similar type. 5130-01

Careful control of surface
patterning when firing
enables this porcelain stone
tile to mimic wood planks.
The porcelain is glazed with
a 12 mm-thick (⅛ in) coat
that is textured and coloured
to give decoration and added
slip resistance. Tiles are
available in various widths
and lengths, which enable
the installer to create the
look of wide-plank flooring.
Applications are mainly for
residential and commercial
flooring. 5182-01

These stiff, non-combustible
inert panels are produced
from geopolymer
compounds. They have
the high temperature
resistance of ceramics
and the processability of
polymers, and are based
on alumino-silicates, with
different properties of the
materials dependent upon
the Al:Si ratio. The material
is available as a sheet and
is processed in a similar
way to FRPs (fibre
reinforced polymer
composites): by pouring
the geopolymer onto woven
layers of ceramic or glass
reinforcement. The
compound is then cured at
80°C (176°F) (as opposed
to over 1000°C (1832°F) for
ceramic firing). The cured
compound withstands heat
of up to 1200°C (2192°F).
The panels are durable,
resistant to extreme
weathering. 5232-01

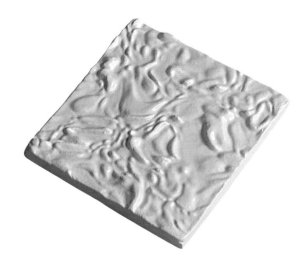

1 5   2 6   3 7   4 8

GLASS

1 A coating applied to woven glass fibre fabrics for tensile membranes, used in interior and exterior tensile membranes.
2 This lamp by Patrick Jouin, features a cascade of blown Murano glass bubbles that are illuminated from above by four spotlights and an optional multi-colour LED, creating a striking visual effect.
3+5 These wall coverings were created from an idea based on the reflective glass beads used in road markings. Applications are for interior residential wall and column coverings and accent design.
4 These woven technical textiles are manufactured from a wide variety of glass fibres and are found in the sports apparel, upholstery, car, industrial protection, packaging and agricultural industries.
6 This machine-manufactured glass has the appearance of handmade glass. It may be applied as a splashback, divider wall, door, ceiling panel, screen, or as a window, in commercial or residential areas.
7 Increasing the proportion of transparent glass to mortar in glass blocks can only be a good thing. Applications are for interior and exterior dividing walls and façades.
8 At the San Manuel Indian Bingo and Casino in Highland, California, patrons walk across a transparent floor made from textured glass panels. The dramatic feature affords vistas over a water and light display some 9 metres (30 ft) below.

Most people might not notice much difference between the glass in their home and that found in the windows of a 16th-century cathedral. Both look the same, both have silica (sand) as the principal constituent and both are produced by melting the sand and cooling it at a certain rate. However, where we have seen innovation, and no more so than in the glass category, is in the additives that can be used to improve processing, the coatings to control the transmitted light and in the decoration now possible both on the surface, and within, the glazing of modern glass.

Thought to be strictly within the category of ceramics (silica/silicon dioxide, is a non-metal oxide), glass actually warrants its own section. Modern glazing is still made from sand, but just about every other element has been added to it over the years in order to alter the properties of the base material. It has the mechanical rigidity of a crystalline material (such as a metal) but the random disordered arrangement of molecules that characterizes a liquid. Molecules are locked in this arrangement by cooling the glass from its liquid state at a high temperature. Heat it up again and it will return to its crystalline state (although it will no longer be transparent). Because of our extended knowledge of the material and its properties, it is rare that completely new applications are found for glass. Most innovation offers slight improvements only in mechanical properties or new aesthetic variations instead.

Increasingly we are seeing the replacement of glass with clear polymers. Moon and sun roofs are manufactured from polycarbonate and even some side windows (at present only the quarter lights on the Smart Car) now use polymer windscreens instead of glass. So is it the end of the road for a material that has been the choice for windows for the last millennium? Well, yes and no. Although polymers offer a forty per cent reduction of weight in automobile glazing and their complete replacement of glass is only a matter of time, we are unlikely to see the same change in architectural glazing until the limited resistance to heat of contemporary plastics is improved. Building specifications require a flame and smoke resistance that most polymers cannot achieve, and the plastics currently used in cars cannot pass these tests.

9   13   10   14   11   15   12   16

As the use of coatings, interlayers and multi-layers are developed, we are also seeing greater creativity in glazing applications. Advances in technology allow for the deposition of ultra-thin transparent layers of metals and metal oxides, reducing transmitted heat without affecting light and producing unique optical effects. Materials as esoteric as Lanthanum Hexaboride nanoparticles that have resonant light absorption in the near-infrared part of the spectrum are used to reduce solar heating of glazing. Yet switchable glass (glazing that changes from clear to translucent or opaque), though a great idea and commercially available, is still some way from mainstream use. Cost and complexity of installation are the normal reasons given for its limited application, so you are likely to still need curtains, even ten years from now.

However, the decoration of glass through printing of a polymer interlayer between two sheets of safety glazing has taken off on a massive scale. The process involves digitally printing onto a clear flexible sheet of polyvinyl butyral (PVB), then laminating this between glass sheets. The result is both aesthetically pleasing and shatterproof. Store windows, restaurant interiors, building façades as well as glazing have all been given unique graphic effects through this process. Taking the decorative impulse one step further, real flowers, bamboo stems and other organic objects have been encased in clear resin and laminated between two outer sheets of glass. Multi-layers that comprise outer glazing and two resin layers separated by a third thin sheet of glass are also possible, with a visual effect that is stunning. Though this has been done in polymers before, the use of glass for the outer sheets allows for larger and architecturally compliant glazing for interior and exterior use.

Despite the continued replacement of glass with polymers, there is still much glass waste. Samuel Mockbee's Rural Studio offered a creative re-use of the material with conservatories made from recycled car windscreens. But most waste glass is crushed for pavement filler, although it is increasingly used as an expanded foam-like structure in non-combustible construction panels, moulded into shapes for interior decoration and used as fillers for resins or as acoustic absorbers.

9, 10 + 14 This recycled glass and granite grit is used in the manufacture of terrazzo tiling. Large, small and random-sized grit is incorporated into resin to create tiles that are available in twenty-one colourways. The tiles are resistant to impact, slippage, water, and abrasion. Current applications include tiling for flooring, walls and other hard surfaces.
11 See caption 3 + 5 opposite.
12 This printing process involves printing a clear polyvinyl butyral interlayer between two sheets of glass with artwork supplied as a digital picture file. Applications are for interior and exterior glazing, shower cubicles, shelving and partition walls.
13 This glass engraving process etches the inside of large sheets of glass without affecting the surface. Applications include text or patterning in tempered or float glass for shelving, doors, mirrors or counters.
15 See caption 6 opposite.
16 See caption 3 + 5 opposite.

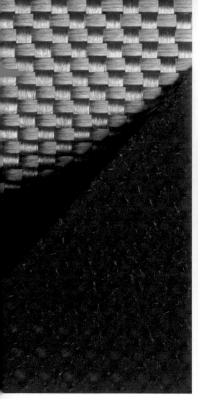

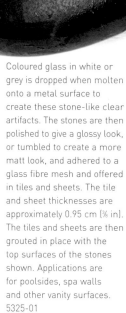

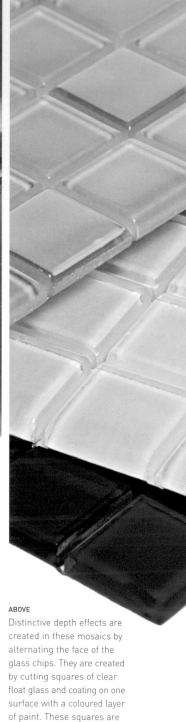

This is a coating applied to woven glass fibre fabrics for tensile membranes. The glass fibre is coated with a thin layer of aluminum on both sides using PVD (physical vapour deposition). It is then coated with a low friction PTFE coating (to reduce soiling) that may be applied in various thicknesses. The PTFE fluoropolymer maintains its optical clarity even in thick coatings, allowing for more efficient light transmission. The woven fabric is available in 2 m (78¾ in) widths and is printable. The light transmission may be specified between 10 and 55 per cent and the membrane is highly UV stable, as well as being fire tested. Current applications are for interior and exterior tensile membranes. 4998-01

Coloured glass in white or grey is dropped when molten onto a metal surface to create these stone-like clear artifacts. The stones are then polished to give a glossy look, or tumbled to create a more matt look, and adhered to a glass fibre mesh and offered in tiles and sheets. The tile and sheet thicknesses are approximately 0.95 cm (⅜ in). The tiles and sheets are then grouted in place with the top surfaces of the stones shown. Applications are for poolsides, spa walls and other vanity surfaces.
5325-01

RIGHT
Created by Anu Penttinen for Nounou Design, these decorative glass vases have been hand-blown and wheel-cut to reveal the white glass base underneath. The variety of colours and techniques that can be expressed in glass make it an infinitely customizable material.

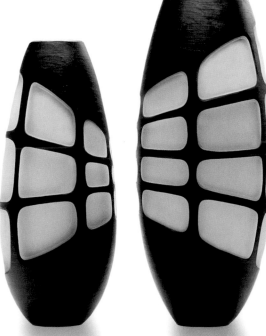

ABOVE
Distinctive depth effects are created in these mosaics by alternating the face of the glass chips. They are created by cutting squares of clear float glass and coating on one surface with a coloured layer of paint. These squares are then adhered to a flexible backing of PVB. Only one colour is possible for each sheet of tiles, but variations in colour are achieved by the surface that the coating is painted onto. Applications are for bathrooms, wall surfaces and countertops in residential and commercial interiors. 5503-01

Such woven technical textiles are manufactured from a wide variety of glass fibres. The properties of the textiles range from rigid and firm to 3-D ductility They are produced in various widths and weights as flexible tubes or webs for applications such as insulation, filters, sporting goods, shoes and lawn-mower bags. The textiles are available as wovens or may be coated, and the fibres dyed (where possible). Applications for these textiles are found in the sports apparel, upholstery, car, industrial protection, packaging, geotextile and agricultural industries.
5218-01

This through-thickness, rough-cut coloured glass is used for mosaic tiling. Transparent or translucent glass tiles, in twenty-one colours including iridescent and metallic-pigmented effects, are available in square and diamond shapes. Current applications include mosaic tiling for flooring, ceilings, walls and other hard surfaces.
5026-01

ABOVE
This wall covering was made based on the reflective glass beads used on roads. It is a flexible wall covering that incorporates millimetre-sized glass beads plus a random array of larger beads adhered to a metallic coated surface. The sheets are available in eight colours including black, white, gold and silver and have a class A fire rating.
2887-04

RIGHT
The unmistakable luminosity of coloured glass enables architects such as Adam Tihany to create striking sculptural objects. Used as part of an interior for a Shanghai rooftop restaurant, these large representations of spirit bottles have been made by fusing together multiple layers of cast glass.

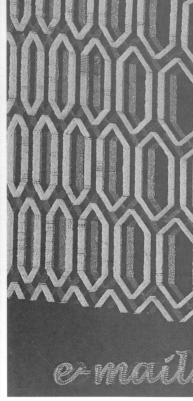

In order to protect the surface of these decorative high-pressure laminates (HPL) sheets against scratches, moisture and chemicals, they are laminated to glass sheets. The glass is available as either float glass or safety glass and the HPLs are available in a wide range of patterns and colours. Applications are for horizontal and vertical surfaces and other architectural accents. 5359-04

This construction board uses expanded glass particles for strength and insulation. One hundred per cent recycled crushed glass is bonded together using an inorganic binder. The outer surfaces are HPLs that have both decorative and functional properties, providing a scratch-, impact- and heat-resistant surface. There are hundreds of HPL designs and colours to choose from, and the boards are used mainly in construction. 5305-01

An interlayer of resin and textile are incorporated into these decorative glass sheets. Textiles of various patterns and styles are laminated between the glass sheets using a polyvinyl butyral (PVB) layer. Customization of the decorative layer is possible, including paper and metals, and the laminated glass sandwich has the same properties as regular laminated glass. The sheets may be curved. Applications are for partitions, shower stalls and wall decoration. 5498-01

ABOVE + BELOW
This glass engraving process etches the inside of the glass without affecting the surface. A laser with a specific wave length is used to devitrify the glass, giving it an etched appearance (although in fact the material is simply crystallized). The depth of the etching may be specified as well as the thickness of the glass. Theoretically there is no limit to the type of design as the image is computer-controlled. Applications include text information or patterning in any type of tempered or float glass for shelving, cabinet doors, mirrors or countertops. 5202-01

At the moment, this is the
only class A glazing that
can incorporate decorative
inclusions such as plants
and other organics. The
system comprises two
outer glass layers and one
or two cast-resin sections
with inclusions. There are
currently over 100 materials
included in the line,
although virtually any
material may be captured
in the resin interlayer,
including 3-D textiles, plants
and grasses, metal and
polymer objects. The panels
are UV-resistant and current
applications are for interior
curtain walls, doors,
countertops, splashbacks
and decorative surfaces.
5089 01

The patterns on these glass
surfaces are produced by
means of an acid engraving
process devised between
1965 and 1968 by Antonio
Bresciani. These float glass,
high-transmission
translucent panels are
available in light colour or,
by request, on coloured
float. They are suitable for
both furniture and
architecture. 4491-04

ABOVE + BELOW
For safety and decoration,
this glazing incorporates
a photoluminescent coating
fused into the surface.
A thin ceramic coating is
baked onto one side of a
sheet of glass that contains
a pigment of strontium
aluminate that, when
activated by UV rays for as
little as ten minutes, glows
for up to eight hours. This
process is currently in the
prototype stage, but
proposed applications
include signage, decorative
curtain walls and displays.
5299-01

Using nanostructured PTFE particulates in this coating for architectural membranes allows for the coating to be printed and heat-welded, both impossible in standard coatings, thus reducing the cost of installation and enhancing creativity with colour. The membrane still maintains the durability required for multiple-year external usage. 4998-02

ABOVE + BELOW
This glass flooring offers slip resistance in both optically clear and textured surfaces. Through a specific casting process, the cast tile is approved in accordance with standards for slip resistance of floor surface materials. The slip resistance is a textured surface effect that is added during the casting process and will not wear off. Applications include shelving, floor tiles, and other surfaces where slip resistance is required in clear glass. 5251-01

Comprising 80 per cent recovered filament glass, with 90 per cent recycled content, this material offers a unique blanket insulation. Long textile-type glass fibres are bonded with a thermosetting resin to produce a strong, resilient insulation that will return to full thickness after compression and can withstand temperatures ranging from -198°C to 232°C (-325°F to 450°F). It does not rot, mould, sustain growth of bacteria or vermin, or corrode metals. It can be easily cut, and has been used for gasket seals between Antarctic research station pods by the United States Antarctica Program and to insulate liquefied natural gas tanks around the world. 5461-01

Two sheets of glass are fused together to capture bubbles in geometric or organic patterns, without the use of interlayers or glues, in sheets of up to 0.9 x 0.9 m (3 x 3 ft) (the size of the manufacturer's kiln). Larger sheets are also possible to manufacture. Colour may also be incorporated into the fused glass and the bubbles may be designed to create words, logos or patterns. Currently this glass is used in decorative objects and interior space glazing. 5258-01

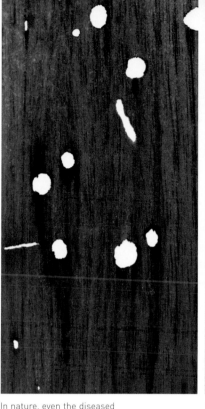

This machine-manufactured glass has the appearance of handmade glass. It is made using a proprietary technique that allows large sections to be produced at a competitive cost in two different styles: one a ribbed surface, the other a mottled surface, both with imperfections built in. Currently the glass is clear. This glazing may be applied as a splashback, a divider wall, as a door, as a ceiling panel, a screen or as a window, in commercial or residential areas. 2721-03

In nature, even the diseased and dead has an aesthetic beauty. These thin veneers have been sectioned from disease-killed, forest-salvaged butternut (white walnut) wood. The holes are from burrowing beetles, and the veneers are sandwiched between layers of plate glass. The approximate hole concentration may be specified within certain parameters and current applications include architectural interior glazing panels as well as for decorative furniture.
4683-02

Loose, expanded glass granules are reclaimed from recycled waste from the glass manufacturing industry. The glass is ground down into powder then made into spherical pellets using water, a binder and expanding agents, then heated to 900°C (1352°F). It is intended for use in construction and as fillers for adhesives and mortar. The pellets are light but have good compressive strength, are heat and chemical resistant, and have excellent acoustic and thermal insulating properties. They do not give off VOCs and are suitable for addition to synthetic resins. They find application as fillers for mortar, plaster, adhesives and in construction boards. They are also used in partition wall systems, as paving and as acoustic absorbers.
5538-01

1
5

2
6

3
7

4
8

METALS

1 Relying on the malleable nature of metal, air is used to 'inflate' these steel pillows. Applications include the production of decorative objects.

2 This process for the seamless, cold-forming of metal sheets uses machinery to produce solid forms with a hollow core. These shapes are used in furniture, in architecture and in industrial design.

3 Architectural metal sheets such as these are die-cut in muntz metal, stainless steel and aluminum. Applications include interior cladding and door panels.

4 This is a dye- and pigment-free colouring for titanium. Applications include outdoor monuments, bicycle, golfing and marine parts, jewelry and housewares.

5 These woven metal textiles are flexible and highly durable, and used for a variety of interior drapery and sculptural uses.

6 Almost imperceptibly fine holes and slits may be made in metal using this process. Applications include medical instruments and aerospace component manufacture.

7 These hot stamping foils are typically used for plastic decoration on consumer products, personal communication devices, frames and car interior panels.

8 This metallic alloy can vibrate at high frequencies in response to changes in magnetic field: a phenomenon known as 'Magnetostriction'.

We have known about almost all of the metals in the periodic table for over seventy years, with most of the useable combinations of different alloys (a combination of two or more metals) tried and tested for their individual properties. Barring the effective use of some new way of combining metals (and it is here that the ideals behind nanotechnology could lead the way) we mostly know their limitations in terms of strength-to-weight, temperature, corrosion and scratch resistance, formability and electrical properties. So have metals had their day? Take a look around you and the answer will be a resounding 'no'. They will continue to be a major part of all architecture, transport, furniture, and manufacturing and consumer products for the foreseeable future. The next steps in the evolution of metal, however, are likely to be in their combination with other materials to create multi-layer materials, metal-matrix composites and other hybrids that utilize the best properties of each constituent part to synergistic effect.

As with many of today's advances in this area, exacting control of the manufacturing process is the key to enhancing such properties. The use of magnesium, one of the lightest of all the metals, has grown enormously with the advent of processes such as thixomoulding and precision casting. Both are techniques that necessitate careful control of both material and mould. Thixo-moulding, most beautifully utilized in the Go chair by Ross Lovegrove (see page 109), involves the high-speed injection moulding of semi-solid magnesium, relying on its thixotropic properties to create near-net shape parts of geometrical complexity. T-Mag casting takes the high pressure casting currently used for the moulding of magnesium engine blocks to the next level: it does not waste magnesium during the process nor does it require either high pressure or a vacuum to fill the die. In addition, it creates exceptionally high quality non-porous castings. As a result, T-Mag can cast lightweight magnesium-alloy engine blocks that will be only two-thirds the weight of current aluminum alloy blocks and less than one third the weight of cast iron blocks.

9   13   10   14   11   15   12   16

Composites of a metal with a non-metal such as a ceramic or plastic are showing promise in the areas of stiff structural parts. Metal matrix composites, where a hard, usually ceramic particle is embedded in a tough metal such as aluminum, offer lighter, more damage-resistant profiles that may be worked like the base metal and are as scratch resistant as a carbide. The particle size, density and composition can be tailored to suit the application, with uses already found in the demanding sports equipment industry.

Proficiency in producing more complex metal structures on a micro and macro level is also advancing. On the micro level, we have seen the creation of glass-structured metals (suppression of the crystallization of metal during solidification promotes an amorphous, glassy structure) that offer improved scratch resistance and energy transfer, making them ideal for luxury mobile phones and tennis rackets. On the macro level, alternatives to honeycomb structures include filament-separated thin steel sheets (that have a much reduced weight for a given thickness), and patterned hydroformed panels offering decorative yet super-stiff steels, aluminums and titaniums.

9 This copper cladding is meant to corrode: it is used for a wide range of construction façades, and is available in sheets, strips, shingles and nets.
10 Mimicking the look of a woven wood slat fence, these metallic embossed panels are used for interior applications, including doors and door inserts, furniture, wall coverings and display counters.
11 See caption 5 opposite.
12 This woven fabric is composed of drawn steel and silver wire and has a rigidity that allows it to be shaped and sculpted into room dividers and screening for interiors.
13 Metal objects such as miniature springs can be produced using this electroforming process with surprising accuracy. Current applications are for flexible springs and high precision funnels and nozzles.
14 See caption 3 opposite.
15 High-performance fabrics such as this one are made from high-strength, high-modulus polymer fibres. Applications for Zylon® include replacement for copper and copper beryllium alloy wires in aerospace applications, as a conductive fibre in electronic textiles, and in computing devices.
16 See caption 3 opposite.

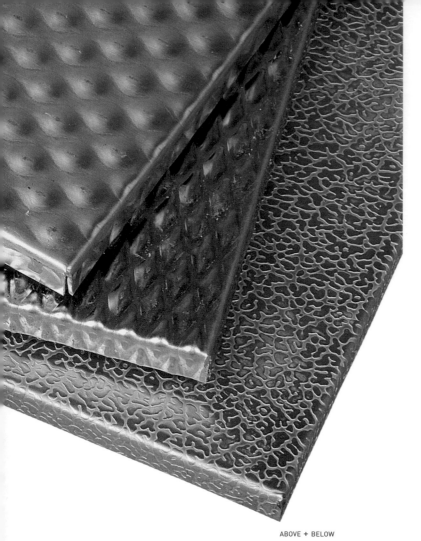

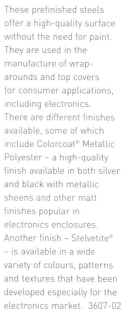

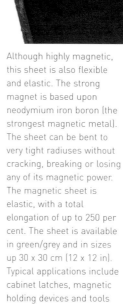

ABOVE + BELOW
These stainless steel-clad tiles come in a range of surface patterns. The 316L sheet is formed over fired ceramic tiles to produce clad tiles that are used for flooring. They are available in twenty-nine designs and four colours, and in various tile dimensions. They are used as flooring in showrooms and reception areas. 5046-02

Although highly magnetic, this sheet is also flexible and elastic. The strong magnet is based upon neodymium iron boron (the strongest magnetic metal). The sheet can be bent to very tight radiuses without cracking, breaking or losing any of its magnetic power. The magnetic sheet is elastic, with a total elongation of up to 250 per cent. The sheet is available in green/grey and in sizes up 30 x 30 cm (12 x 12 in). Typical applications include cabinet latches, magnetic holding devices and tools and appliances. 5403-01

These prefinished steels offer a high-quality surface without the need for paint. They are used in the manufacture of wrap-arounds and top covers for consumer applications, including electronics. There are different finishes available, some of which include Colorcoat® Metallic Polyester – a high-quality finish available in both silver and black with metallic sheens and other matt finishes popular in electronics enclosures. Another finish – Stelvetite® – is available in a wide variety of colours, patterns and textures that have been developed especially for the electronics market. 3607-02

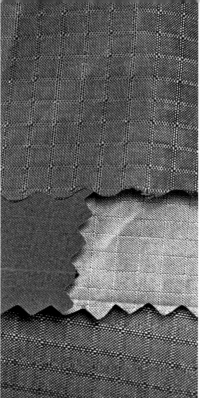

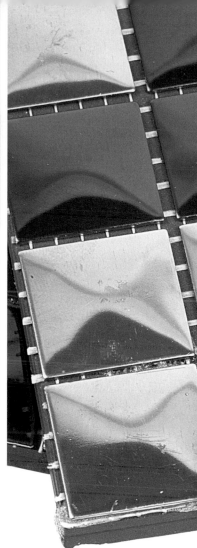

Selective laser sintering such as this, may be the future of custom manufacturing processes: it is able to build complex objects from powder via a CAD platform. The process utilizes selective sintering by computer-controlled laser heating of powdered nylon, nylon alloys, metals and also ceramics. High surface tolerances reduce the need for post-machining. Processing time for a single part takes hours and this process is a quicker and cheaper alternative to photolithography. Applications are for the production of virtually every object imaginable that does not contain mechanized parts. 5201-01

This process can coat textile materials with a fine layer of metal. It uses a proprietary deposition technique that coats textile fibres with an extremely fine (less than a nanometer) layer, which is an improvement on vapour deposition and electro-plating techniques. It can deposit both low- and high-melting point metals as well as metal oxides and metal nitrides such as titanium oxide and titanium nitride, with little effect to the hand of the woven textile. It produces a uniform, electrically conductive surface, protecting against static electric discharge and EMI (electro magnetic interference). The coating can be applied to a variety of natural, synthetic woven and non-woven materials. Applications include heat insulation for greenhouse covers, EMI shielding coatings for surgical gowns and masks, temperature-regulating coatings for outerwear, and discharge coatings for air filters.
5176-02

ABOVE + BELOW

The elastic nature of the Teflon® coating on this steel allows it to be cold-drawn. The coating does not split or delaminate even with deep-drawing processes, and is applied to cold-rolled strip-carbon steel, high-grade steel, spring steel, aluminum, brass or copper. A range of colours and pigmented special effects are available for the coatings. Textured surfaces are also possible, for use in consumer products, engineering components, car interiors and sports equipment. 5394-01

Mosaic tiles like the above example are formed from individual stainless steel tiles held together with a polyester mesh backing. The tiles are slightly bevelled, come in nine metallic colours and forty different design combinations and are highly scratch-, corrosion- and UV-resistant. Applications include splashbacks, countertops, decorative cabinetry and wall-coverings. 5046-01

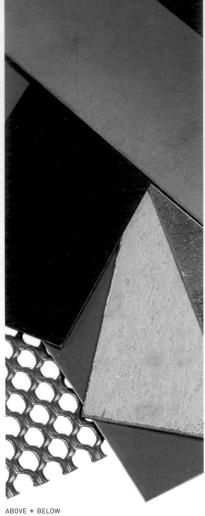

These flexible, lightweight sheets are typically used for point-of-purchase and event displays. The metallic films are adhesive-backed and available in chrome, copper, aluminum and bronze. Polished as well as brushed surface effects are offered and the sheet is available in rolls that are 91.4 cm (36 in) wide. Applications for this sheet include car interior accents, furniture surfaces, point-of-sale and event displays. 5055-01

One hundred per cent 304 stainless steel is stamped into small mosaic pieces and arranged to form scratch-, fire- and stain-resistant tiles which are light and flexible. The tiles are produced in various styles that provide an infinite number of combinations. This collection may be applied in areas of all types, including aquatic environments and even heavy traffic areas. The tiles are created using a patent pending rubber backing system, which provides structural support to the inner shell. Standard tiles use 304 steel, but brass tiles are also available. Applications are for interior floors and decorative surfaces and splashbacks. 5084-01

ABOVE + BELOW
Copper cladding like the above example is meant to corrode: it is used for a wide range of construction façades, and is available in sheets, strips, shingles and nets. Due to the nature of the copper, it is susceptible to rusting. However, unlike the bright green 'verdigris' coatings seen in many architectural façades, this version develops a dark brown matt colouring. 5085-01

Both screen-printing and electroplating processes are used to decorate this steel. It is available in a range of metallic colours and surface finishes such as brushed and polished. The surface is scratch- and UV-resistant and may be applied to flat or curved surfaces. It is used for furniture, elevator cladding and interior and exterior wall cladding. 5136-01

This electroforming process can produce metal objects such as miniature springs with surprising accuracy. It produces the required shape by electroplating a thin layer of nickel onto an aluminum mandrel of any shape. The aluminum mandrel is then chemically dissolved, leaving behind a thin shell of tough nickel, which is known as an 'electroform'. They can be designed and manufactured with unusual shapes, and even made with varying cross-sections and with varying wall thicknesses on a single part. The electroform shape can be used between great temperature extremes. The basic electroform material is nickel, but copper, silver and gold are also available either as complete part or as a surface finish. Current applications are for flexible springs, bellows and high precision funnels and nozzles. 5088-01

Hydroforming (using high pressure water to deform sheet) creates the patterns in these steel sheets and also stiffens the material. Two metal sheets, from stainless steel, copper, titanium, zinc, zinc-coated steel or magnesium, are hydroformed and glued together back to back to create a highly stiff sheet. The top and bottom faces are typically then laminated with a decorative sheet. They are an economical alternative to honeycomb materials, with a good strength-to-weight ratio, good shear resistance, and good torsional and buckling resistance. Coloured, textured or high-gloss-finished sheets are available, with customization of size and surface possible. Applications are for dividing panels, work surfaces, electromagnetic shielding and furniture design. 5519-01

Relying on the malleable nature of metal, air is used to 'inflate' these steel pillows. Two matching squares of metals such as steel or aluminum are welded at the edges and then inflated to create a pillow effect. The resulting form maintains its shape and has good structural strength. It is possible to use this process with a range of simple shapes, though size is limited. Applications for this process are for the production of decorative objects. 5368-01

Taking full advantage of the novel properties of these steel 'pillows', designer Stephen Newby has created a wide range of decorative and functional pieces both for indoor and outdoor use. Also among his creations are fountains, sculptures, furniture and mirrors.

With the stiffness of a standard sheet three times its weight, this steel sheet comprises two outer thin sheets that are separated with a regular array of thin wires orthogonal to the sheet orientation. The wires are each individually bonded using an adhesive to the sheets and constitute only about 5 per cent density of material between the sheets. The configuration allows for much greater energy absorption than standard sheet steel and may be worked like steel. Applications are for rigid structural sections in aircraft and military equipment, as well as proposed applications for cars, consumer products, electronics and sports equipment. 5487-01

ABOVE + BELOW
Crystal decoration is incorporated into these wire meshes, which are woven using drawn stainless steel wire. The weaving process creates wire deformations that have an effect on the surface of the wire mesh. Added to the wire mesh are decorative crystal-like acrylic beads, designed in collaboration with Swarovski that do not compromise the integrity of the mesh. Applications include façades, wall coverings, ceilings, gates, sunshades, displays and exhibition stands. 5033-01

To create these metallic, laminated sheets, thin aluminum foil is laminated onto a rigid laminated sheet (kraft paper impregnated with phenolic resin) and then backed with a second aluminum sheet. The top sheet is then stamped without puncturing the surface to create a decorative mirror-like surface. Applications include interior decorative surfaces for cabinetry, wall panels, doors, splashbacks and store design. 009112

A novel metal mesh adds drama to the entrance of this shopping arcade in Düsseldorf, Germany. Lit from within, the overhangs provide a striking – almost electric – focal point that draws people in off the street.

Chemical etching is a stress- and burr-free manufacturing process with component blanking, holes, fine detail and bend lines produced as part of the single standard manufacturing process. This process for fine precision etching by chemical and physical means can be used on many metals and metal alloys, non-metallic materials and composites. The etched part can be hardened, vibration- or electro-polished, blackened, coated, inscribed or pre-assembled. Applications for this process include electronic circuitry, medical instrumentation and aerospace component manufacture. 5505-01

This high-precision, perforated sheet metal may be used as either a finished or semi-finished surface. A variety of metals are perforated with one of a range of patterns in various hole sizes and spacings. The sheets may also be formed, painted or anodized according to specifications. Applications include speaker grilles, display stands, computer housings, light fixtures, ceiling panels and other consumer product and interior accent applications. 5406-01

Few materials can withstand the direct impact of an explosion but this is one of them. This multi-layer laminate sheet comprises thin layers of aluminum alloy 2024-T3 sheet and unidirectional glass fibre layers embedded in an adhesive binder. There are six different versions, differentiated by the number of aluminum and fibre layers and the orientation of the fibres in the layer. All grades are explosion-proof to some extent, but the thicker grades offer greater resistance. The sheets are available as a standard size up to 2.44 x 1.22 m (8 x 4 ft) but any size is possible due to interlayer splicing. They may be curved and shaped to order, and cut and drilled like aluminum sheet. Applications include blast-proof cargo holds for aircraft, as well as fuselage shells for passenger aircraft. 5203-01

LEFT

For a project at a vineyard in Barolo, Italy, the firm of Archicura Architects wanted to create a structure that would appear to literally grow out of the earth. This vertical tower on the side of the structure mimics a vine pushing out toward the sky, and its surface of zinc sheeting will change its appearance in concert with the exposure to the elements.

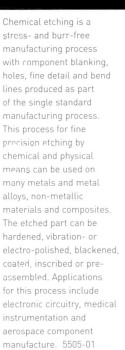

This process deposits ultra-thin layers of metal or ceramic on any surface. Substrates such as metal, glass, ceramic or plastic may be coated, under a vacuum. An electric current is used to vaporize the ceramic or metal into a cloud of ions that are deposited onto the substrate in a very thin layer. Various metals may be deposited, including steel, copper, silver, aluminum, as well as hard ceramics. The surface has a very high hardness, good scratch resistance and good adherence to the substrate. The colour of the coating is dependent upon the material deposited, and applications include machine tools, decorative surfaces and mould interiors. 5124-01

Stainless steel, very stiff in thick sections, can have wonderful flexibility when used as a thin filament. This tubular-knit textile has the properties of knitted fabrics, such as stretchability and softness, but is knitted from fine multi-filament cold-drawn stainless steel yarn. Current applications are for use as a separation cloth between the glass or the metal and the mould in production processes where resistance to high temperatures and mechanical loads is required. This includes the fabrication of complex glass forms like car windows, bottles, TV tubes and stainless steel cooking utensils. 2535-03

This metal mesh acts as security and as a decorative screen. It is a one-axis flexible mesh made from 100 per cent stainless steel and is available in white and stainless colours. The open area is 74 per cent, it has a maximum width of 30.5 cm (120 in) and is available in continuous-length rolls. Applications are for façades, screens and security doors. 1489-04

ABOVE + BELOW
Used as drapery and decoration, this woven metal fabric is composed of drawn steel and silver wire that has a rigidity that allows it to be shaped and sculpted. The fabric is available only in a silver colour, and in 110 cm (55 in) widths and is suitable for residential interiors. Applications include room dividers and screening. 4849-04

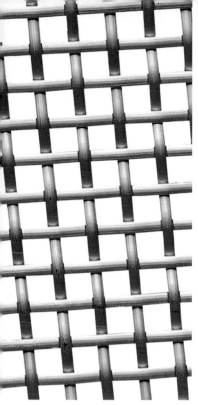

Aluminum wire is used for this open-weave rigid mesh. The surface is chemically treated to give it weathering protection with no visible anodization points. The material is non-flammable and comes only in its natural metallic colour. Applications are stand-building, shop-fitting, displays, event-building, museum exhibitions and signposting. 5256-01

These flexible meshes are woven using thin drawn wire. The weaving process itself creates wire deformations that have an effect on the surface of the wire mesh. The meshes are available in 'plain weave', 'twilled weave', 'plain Dutch weave' and 'twilled Dutch weave', in widths up to 6 m (19.7 ft). These meshes offer decoration in architectural façades applications. 4986-01

Mainly used for aerospace applications, this high-performance yarn is an electrically conductive, low weight, high-strength, flexible polymer/metal hybrid yarn. Zylon® (or polyphenylene bisoxazole, PBO), a high-strength, high-modulus polymer fibre, is coated using a proprietary process with metal, producing strong flexible strands that are wrapped together forming a yarn. Standard metals used include silver, copper and nickel. Applications include replacement for copper and copper beryllium alloy wires in space and aerospace applications, as a conductive fibre in electronic textiles, and in computing devices. 5452-01

This process is for the custom manufacture of knit security mesh for the protection of objects and containers in transit and storage. Copper wire is sheathed in 100 per cent PVC, knitted into wide textiles, and then connected to a continuous-current circuit so that if one section of the wire is cut, an alarm sounds. The textile may also be knitted into a circular format, as well as in shaped structures and smaller mesh produced to order. Moreover, the mesh can be incorporated into polyurethane resins in order to create solid structures. 5358-02

Playing with the idea of the emotional and the industrial, designer Joep Verhoeven created this remarkable fence. By weaving coated wire in a traditional lace pattern and combining it with a standard metal fence, the designer created an innovative barrier.

Developed in Japan, the *Mokume Gane* process uses thin, parallel layers of metals such as silver, gold, copper, and palladium, to form a solid block of metal as the basis for these rings. Once formed, the blocks are then cut, ground and distorted to create unique surface effects. 5260-01

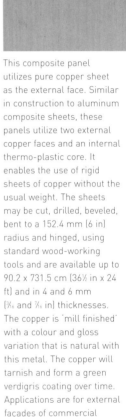

This composite panel utilizes pure copper sheet as the external face. Similar in construction to aluminum composite sheets, these panels utilize two external copper faces and an internal thermo-plastic core. It enables the use of rigid sheets of copper without the usual weight. The sheets may be cut, drilled, beveled, bent to a 152.4 mm (6 in) radius and hinged, using standard wood-working tools and are available up to 90.2 x 731.5 cm (36½ in x 24 ft) and in 4 and 6 mm (⁵⁄₃₂ and ⁷⁄₃₂ in) thicknesses. The copper is 'mill finished' with a colour and gloss variation that is natural with this metal. The copper will tarnish and form a green verdigris coating over time. Applications are for external façades of commercial buildings. 5435-01

Due to the high reflectivity of these sheets, they are typically utilized in lighting applications. The super-bright finish is applied to the sheet aluminum and then coated with a protective film, before being embossed by roller and recoiled. The coils are available in widths of 1000 and 1250 mm (39⅜ and 49⅛ in) and from 0.2–1 mm (¹⁄₁₀₀–¹⁄₂₅ in) in thickness, and in continuous length rolls. Current applications are for furniture, including cabinetry, door and wall panels, consumer products, lighting and marine transport. 5047-01

Used as flooring and furniture design, the thickness of this super-thin embossed stainless steel sheet is as low as 0.5 mm (⁷⁄₆₄ in) but also up to 2 mm (⁷⁄₆₄ in). Maximum sheet dimensions are 150 x 600 cm (59 x 236 in). Alternative surface textures are available as well as mirror, bright, fabric effect and woven effect finishes. The sheet is rigid, highly wear-resistant, corrosion-resistant, and an anti-skid surface is available for some finishes. Current applications are for furniture, industrial design and flooring. 5069-01

The Velcro-like hooks on this material are produced on rolled metal sheets. An intense beam of electrons is focused on the surface of the metal and swiped across, leaving a hole and a corresponding wave behind it, that, if repeated in the same area a number of times, is able to build up a protrusion up to 2 mm (⁷⁄₆₄ in) in height. Currently only steel has been used as a substrate, but other metals may be processed. The limitations of the process have yet to be determined (such as how large an area of metal may be altered, and how quickly this may be done, as well as how long the protrusions may be), but applications for this process include metal/composite bonding, as a heat sink and to modify the speed and pattern of air or fluid flow. 5117-01

ABOVE + BELOW
Comprised of melamine resin, decorative and core paper, and aluminum, these multi-layer, structural solid surfacing sheets have high structural strength, allowing thin sheets to withstand high loads. The sheets may be cut, drilled and milled and the edges may be detailed by lipping, curving and milling. 5206-01

Titanium still maintains its preeminence as the highest performing aerospace metal. This treatment decorates its surface and is achieved using controlled grain growth of the metal when cooling, and anodized colouring. The integrity and properties of the titanium are not compromised. A wide range of colours are available. Special processing treatments impart fingerprint resistance and prevent yellowing. 50 x 100 cm (19¹¹⁄₁₆ x 39⅜ in) sheets are available. Applications include jewelry, decorative applications, houseware and architectural elements. 5548-01

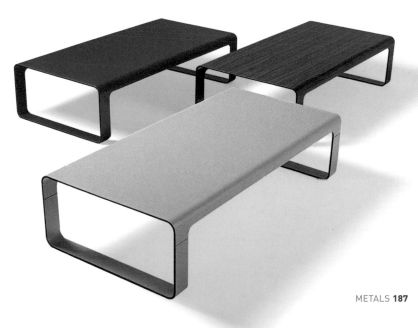

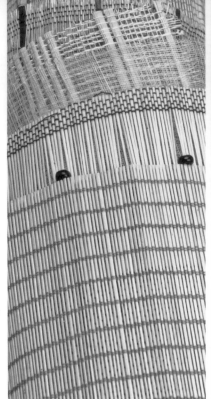

This is a cellulosic matrix impregnated with polyester resin for cost-effective cooling and humidification. The process of cooling and humidifying air is based on the principle of evaporative cooling: when hot, dry air passes at low speed through a wet matrix, it is cooled and humidified. The polyester resin imparts water and allows water absorption. The efficiency of the cooling process is due to the relatively large surface area, enhancing contact between air and water. The UV-resistant structure also acts as a natural filter, removing dust, algae and mineral build-up, and is easy to clean and maintain. An optional protective and strengthening coating is available in customized colours, providing protection against bacteria, algae and other deposits. Applications include cooling systems for green houses and open-air structures. 5514-01

ABOVE + BELOW
Produced from fine strips of bamboo or paper in the weft and natural monofilament in the warp, these handmade window screens are coated with a natural tree lacquer. Variations of light transmission value are available by variations in the number of strips per cm/inch. The fabric is treated with pesticides but as yet is not flame retardant. Applications include window and wall treatments, furniture and tabletop accessories. 4815-02

Solid surfacing from 100 per cent post-consumer recycled paper. Waste paper pulp is mixed with a non-petroleum phenolic resin to produce a rigid, hard, durable and solid surfacing sheet. These sheets are Class A fire rated, but may darken slightly under UV exposure. They may be worked like hardwood and come in eight colours. Approved by SmartWood and the Rainforest Alliance, it contributes to LEED (Leadership in Energy and Environmental Design) certification, using a water-based, non-petroleum phenolic resin with no detectable formaldehyde. Applications for this material are for interior countertops, work surfaces, tables and splashbacks. This material is currently only available in the US. 5518-01

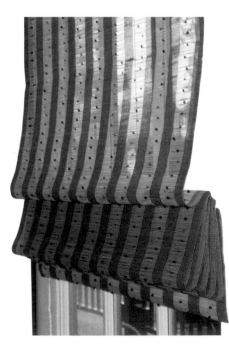

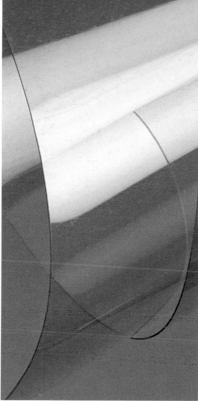

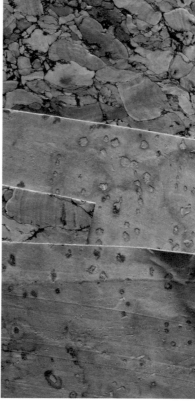

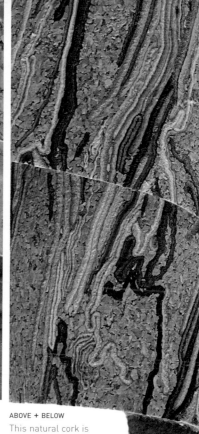

These nanocomposite compounds improve on existing polymers. Nano-sized (less than 100 nanometers) particles are added into polyolefin compounds such as polypropylene (PP) or polyethylene (PE) to increase stiffness, toughness and impact resistance. The particles are thin platelets of a naturally occurring clay-based mineral that disperse in the polymer and impart the improved properties. Only a small weight of the platelets is need to create significant property improvements, to process temperatures, reduce glass fibre content (without losing stiffness) and improve surface gloss. Current applications are for moulded car and consumer product parts. Potential applications include any moulded plastic component that requires better surface gloss, higher stiffness or improved impact resistance. 5008-01

Made from corn and other plants, this compostable polymer film is a biocomposite and requires twenty to fifty per cent less fossil fuel than comparable petroleum-based plastics. These bioplastics are blow moulded to form an environmentally friendly alternative to petroleum- and cellulose-based plastic films, with more stable pricing. After use, the films can be recycled into monomers, polymers or composted in municipal composting facilities. These films are produced from a renewable resource, have a natural dyne level of 38, and have good adhesion properties, excellent optics, are high gloss, scratch-resistant, printable, heat-sealable, die-cutable with good lay flat, rigidity and strong dead fold retention. Applications include film for window, carton, label, packaging, envelope, floral and speciality markets. 5389-01

Laminated onto a variety of textiles, including polyurethane, viscose/polyester and nylon, these thin slices of natural cork create various patterns and colours. The textiles are hypoallergenic, wear-resistant, waterproof and dust and dirt repellent. Teflon® coatings can be applied to increase stain resistance, and a flame-retardant version is available. Applications include footwear, upholstery, book binding and apparel. 5335-02

ABOVE + BELOW
This natural cork is laminated onto non-woven backing. The wall covering is available by the linear metre in continuous rolls with a width of 100 cm (39 in). There are various cork patterns and colours available. The wall covering is hypoallergenic, wear-resistant, waterproof, and dust and dirt repellent. It is also easy to cut, apply and remove. Applications are for interior wall coverings. 5335-01

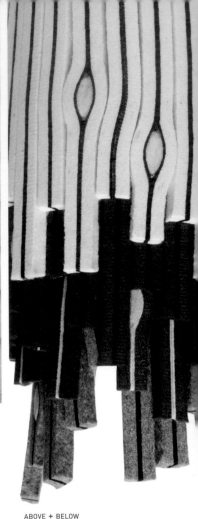

This natural fibre rug has a deep pile height. These 100 per cent New Zealand rugs are woven using felted wool loops in ten patterns. They are backed with a woven jute and cotton mat and are class 1 (class 2 in some cases) fire rated. They are woven 3.66 m (12 ft) wide with a pile height of up to 70 mm (2¾ in). The rugs can be used for residential interior flooring, although they are not recommended for stairs. 4791-03

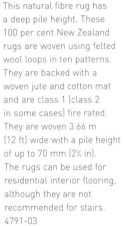

Felt-based fabrics like the above example offer sound absorption, tactile effect and unique visual appeal. The fabrics are handmade from 100 per cent wool felt and woven wool, and incorporate patterns created by twisting and/or stitching different pieces of fabric together. The textiles are sold by the square metre and are available in a standard range of colours and textures. Special orders or commissions are also available with four to six weeks of lead time. The textiles are naturally fire-retardant. Current applications are for wall panels, window blinds, cushions, blankets, ottomans and upholstery. 5453-01

There has been a great push towards more sustainable packaging materials. This corn starch-based, biodegradable packaging foam is one attempt. The foam is extruded into sheets for protective packaging applications and completely dissolves in water. It is available in one colour (off-white) in sheets up to 610 x 1524 mm (24 x 60 in), with thicknesses ranging from 12.7 to 50.8 mm (½ to 3 in). This foam is available at a similar or lower cost than comparable petroleum-based polymer foams. It is water soluble, readily biodegradable and assimilated by soil micro-organisms as food. 5558-01

ABOVE + BELOW

Strips of felted wool are adhered together in this material using a polyester woven backing to create a flexible sheet, and are typically used for carpeting. There are over thirty colours of strip, and the resulting flexible mats are non-flammable, water repellent and breathable; and the mat may be dry-cleaned or wiped clean with a damp cloth. Individual damaged strips can be easily replaced. 5304-01

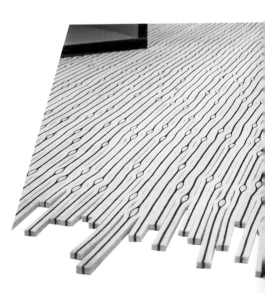

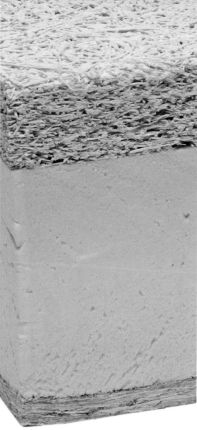

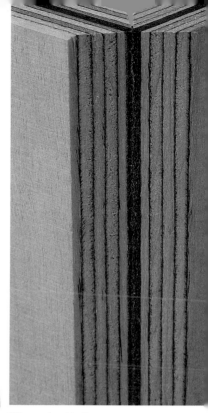

In the above material, a linoleum-based sheet is laminated onto rigid board for use as low-cost durable countertops and desktops. The sheet is available in over 300 colours and patterns and in a matt surface finish. It is durable under mechanical load, permanently anti-static, inflammable, heat resistant, lightfast, elastic and resistant to abrasion, cigarette burns, oils and fats. All marks are easily removable with water and common agents such as detergent. This material can be used for everything from a kitchen counter to a workbench or to a corporate president's desk. 5012-01

These three-layer roofing panels are made from a cementitious wood fibre plank for interior applications. Bonding is possible with standard structural adhesives and nailing is also possible. Panels can be cut using standard wood-working tools, and are abuse-resistant and sound-absorbing. The panels are typically used in sloped roofing applications where insulation and a nailable surface are required. 0493-03

ABOVE + BELOW

As an alternative to hardwood, strands of bamboo are mixed with a low-VOC adhesive, heated and compressed to their specified thickness. The heat and pressure of the press causes tangling of the bamboo fibres, transforming them into high-density, high-strength boards that are cut and planed into tongue and groove flooring. 5171-04

This wood and leather composite allows for easy construction of modular furniture. Leather or rubber is sandwiched between two pieces of plywood or medium density fibreboard (MDF) so that when notch sections on either side of the central leather piece are removed by routing, it creates a flexible hinge. Decorative laminates can be applied to either outer plywood surface and the composite can be processed in CNC-controlled wood-working machines. This low-cost sheet is used as a packaging material, in event displays, furniture and for desktops. 5062-01

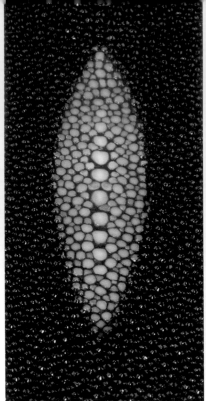

Made from reconstituted leather and synthetic materials, these textured and embossed leather panels are made from a combination of 60 per cent leather, 25 per cent rubber latex and 15 per cent other polymers to produce a leather alternative with the feel and look of leather, but with a polymer surface layer. The leather is obtained from scraps from the tannery floor, which is ground up and added to the latex and calendared to produce thin sheets. The panels are colourfast and have a high breaking strength but a low tear strength. The panels are available in a wide range of colours including custom colours and textures. There are no minimum orders and current applications are for accessories, belts, bags and furniture. 492002

This is an example of woven leather for flooring, walls and upholstery. Leather strips are woven into a range of designs using a broad range of colours. For flooring applications, the leather is backed with synthetic foam. 5014-01

ABOVE + BELOW
These small shagreen hides from stingray have been dyed. The hides are from farmed stingray, and the aniline dyeing which is similar to that of cow hides, uses no chemicals. The hide is tough and highly abrasion-resistant as well as water repellent. There are four standard colours available and customization of the colour is also possible. Applications for these hides are for luxury fashion jewelry as well as boxes, purses and bags. 5157-01

Also made from reconstituted leather and synthetic materials, this sheet is a combination of 70 per cent leather, 10 per cent rubber latex and 20 per cent PU to produce a leather alternative with the feel and look of leather, but with a PU surface layer. The reconstituted leather is again obtained from scraps from the tannery floor, which is then ground up and added to the latex and calendared to produce thin sheets. The panels are colourfast and have a high breaking strength but have a low tear strength. The panels are available in a wide range of colours. Current applications are for accessories and furniture. 5247-01

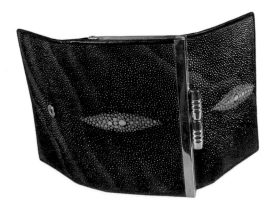

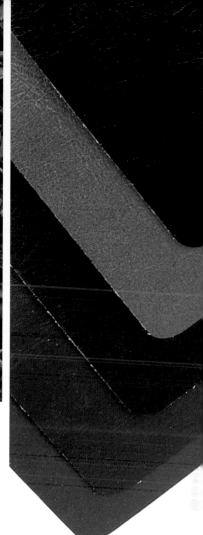

The examples above are leather floor and wall tiles. These waterproof and abrasion-resistant tiles are available up to 300 x 300 mm (11¾ x 11¾ in) in size and in nine colourways, as well as in hexagonal, herringbone and chequerboard designs. Applications are for residential flooring, as wall coverings and for light-use work surfaces. 5014-02

From the bark of Ugandan Fiscus trees comes this mouldable, flexible material. The sheets are transformed by mechanical deformation into a soft, flexible, textile-like material that has mechanical strength and good abrasion resistance. The sheets may be stitched, laminated or moulded into complex shapes and are rigidized using resin. 5257-01

This house insulation is a non-toxic alternative to glass fibre. It is a low-density, non-flammable loose fill made from 100 per cent seaweed that has been harvested from the sea, cleaned, chopped and dried with no additives. This insulation is durable, does not attract parasites, has good absorption and acts as a humidity buffer. It has similar values to insulation materials such as paper, fibreglass and PU foam. Applications are for residential house insulation. 5485-01

High pressure laminate (HPL), like the example above, is made of processed leather fibres from scraps of shoe soles. The resulting leather surface is resistant to hot water, impact and light scratching, and most household stains. Current applications are as work surfaces on home and office furniture. 0421-04

Combining his interest in design and nature, along with his dedication to Uganda, Rene Malcorps became a specialist in barkcloth. He uses the material to create pieces that raise awareness of his principle of 'Art Nature Design' (AND), and to teach of the importance of respecting all three. 5257-01

Lightweight and corrugated, this board is made of 100 per cent wood pulp without an adhesive. It is available in sheets in three thicknesses, each with different corrugation frequency and amplitude, and in a style called 'gamma' with rectangular corrugations. It can be cut with conventional wood-working equipment. It was original used as transformer board but current applications include interior room dividers, decorative panels and sound-absorptive ceiling panels. 5372-01

Low-cost corrugated construction board like this one is typically used for temporary displays. Recycled pulped paper is used to produce card that is coated on one side with clay for easy painting or finishing, then corrugated to form sheets rigid in one direction and flexible in the other. The card can be printed prior to corrugation with a range of designs that may also be customized. It is used for point-of-sale displays, temporary trade show exhibits, to wrap columns and as a screen. 5005-01

This packaging material is composed of waste palm fibre that would otherwise be burned or landfilled. The material is FDA (Food and Drug Administration) compliant for food contact, biodegradable and certified compostable. It breaks down into humus after ninety days outdoors, unlike polylactide (PLA), which requires industrial compost facilities operating at a higher temperature. The material is strong, durable and naturally water and oil-resistant. It is available in a natural 'fibre' and vanilla colour, with other colours possible using vegetable dyes. Pricing is comparable to packaging made from polyethylene terphthalate (PET) or PLA. Current applications include fresh produce packs and fast-food packaging. Fresh meat trays and garden pots are currently under development. Custom packaging solutions are also available. 5415-01

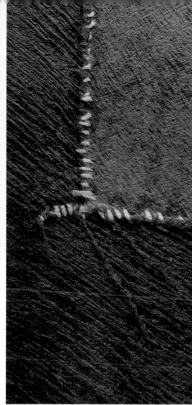

An example of biodegradable string and rope that has been manufactured from corn. Derived from lactic acid that is made from fermented corn starch, this material is a non-petroleum braided and twisted rope and string. It is currently available only in white. The ropes are used in greenhouse cultivation, as it is biodegradable over time. 5279-01

These customized hand-knitting yarns can be made with specifications on fibre content, blends, texture and colour. The types of yarns available are craft, apparel, and high performance yarns that are usually blended with anti-microbial fibres. End uses can be various across the textile industry. 5272-01

ABOVE + BELOW
This weaving process increases the strength of low-cost yarn simply by twisting it. The yarn is twisted twice around each thread to achieve an increase in tensile strength for the same amount of material. It is used to make low-cost sacks for food packaging, although it can be applied to any textile. 5066-01

Removed from Ugandan Fiscus trees, rigid laminate sheets are actually tree bark. The bark is transformed by mechanical deformation into soft, flexible, textile-like sheets that are then laminated onto a high-pressure laminate (HPL) sheet. It is available in dark 'natural' colours including black, light and dark brown and red, and has good stain and abrasion resistance (it is coated with a varnish, oil or overlay) as well as being fire-resistant. The laminate may be used anywhere a standard laminate sheet is used. 5359-01

Natural felt such as this is used for a range of industrial and commercial applications. The felt, derived from sheep's wool, has been pressed, heated, moistened and vibrated to create dense, mechanically adhered non-woven pads. Density, colour, thickness and overall dimension may be specified. Applications are for sound and vibration damping, for filtration, as a polishing surface and as a flooring and upholstery surface. 5156-01

This handmade paper results from cleaning contaminated soil in Detroit, Michigan. In a process called phyto-remediation, plants (switch grass and sunflowers) are grown to extract contaminates, including lead, from the ground. After each season, the plant is harvested and made into paper. The colour and texture varies based on content. It is tree-free, biodegradable, has zero VOCs and is chlorine-free. Applications are for art, graphic design, printing and wallpaper or lampshades. 5473-01

Produced from shredded, recycled newsprint, this insulation batting is a sustainable alternative to glass fibre, and is bonded with a polyolefin resin and a boric acid fire retardant. The batting is semi-rigid, allowing for compaction and compression for variable size openings. The sheets are as insulative as equivalent volumes of glass fibre batting. It is typically used as interior house insulation. 5060-01

These perforated veneer panels are available in a range of designs. Veneers of various types, including beech, maple and stained birch are adhered onto thin fibreboard and perforated. Alternative wood species veneers are also available, as well as metal and other laminate surfaces. The boards are available up to 263 x 122 cm (104 x 48 in) in double-sided and single-sided veneer options, and up to 7 mm (¼ in) thick, depending on format. There are eleven different standard hole patterns and the sheets may be incorporated into an acoustical system with a suitable inner core. Current applications are for furniture. 4891-03

LEFT + FAR LEFT
Exhibiting the true flexibility of paper, this novel lamp by Kouichi Okamoto takes the material that we usually think of as merely two-dimensional, and gives it one more. Using locally sourced Denguri paper, the designer has created a lamp that ships in a flat form some 2 cm (¾ in) thick, but then unfurls to reveal its delicate honeycomb structure.

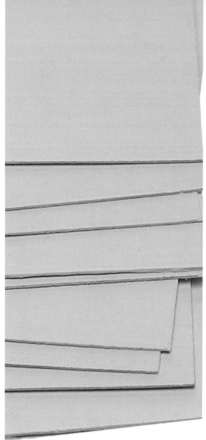

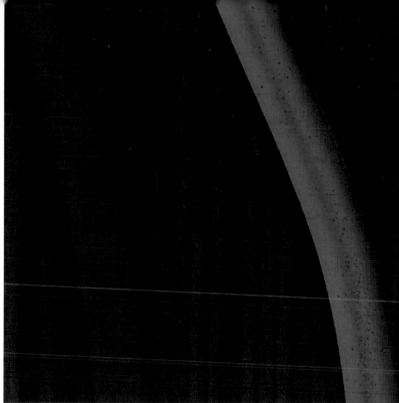

Though not new, this flexible barkcloth has rarely been used outside of Africa. Flexible and soft, it is made by a process in which the bark from dead trees is moisturized, cut into strips, hand-pounded, and finally dried. The sheets are not dyed, so each one slightly varies in its natural colour. They can be fire-proofed and are acid-free. They can be sealed with a clear polyurethane finish and are available in satin (matt) or gloss finish. Stains and other products compatible with wood can be used as well. Uses include wall coverings, furniture, lampshades, book binding, framing and stationery. 5276-01

These fire-retardant, non-toxic paints are available in 109 colours. These paints do not contain any VOCs and are suitable for the most demanding of applications, including use in enclosed vertical exitways for commercial interior walls. 5409-03

ABOVE + BELOW
This is a unique method of creating translucency in wood panelling. Various types of hardwood, such as cherry or oak, are produced as panels and then sectioned along straight or curved lines. At the final stage of production, transparent resin is inserted at a thickness of between 0.32 and 5.1 cm (⅛ and 2 in) into the gap. The acrylic is available in a range of standard colours, including clear. The acrylic layers may be straight or curved, in any specified pattern, and different colours may be used on the same panel. 5042-01

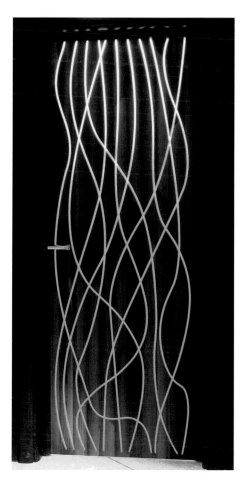

Unlike other pulped paper materials, this version has a super-smooth outer surface. It is created by foaming the 100 per cent paper pulp, generates no dust, and precludes the need for plastic bags around the product, which improves look and cost. The product is recyclable with other paper products and is also biodegradable. It may be moulded into an almost unlimited range of patterns and shapes and may also be coloured. Applications for this technology include packaging for delicate components and as decorative packaging. 5281-01

Made entirely from agricultural waste, this mouldable resin/fibre composite compound is biodegradable and has good acoustic properties. Any raw material containing cellulose in sufficient concentration can be used for the production of this rigid, dense compound. Additional materials such as stones or glass chips may be inlaid into the moulded piece and it can be finished, glued, screwed and worked like a hardwood. 5460-01

This sheet acts as cushioning in flooring and for model production. This composite tile is produced by adding rubberized wood and cork granulate (latex is used to coat the particles) to polyurethane (PU) foam during extrusion. This creates a composite sheet with good cushioning properties that can be coated with a polyurethane sealant to provide water and scratch resistance. The sheet is available as rolls, and in a wide range of binder colours (the cork and wood granulate are only available in their 'natural' colour). 5064-01

Finished with an iridescent pigmented coating to create decorative packaging, this cotton cloth may be embossed, screen-printed onto, foil-stamped and stitched. There are thirteen standard colours with custom matching of colour available for larger orders. The textile is available in rolls but may also be sold as sheets. Applications are for packaging and stationery, book covers and boxes. 5158-01

These speaker cabinets are made from an ecological, wood-like, mouldable material processed solely from plant fibres and water by means of a sustainable process. The fibres may be hemp, flax straw or sugar cane, and the material has excellent acoustic properties while being completely biodegradable. 5460-01

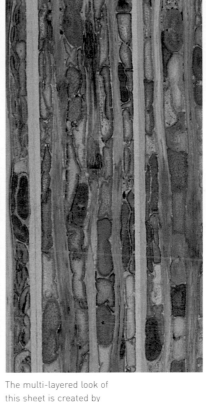

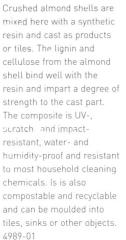

Crushed almond shells are mixed here with a synthetic resin and cast as products or tiles. The lignin and cellulose from the almond shell bind well with the resin and impart a degree of strength to the cast part. The composite is UV-, scratch- and impact-resistant, water- and humidity-proof and resistant to most household cleaning chemicals. Is is also compostable and recyclable and can be moulded into tiles, sinks or other objects. 4989-01

This fibreboard panel uses a revolutionary resin binder that emits no VOCs. The MDF also has a coloured surface so that no laminate sheet is needed. The panels comply with LEED certification in a range of different categories including VOC and formaldehyde emissions. The sheets may be treated similarly to wood-veneered panels and are typically used in residential and commercial interior applications. 5091-03

The multi-layered look of this sheet is created by stacking stalks of the Sorghum plant. The raw stalks are compressed, washed, woven into sheets, then stacked and heat-pressed into this form. They are bonded with a formaldehyde-free adhesive and cut to the desired sheet size. It has good dimensional stability, is resistant to warping and may be finished using standard wood finishes. Current applications are for furniture, wall panels and countertops, as well as for cabinetry and flooring. 5034-01

This fibreboard panelling incorporates agricultural fibre instead of wood. One hundred per cent wheat straw is used that also creates the surface texture. It is finished with a zero-VOC UV acrylic. The surfaces of these panels are also pigmented and have a smooth surface texture, precluding the need for a laminate. The panels comply with LEED certification in a range of different categories including VOC and formaldehyde emissions. There are seven colours available: storm cloud, natural, charcoal, straw, taupe, olive and zinfandel. The sheets may be treated similarly to wood-veneered panels and are typically used in residential and commercial interiors. 5091-02

Created by Achyut Kantawala and Edward Ng, this partition is fashioned from simple panels made from plywood. The screen is easily assembled without tools, and can be expanded vertically and horizontally. The finished piece belies the simplicity of the design and the assembly.

This is a simple idea that offers a different look to MDF. The panel is through-dyed and also utilizes a formaldehyde-free binder. The pigments used to colour the board have good fade-resistance. It is available in seven colours: black, blue, brown, green, red, yellow and orange. Applications include furniture and interior surfaces including cabinetry, work surfaces and interior cladding.
5228-01

These recyclable, shaped, wood components are made of 95–97 per cent soft wood chips and sawmill waste. The chips are shredded, dried, and graded, and then 3–5 per cent isocyanate adhesive is added. The moulded wood is shaped by compression in a heated, metal mould and can be waterproofed during production. Applications include furniture, packaging, and freestanding displays.
5240-01

Individual users can curve this oriented strand board (OSB) into complex shapes. The OSB is available as flat sheets. From the flat sheet, the board may be curved using heat and pressure, hardening the resin and creating complex curves. This product is currently a prototype, but possible applications include furniture, interior design and column cladding.
5261-03

This spectacular example by Andreas Wenning is but one of a growing trend of bespoke tree houses. Ample use of warm-toned wood gives the structure a look that complements the foliage of the two trees supporting it.

These types of composites are increasingly used in the car industry. Typically used as door panels, this composite is made from a blend of natural fibres and polypropylene. This material was created as a substitute for existing wood fibre, wood flour and fibreglass plastics and is mouldable to 3-D shapes. The material is half the weight of glass-filled polypropylene and easier to recycle. It may also have a laminate added to the surface during the moulding process. Applications include doors, moulded work surfaces and other surfaces that need a rigid, mouldable, sound-absorbing surface. 5418-01

Here is an example of construction board made from hemp waste. This formaldehyde-free, medium density fibreboard (MDF) has zero VOC (volatile organic compound) emissions. It is composed of hurd, a product reclaimed from hemp textile manufacturing. Applications include furniture, shop fixtures, work surfaces, shelving systems, custom mouldings, soffit and trim fixtures. 5449-02

This wheat-based structural material is an alternative to oriented strand board (OSB) that is hurricane resistant. Lignin in the wheat straw acts as a binder, only needing water, heat and pressure during production. Boric acid (a low-toxicity mineral) is added to provide resistance to termites, carpenter ants, other pests, mould and mildew. An optional ceramic and fibreglass exterior coating resists impact, moisture and UV radiation. Some current applications include construction panels for residential homes and commercial buildings. 5379-01

Rooms that contain sensitive electronic equipment require static control. This decorative laminated particleboard contains electrically conductive particulates to minimize static buildup. The sheet comprises an inner core of particleboard that includes carbon powder introduced with the binder as well as outer faces of decorative high-pressure laminate. The laminate may be specified from a range that the manufacturer produces, including coloured, patterned and textured. They are typically used in micro-electronics labs, control centres and for housing electronic medical equipment. 5305-03

Sometimes, simplicity can astonish much more than complexity. In this folding chair design, Hannu Kähönen has transformed a simple sheet of birch plywood into a chair produced with virtually no wasted wood. The chair (which features black paint on one side and white on the other), has hidden mechanical parts and can fold in either direction.

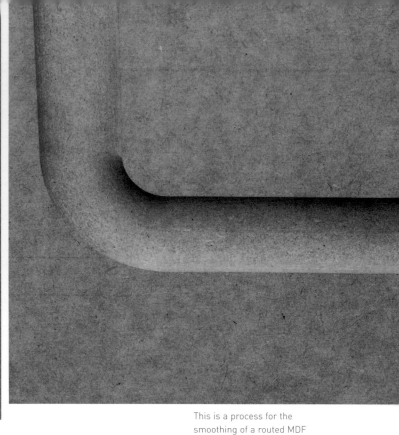

Manufactured with phenol formaldehyde (PF), with emissions of 0.00–0.04 ppm formaldehyde, this is one of the few low-emission particleboards that uses no urea formaldehyde. It is made from western softwood fibres and is Green Cross certified by Scientific Certification Systems as being made from 100 per cent recycled wood fibres (a post-industrial waste product from lumber mills). The sheets may contribute to LEED points. 5369-01

Made from hemp and used for skateboard ramps. This smooth, non-porous surfacing material is made of abaca fibre derived from the banana plant from certified managed forests in Ecuador and the Philippines. The fibres are oriented and compressed with a binder resin to create a hard, durable weather-resistant surface that may be bent. The sheets are available in three colours: nutmeg, camel and slate black. Applications include residential, corporate and workshop counter surfaces as well as interior and exterior skateboard ramp panelling. 4798-03

This is a process for the smoothing of a routed MDF surface directly following the routing process. The technology immediately 'follows' the routing tool and smoothes the MDF to a highly polished surface. With the smoothening technology, non-cutting tools compress the profile surface by means of pressure and heat to durably compress the fibres. The smoothening tool can be used as an additionally mounted module or directly in the spindle of the CNC centre. The tool does not rotate, but is fixed. Applications include cabinet doors and any MDF surface that needs routing. Exterior and interior profiles can also be handled. 5261-02

Designed by Gerard Minakawa for Ukao, the Yolanda chair is the first bamboo-laminate chair designed specifically for the contract furniture market. The chair's distinctly contemporary lines are well suited to the multi-ply laminate material, giving the chair a solid, but not bulky, form.

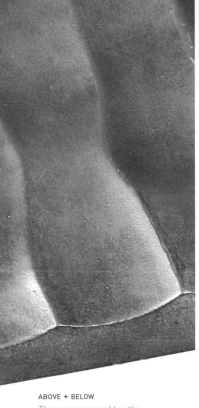

Utilizing unique waste materials, these natural fibre rigid panels are manufactured using vetiver grass, rice husk, wood chips, lemon grass or orange skin in a resin binder. The sheets compare to standard particleboard in strength, screw pullout, water resistance and surface roughness. The resulting colour depends upon the raw material and ranges from yellow to green, to brown to red. The orange-skin board has a natural orange fragrance. Applications are for flooring, wall covering, partitions, shelving, tables, countertops and ceiling panels 5496-01

ABOVE + BELOW

This process enables the creation of organically shaped, sculpted surfaces on fibreboard. CNC routing of the MDF is accurate up to 0.13 mm (⅟₂₀₀ in), allowing for edge-to-edge mounting of two panels with near-perfect alignment. This product offers a broad variety of patterns, materials, finishes and installation options; in addition to MDF panels, HDF, solid wood, and cast acrylic sheets may be used. 4891-02

Based on the natural mineral mica, these metal flakes are covered with a thin layer of metal oxides, for example titanium dioxide and/or iron oxide. The interference of light and the coated platelets creates silver-white, gold and metallic lustre effects. All the pigments can be used alone or in combination with other colours. These pigments find use in the car industry, in after-market applications. 4991-02

By incorporating a polymer layer in this plywood, it effectively dampens sound. Finnish birch is used as the wood, with a thin layer of rubber as the constrained layer. It is primarily intended for insulation of airborne sound, but it also has some structure-borne, sound-damping properties, especially at low temperatures. It is suitable for interior and exterior use, and applications for this sheet material are for transport vehicle floors in trucks, buses, ships and trains. 4868-02

Multi-laminar wood is created by gluing together multiple veneers of different colours and species then cutting at different angles. This process creates a dense, multi-layered wood veneer that may be worked like wood but has unique visual appeal. The number of sandwich layers may be varied to create different physical and aesthetic properties. The colour and pattern of the surface is dependent upon the type of wood used in the sandwich. Most applications are found in interior design. 1632-03

The process of multi-layering wood into these sheets creates a very hard, dense, multi-layered wood composite. The colour and pattern of the surface is dependent upon the type of wood used in the sandwich and current applications are for interior residential and commercial door panels. 1632-05

This plywood is a revolution in low-VOC materials. The binder used is a non-toxic, virtually VOC-free adhesive based on soy. The panels are comprised of one of four core materials, faced in veneer. Core materials include: FSC (Forest Stewardship Council)-certified MDF, FSC-certified particleboard, FSC-certified plywood, and wheat straw. The wheat straw fibre is annually renewable and was historically considered to be agricultural waste. The building panels are available in 1.22 and 1.52 m (4 and 5 ft) widths, in various lengths to 3.05 m (10 ft) and in thicknesses between 0.64 and 3.17 cm (¼ and 1¼ in). The panels can contribute to LEED green building points in a number of different categories and are currently used for furniture, door panels and other architectural panelling. 5091-04

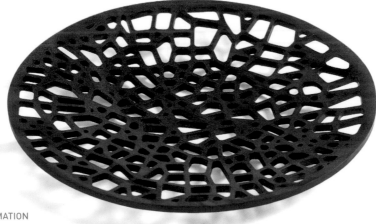

This elegant and organic bowl by Janet and Joe Doucet is cut first by robotic process, but later finished by hand. In an interesting juxtaposition of natural and technological, a single piece of black walnut is transformed through a high-tech milling process.

Here is a 3-ply woodboard that incorporates a lightweight balsa sheet at its core. This laminated woodboard is available as a high-pressure laminate veneer-faced board. Standard sizes are 1.22 x 2.44 m (4 x 8 ft) for the veneer-covered sheet. Alternative sizes are available on request. These boards are lightweight and strong. Applications include door panels. 5288-01

Custom composite timbers (also known as 'Glulam') are created when solid, stable timber is required to meet the design brief. There are three processes to fabricating composite timbers. All processes use inert, clear, water-based poly-isocyanate glues and a low VOC resin. These composite timbers can also be curved without losing structural integrity. The wood used can be specified as reclaimed or sustainably harvested, which can be used for LEED credits. This material is used in load-bearing architectural applications. 5361-03

ABOVE + BELOW
Timbers are used when strength and appearance are paramount. These are made from structurally graded, engineered wood core (Glulam) and veneered with sliced or sawn veneers. Virtually any species of wood may be used for the veneers so it is possible to mix solid material with engineered wood and still meet visual requirements. Sustainably harvested wood is available for the Glulam core or the veneer. Applications are in interior and exterior architecture. 5361-02

Though simply produced, these textured surfaces are unlike any other wood available currently. The soft wood is formed in a metal die at high pressure. There is an MDF core surrounded by paper that provides structural strength for the lightweight panels. They find application as vertical surfaces in interior design.
2239-05

This printing process for wood has the appearance of high-quality marquetry. It uses sublimation printing to create realistic images on wood surfaces that mimic inlaid patterns. The printing process uses a thin film to transfer the image with a heat cure, opening the pores of the surface and allowing the ink to soak into the substrate, creating an indelible image. This process may be applied to metals, polymer laminates and glass, and offers a low-cost alternative to inlaying and marquetry and may be used on wall surfaces, doors, flooring and desks.
5160-01

ABOVE + BELOW
The inherent softness of certain species of wood allows this surface texture to be formed. It is achieved by pressure in a die and is formed on both sides. It has an MDF core that is sandwiched and moulded with a lacquered paper or veneer. Maximum sheet dimensions are 2.45 x 1.05 m (8.03 x 3.44 ft) and range from 4 mm to 30 mm-thick (⅛ to 1³⁄₁₆ in) thick. The pattern may be customized, and applications include walls, ceilings, furniture and display counters.
2239-04

This durable interior flooring is a blend of recycled tyres, post-industrial waste and virgin rubber. There are two versions; a standard version is available in twenty-eight colours, while the 'Chunks' version has larger coloured particulates and is available in ten colours. The flooring is maintained with regular damp mopping and periodic buffing if desired, and the manufacturer recommends coating the floor with a mop-on acrylic emulsion finish to further protect and enhance it. The floor will typically need to be resealed twice a year. Applications are for high traffic commercial flooring surfaces. 4571-02

ABOVE RIGHT + LEFT
Insulation batting is made from wood chippings and is an alternative to glass fibre. A polyolefin binder is used to bind the chips; ammonium polyphosphate is used as a fire retardant. The batting is semi-rigid, allowing for compaction and compression for variable size openings. The sheets have a very low thermal conductivity and are typically used as interior house insulation. 5060-02

BELOW
Design group GAMplusFRATESI's novel approach to seating with these felt and wood 'pillows' was inspired by a fairytale. Strips of felt are bolted between the slats of wood providing the decorative design on the top, and a flexible cushioning loop on the bottom.

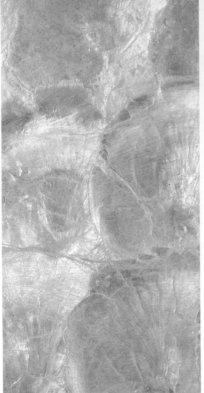

ABOVE

This material was originally created as an aid to visualizing 3-D structures. It is a laminated sheet consisting of two or more layers of thin rigid veneer and a flexible textile or film. The sheet is then CNC-milled to create a tear-resistant hinge. The flexible layer can be specified, with options including leather, linen or mirror foil. The rigid, thin veneer layer can be finished using veneers, stains or paints. Two thicknesses are available and panels are available in sizes up to 140 x 210 cm (55⅛ x 82¹¹⁄₁₆ in). The panels can be used during the ideation process, or for model-making, lighting or folding products. 5301-01

Unmistakably for the luxury market, layers of genuine shell are hand inlaid on these sheet tiles that have a stain-resistant coating. They are easy to install, naturally UV-resistant, and can be bent around corners. The standard tile size is 30.5 x 61 cm (12 x 24 in) and they are currently available in white (natural) and gold. The decoration may also be used as an inlay for furniture. 2687-05

ABOVE + BELOW

Sheets of these stones are backed with a mesh that creates textured flooring and wall tiles. There are ten colourways available, with sheet sizes up to 30 x 30 cm (11¹³⁄₁₆ x 11¹³⁄₁₆ in) though customization of pattern and sheet size are available for larger orders. The tiles can feature in residential and commercial flooring and wall coverings in bathrooms, showrooms and other display areas. 4268-02

This compression moulded composite sheet is a mineral-filled thermoplastic polymer with fibre reinforcement that is finished to a smooth surface. Currently there are over fifty colours that include solids, granite, marble and high-gloss effects. The surfaces are scratch-resistant, promote no bacteria growth, are highly impact- and thermal shock- and burn-resistant. The compression moulding process also allows these materials to be made into sinks and other shapes. Current applications are for residential countertops, sinks and kitchen work surfaces. 4377-01

Made lower cost for low volume runs, this is an economical type of pulped paper. Recent processing innovations allow a large number of moulds with different vacuum, paper amounts and drying times on the platen at once. This permits cost-effective manufacture of a number of dissimilar low-volume products at the same time. The material is strong yet flexible and recycles with newspaper at existing curbside and community programmes. Products are available with a clamshell shape, with a more finished look, as can be embossed with a logo, recycling symbols or other relevant information. Current applications include packaging for shipping and secondary packaging for cosmetics and personal care products. 5391-01

ABOVE + BELOW
A thin glass sheet is used to protect these water-absorbing stones in wet areas. Flat, polished float glass is adhered to marble, sandstone or limestone to allow use of marble and other absorbent stone in bathrooms. The top glass surface may be specified 2.2 or 4 mm (⅒ or ⅛ in) thick with four ground edge types available. There are ten stone types to choose from and the surfaces are typically used as bathroom and bar countertops. 5365-01

This tile is made from recycled granite, marble and glass chips. It also comes in versions that include mother-of-pearl. It is highly abrasion-resistant, frost-resistant and is low-cost. The colour and chip inserts can be customized. Applications include flooring, countertops and splashbacks. 4961-02

Interior designers are continually looking for more sustainable alternatives to traditional wall coverings. This 100 per cent twisted, coloured paper is woven into textiles that are backed with a non-woven synthetic paper for direct adherence to walls. Two weave patterns are available; a 'Tweed' using multicoloured yarns, and 'Paper Shift', a more linear weave. There are a total of eleven colours, measuring 137 cm (54 in) wide.
1940-07

ABOVE + BELOW
Energy-absorbing material is incorporated into the 'bubbles' in this film that are capable of absorbing massive amounts of energy. The pouches are filled with volcanic glass beads and the material is available with an extinguishing coating that offers a revolutionary blast protection system against all blast and fire or burn threats. Current applications for this wrap are for rubbish bins capable of absorbing the energy of a backpack bomb, and it can also be used in the walls of buildings to reduce the impact of explosions.
5390-01

These papers incorporate natural materials such as grass cloth, wood veneers and rice papers that are manufactured using processes that attempt to reduce their energy footprint. They are class A fire-rated and are breathable and permeable too. The wall coverings may be cleaned by vacuum but are also treated with a PTFE coating for stain-resistance. The rolls are 137 cm (54 in) wide and find application in residential and commercial interior wall coverings.
5053-02

Wood veneer that glows in the dark? This multi-laminar veneer incorporates fluorescent pigments in the non-coloured veins of the grain. It fluoresces when exposed to UV light or 'blacklight'. The veneer colour and texture is customizable, and current applications are as decorative laminates in nightclubs and other entertainment venues.
1632-11

This lumber is harvested underwater using a logging machine to cut old growth timber submerged by hydro dam reservoirs. The submerged wood is in good condition since it has not been exposed to oxygen, wood-decaying fungi or insects. A patented submarine called 'The SawFish', operated by remote control, clasps onto the truck, attaches airbags, cuts the tree underwater and then releases the timber, which rises to the surface of the water. The cut trees are towed by a tug, avoiding the need to build roads. The waterlogged trees are easier to mill than above ground trees, dry easily in a conventional wood kiln and stain better. The wood has Smart Wood Rediscovered Wood certification. Species include Douglas Fir, Western Red Cedar, Western White Pine, Lodgepole Pine and Hemlock. Applications are for any wood requirement. 5384-01

FSC-certified softwoods such as these have been chemically treated to act as hardwoods. This formaldehyde-free process enables softwoods such as pine to take on the characteristics of Brazilian cherry, mahogany or ebony. In this process, starch is pressure-impregnated into the wood, then kiln-dried to remove the moisture and set the polymer. The process can also be used to colour the wood and can be used on any type of softwood for cabinetry, flooring, windows, doors and architectural trim. 5366-01

This material has come from an 81,000-hectare forest in north-west Argentina that was the first area of Argentinean native forest to be certified under the Forest Stewardship Council (FSC) principles and criteria. The forest offers hardwood and available species suitable for furniture include Afata, Cebil, Cedro Orán (Spanish Cedar), Cedro Rosado (Spanish Red Cedar), Nogal Walnut, Quina, Tipa Blanca and Urundel. 5385-01

This tongue-and-groove flooring is from disease-killed, forest-salvaged butternut wood. The approximate hole concentration may be specified within certain parameters. The planks stain, dye and oil very well and are dimensionally stable. It is a medium hardwood. Current applications are for residential flooring. 4683-03

There is no question that liberal use of natural materials integrates architecture into natural surroundings. Here, the Wingårdh architectural practice has used both raw and finished woods to create a tranquil and sympathetic country retreat in the Swedish countryside.

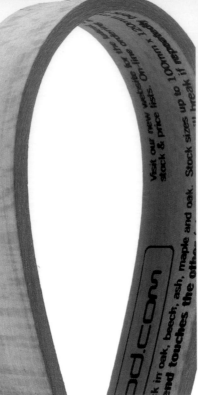

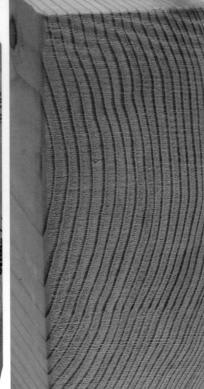

ABOVE + BELOW
Weaving natural materials
such as jute and twisted
paper creates durable
matting for rugs. Jute, paper,
sisal and cotton are woven
into mats that are latex-
or jute-backed in a wide
range of colours and designs.
The mats may be woven
up to 3 m (9.8 ft) wide in
continuous lengths. These
mats are currently used
as residential rugs.
5056-01

When steamed and
compressed along its
length, this solid hardwood
becomes a highly flexible
material. The process uses
no additional chemicals or
resins and the wood can be
bent to a radius ten times
its thickness. This material
has found application in
handrails, decorative
profiles to finish curved
tables and worktops,
glazing beads and sculpture.
4988-01

This process for kiln drying
timbers reduces shrinkage
and warping. Dimension
lumber can be dried using
conventional kiln drying
methods. But typical kilns
extract moisture from
the lumber, twisting and
warping the timber beyond
any useful parameter. The
radio frequency vacuum
kiln drying (RF/VKD) solves
that problem. Combining a
hydraulic restraining system
in a near-perfect vacuum,
radio frequency waves are
applied to the timbers. The
agitated water molecules
cause friction, which in turn
creates heat. The water
expands as it boils and
moves along the longitudinal
direction of the wood
because of its higher
permeability. In RF/VKD,
most of the moisture exits
the ends of the timbers
as opposed to the sides,
reducing checking, splitting
and twisting, which reduces
the amount of raw material
needed for a straight board.
Applications are for load-
bearing timbers or
decorative elements.
5361-01

Mainly used in packaging
applications, this scrim-
reinforced paper is
composed of various
materials including cotton,
bitumen, jute, polyethylene
(PE) film, aluminum,
paraffin and raffia.
The papers are available in
50 m (164 ft) lengths or cut
to A4 sheets in packs
of fifty sheets. Current
applications are for point-
of-sale displays, event
displays and packaging.
5644-01

ABOVE + BELOW
This type of wallcovering has been used for many years, due to its distinctive look, durability and breathability. Woven grasscloth is now also produced as a wallcovering. A range of decorative designs and textured finishes have been created. The grasscloth is available in rolls 58.6 cm x 4.57 m (27 in x 15 ft) long with a minimum order of six rolls. Current applications are for residential and commercial wall coverings and upholstery. 5061-02

Woven paper is durable enough for flooring, so equally suitable for walls. This paper is composed of 40 per cent paper, 20 per cent cotton, 8 per cent polyamide and 27 per cent backing, woven in four different patterns. The surface is coated with an acrylic that is colour and stain-resistant. The colours and weaves can be customized, and this paper can be used for upholstery, screens, lampshades and seating for domestic/light contract use. 4873-03

It may be a little hard to believe, but paper is an exceptionally durable flooring material. This is matting woven from twisted paper. The weaving process creates dissimilar coloured surfaces on either side of the piece, creating a 'reversible' rug or mat. The rugs are hand-washable at 40°C (104°F) and available in blue, black, white, dark blue, grey green and red, all with a 'natural' colour on the reverse. They are used for residential flooring. 4849-05

Made from organic cotton, these textiles are grown without synthetic chemical fertilizers, pesticides or defoliants. It takes 255 g (9 oz) of cotton to make one t-shirt. Of that 255 g, 80 g (2.8 oz) of synthetic fertilizers and 2.8 g (0.1 oz) of active ingredients such as pesticides, herbicides, insecticides and defoliants are used. These pesticides are classified among the most toxic by the EPA. In organic cotton farming, composted manures and cover crops replace synthetic fertilizers; weeding strategies are used instead of herbicides; insects and trap crops control pests; and alternatives to toxic defoliants prepare plants for harvest. Organic fibres are grown and milled in the US without sweatshop labour. Available in fleece, French terry, interlock, jersey, ribs and textures. Current applications are for apparel. 5450-01

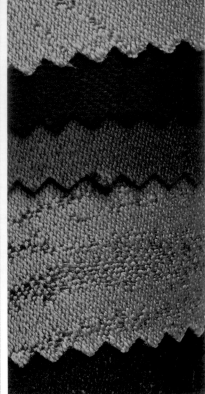

Incorporating cotton fibre and yarn for decorative effect, bunches of cotton fibres in this fabric are woven in parallel lines into non-coloured cotton to create fabric that is 500, 600, 700, 800 or 900 cm (196⅞, 236¼, 275⅝ 314¹⁵⁄₁₆ or 354⅜ in) wide. The fabric is available in blue, red, black, green and other colours. Applications are for interior drapery, apparel accents and room dividers. 5462-02

These sustainable textiles are composed of eco wool™ and organic wool from Australia and New Zealand, and minimize environmental impact over the lifecycle of a textile, including raw material selection, production, usage and disposal. They are made from a rapidly renewable resource, with minimal energy, water input and waste, and without using toxic chemicals during processing. The textiles are reusable, recyclable and biodegradable, and naturally fire retardant and anti-static. Applications are for upholstery. 5451-02

Grown without the use of synthetic chemical fertilizers, pesticides or defoliants, these textiles are composed of organic hemp fibres. The synthetic chemicals in conventional hemp farming harm the environment, farm communities and workers. In organic hemp farming, composted manures and cover crops replace synthetic fertilizers; innovative weeding strategies are used instead of herbicides; beneficial insects and trap crops control insect pests; and alternatives to toxic defoliants prepare plants for harvest. Organic fibres are grown and milled in the US without sweatshop labour. Available in blends, fleece, French terry, interlock, jersey, ribs and textures. Current applications are for apparel. 5450-02

This is one of the ranges of newer sustainable textiles available. Bamboo pulp is refined through hydrolysis-alkalization and multi-phase bleaching, followed by processing into fibre. Bamboo is recognized as a green material because it matures in three years, regenerates without replanting and requires minimal fertilization or pesticides. 5392-01

Instead of heavy woods or metals, German casket manufacturer Uono has turned to an impregnated jute material to create its Cocoon coffin. Aside from being lightweight, the enclosure is completely biodegradable.

Bamboo fabric such as this one has all the properties of cotton with other advantages including natural anti-bacterial properties. It is breathable and cool with the ability to absorb and evaporate moisture. It can be used in any application where cotton is currently used. 5392-01

Similar to organic hemp, these textiles composed of bamboo fibres are grown without the use of synthetic chemical fertilizers, pesticides or defoliants. The manufacturing process does not generate pollution and is certified by the International Organization for Standardization for quality and environmental management. The textiles are available in blends, jersey, ribs and textures; coloured textiles use low impact dyes. Bamboo fabric has all the properties of cotton with other advantages including natural anti-bacterial properties. It is breathable and cool with the ability to absorb and evaporate moisture. Current applications are for apparel. 5450-03

Another sustainable alternative to cotton. These textiles are composed of 100 per cent hemp, as well as hemp blended with cotton, tencel, flax and/or satin. Hemp textiles are fabricated using an enzymatic process to remove lignin from the hemp fibre without compromising its strength. Hemp textiles are highly durable, age well, and are naturally mould- and UV-resistant. The porous structure and water absorbency of the fibre facilitates the dyeing process and retains colour better than any fabric, including cotton. The porous characteristic allows hemp to 'breathe' so that it is cool in warm weather and traps air warmed by the body, providing insulation in cooler weather. Available in jersey, French terry, fleece knits, fur, twill, muslin, corduroy, linen, denim, canvas, herringbone, and silk satin. Applications are for apparel, accessories, furniture and furnishings. 5449-01

ABOVE + BELOW
Flame-retardant, compostable, environmentally sound, this textile is made from the renewable cellulose fibre ViscoseFR™ and wool. Its lifecycle meets environmental standards including the use of environmentally friendly dyes, a chemical-free washing process and coating-free warp yarns. Custom colours are available. It is used for upholstery in commercial and residential interiors. 5255-01

1   5

2   6

3   7

4   8

POLYMERS

1 These thermo-plastic elastomers can be overmoulded onto nylon and have been developed to bond onto a broad range of nylon grades. Applications are for kitchen utensils, gardening equipment and tools.
2 This hand-loomed 100 per cent recycled rubber rug is made from recycled bicycle tubes woven onto a wool backing.
3 This laminated resin incorporates a decorative inner layer. Applications include partitions, windows, lighting and furniture.
4 This broadband sound- and heat-absorbing insulation is made from recycled polyester fleece and can be used for vehicle and construction insulation.
5 Based on the colour illumination of the Morpho butterfly wings, this decorative, self-illuminating filament is composed of nylon and polyester and has applications for pigments in coatings for cars, sports goods, cosmetics and printing.
6 Natural (wool) and synthetic (nylon) fibres from post-consumer carpet scraps are bonded using a synthetic resin to create rigid panelling for construction.
7 This high-pile, laser-cut faux fur is used to create 3-D patterns. Applications include interior decoration and apparel.
8 This decorative nylon fabric is semi-transparent and tear-resistant and is used for residential drapery.

The latter part of the 20th century could justifiably be described as an age of plastics. Although usage of all other materials continued to grow throughout that period (and still does), it has been nothing compared to the explosion of the use of plastics and the proliferic creation of various types of this versatile material. The number of different plastics now runs to tens of thousands, and there are very few areas of our lives that are not awash with the stuff. In many ways this has been a boon, with so much of our daily lives made better through the use of plastics that are lighter, smaller, softer, less expensive, safer and more colourful than alternatives. And although it is unlikely that our use of polymeric materials will lessen in the years ahead (indeed they will probably continue to replace other materials in many applications), the source for polymers most likely will.

Yet as we start to see the beginning of the end for the oil-based economy, so the same is feted for these plastics, thanks to the fact that ninety-five per cent of plastics are derived from oil. As oil becomes more expensive, so do the plastic raw materials, and low cost has always been one of the major advantages for polymers in the past, as well as one of the main reasons for their massive increase in use over the last thirty years. This price increase has forced manufacturers to look elsewhere for low-cost alternatives, with one area that appears to offer a promising future being biopolymers.

Though still very much in its infancy, this category of materials has the great advantage of having a raw material that can be grown rather than extracted, thereby offering an annually renewable resource; so long as there is soil, rain and sun, these biopolymers can be easily produced. Possibly one of the most amazing images to illustrate this process shows tiny polymer pellets growing inside a plant structure designed by Metabolix, a company developing PHA polymers from sugar.

The changeover from oil-based to plant-based plastics will be a gradual one though, and innovations within existing plastics technology continue to enable the next generation of products to be a step ahead of the last. Noticeable advances have

9 13   10 14   11 15   12 16

been made in the areas of foams, conductive polymers and coatings, though perhaps the biggest trend in plastics technology has been to improve versatility in processing, which allows for a wider range of applications to be met through different moulding and finishing techniques.

The sheer number of polymer foams available is staggering, with the density, hardness, mouldability, self-skinning properties and printability also customizable for many of them. We are seeing more applications for polyolefin-based foams that are often moulded into complex shapes with integral textiles or hardware. Variations in the pore density through the thickness of a foam sheet has also allowed for customization of properties. Conductive polymers spun into yarns will prove advantageous for electronic textiles, negating the need for metal wiring and thus creating a more natural-feeling woven structure. We have also seen them used as connectors for tiny LEDs in laminated glass to power the lights with no visible sign of connection (conductive polymer films are clear).

If more control of the electrical properties of these materials is achieved, then flexible, clear polymer displays should become a tangible prospect. Flexible light-emitting polymers also continue to be more adaptable and have the potential to emit more light. The range of possible applications of polymer coatings is also increasing, along with tougher soft touch coats, harder clear coats, glossier lacquers and more realistic faux patterns. It might be hard to visualize the end of the age of plastics given the myriad new solutions created by these existing versions, but it will no doubt arrive, and this move to biopolymers will be a good thing, though with any luck, we will not even notice the difference.

9 This translucent honeycomb sheet 'pixelates' the transmitted shadow/image from behind it. Current applications include curtain walls, room dividers, cabinet doors, work surfaces and bathroom surrounds.
10 + 13 Moulded silicon is durable, heat- and chemical-resistant and feels wonderful, and can be used in vehicle and household industries and industrial seals.
11 This technology moulds knitted textiles of different types with 3-D designs, creating a unique 3-D design that maintains almost perfect memory and returns to its original shape when compressed or distorted.
12 This polymer skin surface can be laminated onto irregular surfaces instead of car paint. Applications are for the coating of car doors, aluminum and steel extrusions and moulded polymer products.
14 These 3-D knitted textiles may be varied in terms of density, thickness, type of fibre and surface pattern. They are currently used for sneakers and as cushioning as well as for textile spacer applications.
15 This self-supporting, flame-retardant woven textile is used as office upholstery.
16 This hand-poured resin surface panel is made by moulding opaque-coloured resin to create a flat sheet, and sandwiching it between two clear sheets and can be used for counter and bar tops, tables, screens, partition walls, flooring, wall cladding, stair rails and light panels.

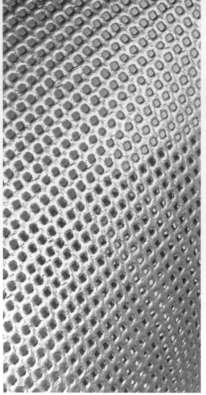

This is a super-wide coated woven mesh for printable signage. It is dimensionally stable, weather-resistant and very uniform in look. These polyester textiles and mesh are coated with PVC (polyvinyl chloride) to produce durable, light-fast surface for exterior flexible signage. The textile is available in widths of up to 406 cm (160 in). Applications are for interior and exterior banners and signage. 1440-04

ABOVE + BELOW
This process creates lightweight, stretchable, 3-D display frames for use in exhibitions. A range of sheer, opaque and translucent meshes and textiles may be used, that are available in fire-retardant and high-tenacity grades. In store and exhibition design, using stretched fabrics makes a lot of sense as they are lightweight and can provide dramatic visual impact. 5230-01

Embossing creates this regular patterned surface. A 100 per cent polyvinyl chloride is backed with a polyester knit textile and embossed with a raised pattern. The textile is available in rolls 137.2 cm (54 in) wide and withstands over 75,000 double runs in the Wyzenbeek test. Available in nine colours, this textile is currently used for contract and residential upholstery. 1940-08

Mimicking hardwearing diamond plate, this upholstery textile is suitable for contract use. Made from 100 per cent polyvinyl chloride (PVC), it is backed with a polyester knit textile and embossed with a raised diamond pattern. The textile is available in rolls that are 137.2 cm (54 in) wide and withstands over 75,000 double runs in the Wyzenbeek test. It is available in nine colours. 1940-09

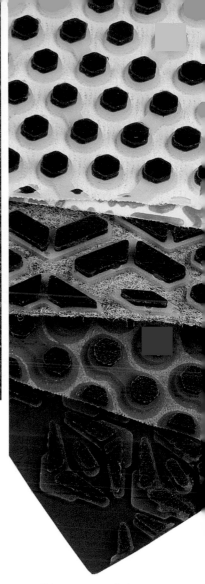

Outerwear apparel fabrics require lightweight, exceptional durability and breathability. These heavyweight, high wear-resistant textiles incorporate a 100 per cent woven 300-denier polyester base with a 100 per cent polyurethane (PU) coating. The coated textile is then top-coated with a fluorocarbon (PTFE) layer to impart stain resistance and moisture barrier properties. Colours include green, black, red, blue and fluorescent yellow as standard. Applications for these textiles include outer-wear for manual workers and mountain sport apparel. 5448-02

Disguised as regular coated fabric, this textile actually incorporates hardened stainless steel wire for security. It comprises two outer layers of PVC-coated 1000-denier polyester that sandwich a central layer of woven stainless steel. It has twenty times the cut strength required for the fabric alone but weighs less than 2 kg/sq m (0.6 lb/sq ft). The fabric may be stitched or high-frequency welded but requires metal shears to cut it. Applications are for outdoor tarpaulins, truck covers and stall awnings. 5356-01

A use for discarded computer chips? This polyester-based tiling uses silicon as crushed agglomerate. The resulting composite tile is hard, abrasion-resistant and dimensionally. It has high impact strength and good resistance to water. Larger slabs may also be produced, in dimensions of up to 140 x 305 cm (55 x 120 in), by 'vibro-compressing' the composite mixture under vacuum in a high-pressure mould. Current applications are for countertops, flooring and splashbacks. 1715-02

Developed by DuPont as a superior solid surfacing material, Corian® offers durability, scratch resistance and unlimited variations in colour. Combining the functions of tabletop and computer, this Corian® desk incorporates embedded computer drives, USB ports and other computer controls fitted seamlessly into Stephen Johnson's design.

This process was first developed for replacing the rubber soles on athletic shoes during the 1988 Seoul Olympics because it reduced the weight of the sole by 50 per cent. It is now being rediscovered by designers for other applications. Through the proprietary process, the polyurethane (PU) projection is melted onto a base fabric. There are stock projection patterns and customization is available upon request. The base textile can range from regular textile to synthetic leather, neoprene or jersey, as long as it allows melted PU to penetrate. It has potential applications in cars, housewares, accessories, apparel, bags, wristwatches, packing material, stationery and sporting equipment. 5086-01

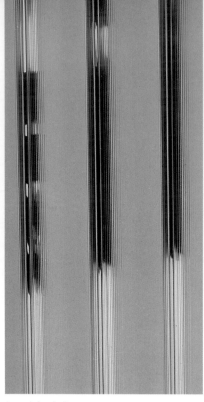

In certain glazing applications, this is a lightweight alternative to glass. It is a standing seam, translucent, polycarbonate dry-glazing system. It is available in several configurations for a diverse range of buildings. These include a homogeneous, insulating single panel with two isolated air spaces that has insulating values comparable to 2.54 cm (1 in) insulated glass but at a lower weight. 3544-01

This material is from a range of drapery textiles that combine two dissimilar yarns. It includes woven elasticized viscose of widths of 140 cm (55 in) for drapery and panels. 4925-05

This synthetic coating for upholstery protects against staining. A PTFE (Teflon®-like) coating may be applied to both synthetic and natural woven textiles as a stain-resistant coating that also protects against microbes. However, this coating also acts as a moisture barrier (unlike Teflon® coatings) and protects the seating foam from the ingress of water or oil-based soiling. Applications are for commercial and residential upholstery fabrics. 2277-03

Used for display applications similar to optical fibres, this is a synthetic light guide. Light entering the end of the rod is reflected off the white reflector strip and emanates from the entire rod, creating a 'neon sign' effect. The rod is low-cost and can be thermo-formed into complex shapes. It is also waterproof. Applications for this material include lighting situations of high vibration or where direct human contact is expected. 5070-01

This skylighting system combines twinwall sheets with mechanical louvres. The impact-resistant polycarbonate twinwall has channels running the length of the sheet which incorporate translucent half cylinder rods with an opaque face that can rotate to admit between 6–60 per cent of transmitted light. The panels are available with a light-diffusing frosted outer face and a clear inner face. 3544-01

Producing caps that have good abrasion resistance, this process creates moulded end caps for securing and protecting metal rods that are self-extinguishing, have a 300 per cent elongation, are resistant to most acids and alkaline solutions, and can be used in heat. They are FDA-approved for food contact use and are available in a wide spectrum of colours. Applications are for axle and valve handle covers, handle grips and decorative and alligator clip covers. 5270-01

Conductive polymers are plastics that have the electrical properties of metals. Individual fibres within this fabric are coated with a conductive polymer. Substrate fibres include polyester, nylon, glass fibre or Kevlar® and can be woven or knitted. The coating process does not significantly affect the strength, hand, drape, flexibility or porosity of the substrate fibres. However, it does darken the yarn. The conductive coating imparts microwave absorption, static dissipation, and conductivity. The coating is insoluble in water, stable in air but is degraded by oxidants and alkalines. It is non-toxic, non-irritating and non-mutagenic. Applications are for microwave and radar absorption, resistive heating in gloves, trousers, shoes, car seats, plastics welding and blankets. 5521-01

This was one of the first commercially viable e-textiles. It is a woven textile that translates a physical touch to a digital output. The textile comprises a 5-layer construction; the top and bottom layers are carbon conductive fabric with a partially conductive central fabric, separated from the top and bottom layers by insulating textiles. The textile is washable and may also be made waterproof, allowing it to be integrated into products. The sensing technology is also able to monitor bending, stretching, and moisture levels. Current applications for this technology are wearable computers, fabric keyboards, flexible personal communication devices and upholstery-mounted sensors. 5138-01

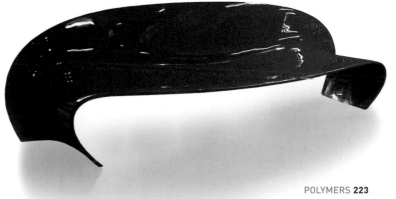

The use of glass-reinforced polymer forms enables designers to create thinner, tougher sections as this chair and couch by Assa Ashuach shows. The woven textile is imbedded in the polymer, adding significant strength without adding bulk.

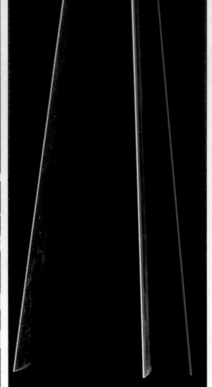

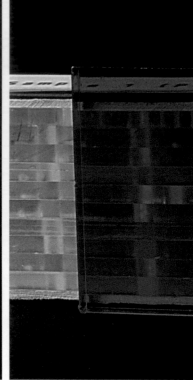

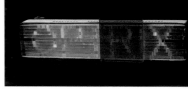

This process enables a bull-nose edge to be created on variable thicknesses of twin-wall polypropylene (PP). A scratch-resistant epoxy coating may be applied to give a more abrasion-resistant surface, making it useful in the edging of low cost desks and countertops. 5097-01

Composites may be the future of materials but they are not always sustainable. Yet these thermo-formable composite sheets are fully recyclable, low-cost and use woven polymer fibres for strength. No mineral or glass fibre is used, so the sheets may be post-formed using low pressures and moderate temperatures. The sheets may be ultrasonic-welded and cut using standard wood-working tools. Applications include car components, suitcases and speaker cones. 5398-01

Known as 'edge-bright' sheet, this polymer is a 100 per cent polycarbonate extruded sheet that incorporates dopants to create the 'edge-bright' effects. These dopants alter the wavelength of absorbed UV light to that of visible light, giving the appearance of more light emitting from the edges than is absorbed. Current applications are for printable graphic sheets, decorative packaging and point-of-sale displays. 4990-01

Through the inclusion of 'light pipes', similar to fibre optics, but rigid, these blocks create dramatic effects. Colours and shadows seem to jump randomly across its surface. The acrylic block is available as custom blocks and sheets and may be used as splashbacks, decorative surfaces and countertops. 5058-02

Polycarbonate is one of the toughest polymers on the market and, as such, it finds applications in a range of diverse products including CDs and DVDs, riot shields, and this decorative table by Janet and Joe Doucet. The top layer of polycarbonate will resist scratching and provide a long-wearing surface.

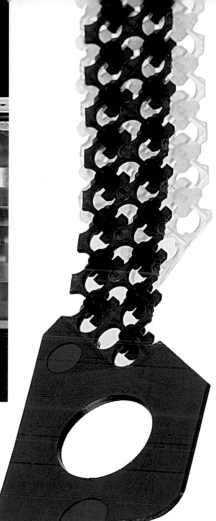

ABOVE RIGHT

Velcro has limitations with regard to dirt accumulation, thick profile and its attachment to other fabrics. This moulded sheet is a cleaner, thinner alternative to Velcro. The main portion of the device has a profusion of fastening elements on its outer surface, interspersed with perforations. The fastening system includes low-profile, self-aligning islands, which interlock when engaged, but are easily disconnected by peeling, providing a strong, durable, non-grabbing, easy-to use system. Areas of the structure not utilized for fastening are perforated in a similar geometric pattern. The interlocking system might be applied for any need where Velcro is used, but where it is important to maintain cleanliness. 5321-01

These adhesives are based on 'Post-it®' technology. They allow for repeated repositioning of labels on any surface. This glue consists of microspheres that are tiny particles measuring between 10 and 250 microns in diameter. Although microscopic in size, these spheres are still larger than the emulsion particles found in conventional adhesives. By forming a discontinuous film, microsphere adhesives limit the total physical contact, resulting in low peel, repositionability, removability and stable tack over time. Applications for these adhesives include wall and window graphics, book coverings, film labels and stencils. 5427-01

The versatility of polymers is highlighted in this art installation by Thom Faulders, with the three reoccurring elements; bungee cords, acrylic panels and stamped urethane connections are all from basically the same building blocks – polymer resins. From these resins come all of the shown elements, as well as the myriad other forms plastics can take.

These zippers are intended for the most demanding conditions. Composed of nylon and a thermoplastic elastomer, they are waterproof and airtight to a pressure of 25 psi (1.7 bar). They are available in eight colours, which may be mixed and matched between tape, zipper teeth and zipper slider, and are also UV- and abrasion-resistant. 5211-01

This is a technology that imparts decals and labels on rigid parts that cannot be removed. The label or decal film is statically charged to allow positioning by robot and is incorporated into a moulded part during injection of the plastic, forming a bond with the part. This creates a 'zero profile' attachment that when applied, has a profile of the thickness of the decal. These films may also be applied in blow-moulded polymers. The film is UV-stable, has a high abrasion resistance and high resolution images may be reproduced from it. Current applications are for warning and information signs on tools, all-terrain vehicles, ships and cars. 5009-01

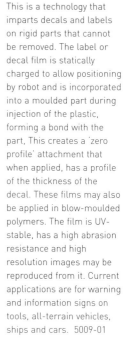

ABOVE LEFT + BELOW
Pultrusion is the production of continuous fibre-reinforced thermoset composite materials. This new technology responds to the need for a resin/fibre composite with the strength and rigidity of traditional composites and the processability of thermoplastics. It permits the production of high-performance, continuous-fibre composites with the workability of a thermoplastic and strength comparable to high-performance thermoset compounds. Applications include sports and electrical equipment, car components and building materials. 2044-01

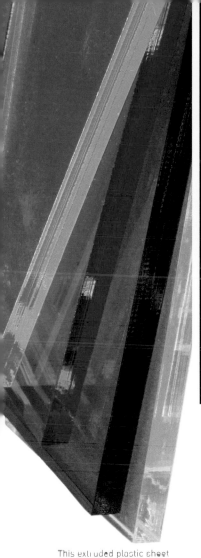

ABOVE + BELOW
This is definitely a bespoke process. The weaving of plastic fibre optics creates textiles and objects as well as signage that emit light. The woven fibre optics are gathered at one end and receive light from a small LED source that is able to change colour. Forms as complex as lingerie or decorative costumes may be woven using this process, though the robustness of such garments is limited. Current applications are for decorative art and apparel. 5120-01

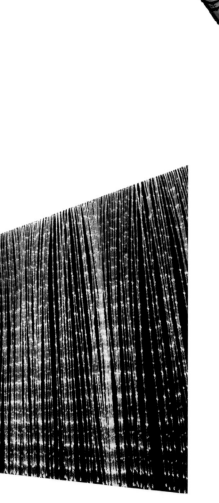

This extruded plastic sheet appears to emit coloured light. The sheet is composed of 100 per cent acrylic (PMMA) that absorbs energy, largely from the non-visible part of the spectrum, shifting it to longer visible wavelengths (red, amber, green and violet), and emitting it from the sheet edges. The sheets are available in orange, yellow, green, red, ruby, blue, red/orange and black. They are used for light transmission, illumination, radiation detection and decoration. 1011-03

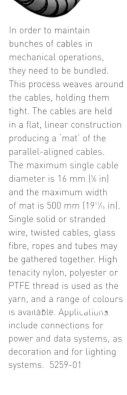

In order to maintain bunches of cables in mechanical operations, they need to be bundled. This process weaves around the cables, holding them tight. The cables are held in a flat, linear construction producing a 'mat' of the parallel-aligned cables. The maximum single cable diameter is 16 mm (⅝ in) and the maximum width of mat is 500 mm (19¹¹⁄₁₆ in). Single solid or stranded wire, twisted cables, glass fibre, ropes and tubes may be gathered together. High tenacity nylon, polyester or PTFE thread is used as the yarn, and a range of colours is available. Applications include connections for power and data systems, as decoration and for lighting systems. 5259-01

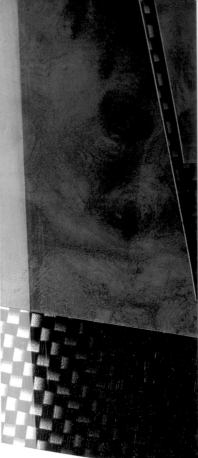

Typically used for packaging, this clear copolyester extruded polymer film has high transparency, high gloss, low haze, good chemical resistance and high impact strength. The film may also be printed onto and is available in film thicknesses from 0.2–1.2 mm (⅟₁₂₅–⅟₂₀ in). Current applications are for medical packaging films, for food and non-food packaging, decorative laminates and for the graphic arts. 5121-04

ABOVE + BELOW
This PVC film can be printed with a wide variety of faux surfaces and backed with a pressure-sensitive adhesive. The printed surfaces can resemble metal, stucco, marble and leather, and more than 150 types of wood. The deformable nature of the cladding allows the material to be applied to complex curved surfaces. The film can be used as exterior and interior cladding, interior column wrapping, elevator and display surfaces. 5048-01

Allowing moulding of the hook into an injection-moulded part, this version of the hook and loop fastener (Velcro) consists of integrating one or more gripping areas onto a plastic part during the moulding process. The process requires no moving parts and can be economically applied to a standard two-plate mould. A wide range of plastics can incorporate this hook surface including polypropylene, polyethylene, nylon and some elastomers. There are three different hook designs, based on the nature of the woven, non-woven or knitted loop material used. The insert is the same material and colour as the moulded part it is incorporated into, eliminating the need for adhesives. Current applications are for fasteners. 2984-02

With their transmission wavelength specifically created to match the wavelength of coloured LED and neon lights, these 100 per cent acrylic (PMMA) sheets are available in blue, red, green and yellow, each with the same wavelength as the corresponding LED coloured light. This allows for unaltered transmission of the coloured light, giving lower energy consumption and also unaltered colour from day to night illumination. 4994-05

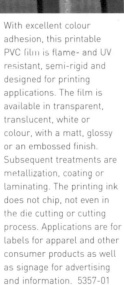

This could be classed as a true 'smart' material. It is a label based on blister packaging that automatically monitors lapsed time. Tinted food grade oil (corn or soy) migrates by capillary action through a micro-porous polymeric membrane at a consistent rate over a period of time, ranging from one day to six months. Labels start measuring time by pressing a bubble or can be activated when the package is opened. Applications include food products, medicines, ointments, perishable general goods, and general reminders 5401-01

®PENTAPRINT DYNOX
für glänzende Oberflächen:
- Offset und Siebdruck UV
- Langlebig / konstant hohe Oberflächenspannung
- Optimale Farbannahme / einzigartige Farbhaftung
- Primer / Schutzlack kann eingespart werden
- Hervorragende Schneid- und Stanzeigenschaften
- Kein Brechen oder Absplittern an den Kanten

With excellent colour adhesion, this printable PVC film is flame- and UV resistant, semi-rigid and designed for printing applications. The film is available in transparent, translucent, white or colour, with a matt, glossy or an embossed finish. Subsequent treatments are metallization, coating or laminating. The printing ink does not chip, not even in the die cutting or cutting process. Applications are for labels for apparel and other consumer products as well as signage for advertising and information. 5357-01

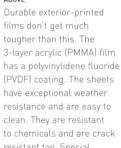

ABOVE
Durable exterior-printed films don't get much tougher than this. The 3-layer acrylic (PMMA) film has a polyvinylidene fluoride (PVDF) coating. The sheets have exceptional weather resistance and are easy to clean. They are resistant to chemicals and are crack resistant too. Special colours and designs are available on request. Standard variations are solid colours and wood imitations. Current uses include the lamination of window profiles, panels and other external uses. 5287-01

By using special combinations of polymers, this material creates a durable coating for a variety of surfaces. The coatings give the surfaces resistance to chemicals and cracking, and also make them easily cleanable using common detergents.

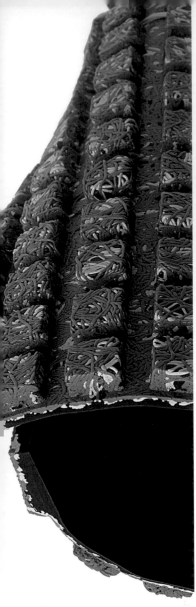

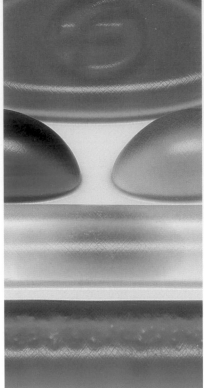

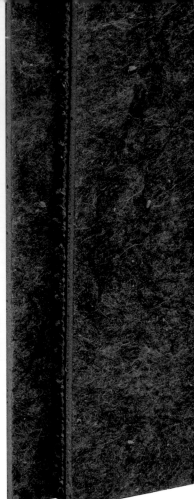

By incorporating strands of pre-coloured vinyl continuous fibre onto a nitrile rubber base to produce a textured surface that may be built up to any desired thickness, this process creates non-slip textured floor mats and tablemats. The surface may be used inside and outside, will withstand UV degradation and is washable. Current applications for this type of process are for high-traffic floor mats as well as decorative tablemats. 5036-01

This PVC insulating tubing shrinks when heated, proving a protective and insulating coating for objects of various shapes. Offered in special-effect pigments (fluorescents, metallic and iridescent) and colours, it is available in several varieties, and supplied in a range of diameters and in different colours for coding. Applications for this material include insulation for wiring as well as a protective, waterproof coating for any object. 5436-01

There is nothing like the look and feel of gel. Polyurethane is custom-moulded and skinned to create these cushioning pads. The colour, mould pattern and design may be customized. Although the skin has good cut-resistance, the material is not recommended for commercial seating. Applications include decorative surfaces and sports cushioning. 4817-04

With a high-friction surface applied to the back of this wall-to-wall and modular tile carpet, no adhesives are needed. The backing has a lifetime guarantee. 1949-06

The simple addition of a soft polyurethane gel seat makes this stainless steel bar chair a comfortable place to perch. Designed by Fabrice Covelli & Farah Salehi, the seat is perfect for outdoor use since the gel cushion is both UV-resistant and completely waterproof. 4817-04

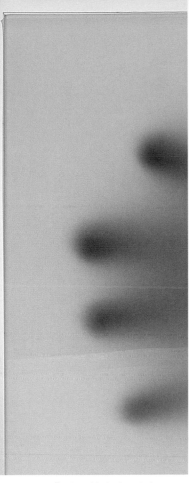

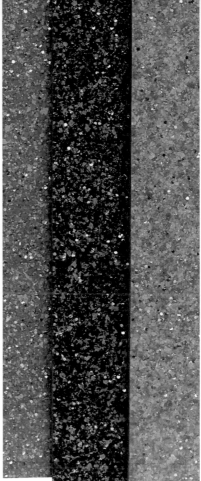

Designed to be inserted between two sheets of glazing, this flexible, strong, 3-ply interlayer resin film has been engineered to reduce wind noise and high frequency sound to create quieter vehicle and building interiors. The films are highly impenetrable, so glass laminated with this film rarely breaks. Applications are currently for architectural glazing, dividing screens and vehicle windshields. 5554-02

Pourable floors are durable, non-skid and can be easily applied to aircraft hangar-sized areas. This one incorporates small flakes of three different sizes with the appearance of bronze, copper, silver or gold spread through the resin, then coated with a clear finish. This clear coat is available in a gloss or matt finish and is chemical- and scratch-resistant. Applications are for school, restaurant, airport, hotel, shop and showroom floors. 5402-02

This is the next generation of pourable floors. It is a durable resin flooring that has a pearl flake effect. Small flakes of three different sizes with the appearance of pearl are spread over resin, then coated with a clear finish. This clear coat is available in a gloss or matt finish and is chemical- and scratch-resistant. There are ten colours available. Applications are for school, restaurant, airport, hotel, shop and showroom floors. 5402-01

Using a proprietary technique, this pattern is created through selective bleaching of the colour. The modular tile is tufted, textured, loop-piled and backed with a PVC-free cushion. The carpet is a modular tile, 914.4 x 914.4 mm (36 x 36 in), with a nominal thickness of ⅓ in (7.49 mm). There are nine repeating patterns available, each in six colours: lava, lake glacier, bedrock, meadow and asphalt. Applications are for interior contract flooring. 1949-07

Poured polymer resins are unequalled in the number of applications that they can be used for. Here, design group Citizen:Citizen has used some ten litres of urethane to create a soft, flexible mat called 'Lovers' that graphically recreates the contents of the human vascular system.

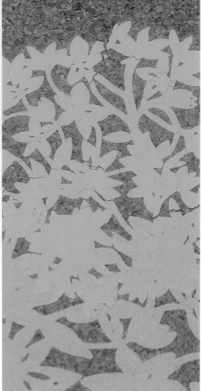

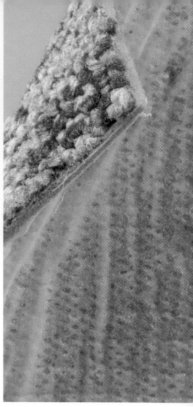

Used for interior wall and counter surfaces, these polymer mosaic disks are 100 per cent polyester (PET) coloured (both disks and squares), are an alternative to glass or ceramic, and are offered in eighty basic, and twenty-six marble, colours. There are two shapes, four sizes and five finish types, and they may be cemented in place using a cement-based adhesive. Applications are for interior wall coverings, partitions, countertops, desktops and other furniture surfaces. 5463-01

These are laser-cut, polyvinyl chloride (PVC) stickers for interior applications. These stickers are designed to be used either in lieu of, or in conjunction with, traditional wallpaper. The vinyl decals have no solid ground (and are similar to a doily). They are applied with pressure (using an application paper that keeps the decal intact) to any substrate including glass, plastic, metal, wood, cork, paper, ceramic or textiles. With proper application, the stickers remain in position for up to seven years. They are available in eleven opaque and six transparent colours, gold and silver foils and seven patterns. 5411-01

ABOVE + BELOW
Adhesive-backed and composed of an elastomer that has a pockmarked surface, this film has a highly grippy face. The adhesive is repositionable and the entire thickness of the film is 0.43 mm (⅟₆₀ in). A range of different colours and patterns is available. The film has been specifically designed for use with PDAs, mobile phones, MP3 players and other electronic devices. 5179-01

As a step towards more sustainable flooring, this carpet backing is a less toxic alternative to polyvinyl chloride (PVC). It is actually produced from used polyvinyl butyral (PVB) that has been collected from safety glass film from recycled car windows. The backing is 96 per cent post-consumer recycled PVB, resulting in a total recycled content for entire carpet at 40–60 per cent. This backing finds application in all residential and commercial carpeting as well as car carpeting. 5159-01

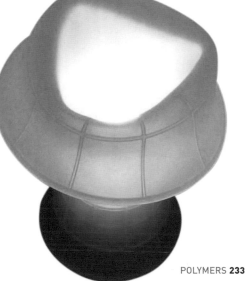

This process moulds and laminates a variety of foams and decorative and protective films to create cushioning and packaging surfaces. Thermo-forming and compression moulding are available for polyolefin, vinyl PVC or EVA foams. Decorative and functional polymer films as well as virtually any fabric can be laminated to the foam. Multi-layer, multi-density, and multicolour composites can be laminated as well. Current applications are in the medical, recreational, marine and industrial fields. 5278-01

Cross-linked polyolefin foams have been available for a while, but never this soft. The open cell continuous roll sheets are ten times softer than closed cell polyolefin foams, offering softness closer to polyvinyl chloride (PVC), polyurethane (PUR) or ethylene propylene diene (EPDM) rubber. The use of polyolefin makes them less toxic and thermo-formable into 3-D parts. The sheets are durable, hydrophobic and skinned on both sides. They are offered in a range of colours and softness, with variant recovery speeds, mechanical and physical properties and flame retardancy. They may be die-cut, adhesive-coated, needle perforated, laminated or thermo-formed. Applications are for sporting goods, shoes, health care and protective padding. 5539-01

Vinyl flooring is still hard to beat for high-traffic areas. In this case, the PVC is compounded with plasticizers and stabilizers to produce a highly wear-resistant flooring with resistance to most acids and alkalis. It is available in a wide range of standard and also custom designs, as well as tile shapes. The company complies with US regulations for quality and environmental management. 5269-01

Moulded silicon is at once durable, heat- and chemical-resistant and feels wonderful. Here, the silicon is compound moulded into custom shapes for high heat- and solvent-resistant applications in industries such as car, household appliances, and industrial seals and gaskets in the chemical industry. A range of grades of silicon is available, depending upon the desired application. 4999-01

This silicon lamp designed by Carlo Forcolini and Giancarlo Fassina for Luceplan is flexible, translucent and heat resistant. The shade can be bent into limitless shapes, allowing more or less light where it is desired, and is virtually unbreakable.

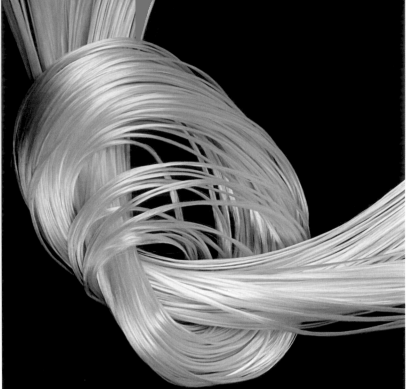

Designed around the themes of 'nature' and 'element', these hand-poured resin panels incorporate natural materials. The resin panel is then sandwiched between two clear sheets of PC (polycarbonate) or acrylic and is approved to be used as a food preparation surface. It is scratch-, stain- and impact-resistant. Current applications include counter and bar tops, tables, flooring, wall cladding and stair treads. 4955-01

This high-strength fibre is for medical implants and sutures. Available in a wide range of deniers, it is resistant to most acids and alkalis and does not absorb water, allowing it to be used in implant devices, requiring much less material than other metal or polymer alternatives (resulting in shorter hospitalization and faster recovery times). It also leads to a lower cost of care. 5041-01

Constructed from high tenacity oriented polyethylene (PE), this strong, single-braided rope is composed of twelve strand-braided 100 per cent Dyneema® yarn coated with polyurethane (PU). The ropes have excellent abrasion resistance, very low stretch, very high strength-to-weight ratio and a high-energy absorption capacity per pound of rope. The rope is available in seven diameters ranging from 9.6–22.4 mm (⅜–⅞ in) and is used in marine applications. 5207-01

The interior of E4, a cocktail lounge in Scottsdale, Arizona, features a series of spaces that correspond to the ancient elements of earth, air, fire and water. For their 'Earth' area, the designers poured resin over grasses to create a dramatic and evocative translucent bar. 4955-01

These silicon gels are specifically designed for vibration damping and shock absorption. They contain no harmful additives and are therefore toxic-free if combusted. They are available as sheets, tapes and chips, and shape and hardness are adjustable. These gels are currently used in mattresses, as cushioning in packaging, for sensitive electronics packaging and in sports apparel and equipment. 5086-02

ABOVE + BELOW
Used for construction, this lightweight rigid foam core sandwich panel is a support element made of polystyrene hard-foam with a mortar coating reinforced on both sides with glass-fibre and blunted edges. The thin boards up to 20 mm (⅞ in) thick serve primarily for the production of substrates. The thicker elements are ideal for lining, constructing, forming and insulating. Applications are for construction. 5192-01

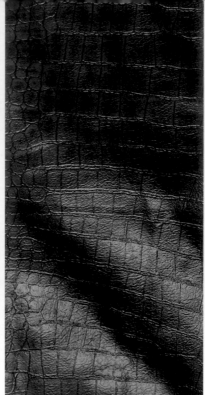

These are fluorescent retroreflective signage used for transport applications. These sign materials are made out of reinforced microprismatic retroreflective sheeting bonded to a heavy-duty, fibre-reinforced vinyl material. Applications are for outdoor road signage in low light conditions. 3908-02

Like highway markings, this signage material is great in low light conditions. This sheet is available in rolls or cut strips. It utilizes a unique microprism design that retroreflects more than 70 per cent of incoming light back to the source, even under poor visibility conditions. A screen printable version of this material is available on request. Applications are for vehicle signage. 3908-03

Changing colour when exposed to variations in temperature, this flexible upholstery and apparel textile is made with a polyurethane coating incorporating a liquid crystal emulsion. Wall coverings, upholstery, apparel, footwear, stationery, accessories and swimwear can all become heat-responsive with this unique material. 2604-13

This yarn woven into textiles reflects incident light. It is composed of glass beads adhered to a yarn that has a silver colour in daylight but is visible under lights up to 100 metres (328 ft) in low light conditions. Current applications are for work-wear, outerwear and sportswear, and for gloves, pants, jackets bags, backpacks and accessories. 0139-07

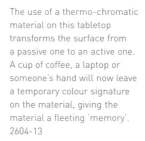

The use of a thermo-chromatic material on this tabletop transforms the surface from a passive one to an active one. A cup of coffee, a laptop or someone's hand will now leave a temporary colour signature on the material, giving the material a fleeting 'memory'. 2604-13

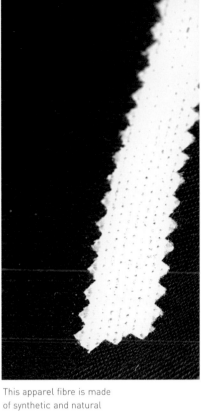

This apparel fibre is made of synthetic and natural fibres that have been treated with an ETFE coating (also known as Teflon®) to reduce friction and therefore heat, abrasion and fatigue. The coating will not wash or rub off of the fibres. These fibres are woven or knit into textiles and used in applications such as sport socks, vests and bras, and walking socks. 5178-01

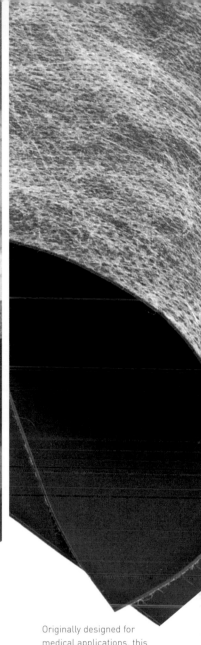

Spinnaker sails need to be super-strong, durable and weather resistant. This composite fabric is made from a polyester (PET) film laminated with 2-ply, rip-stop polyester or nylon. It is reinforced with cross-ply aramid fibres. They are available in a wide range of standard colours as well as custom colours and finishes. Applications for this textile include spinnaker sails as well as sports apparel. 4250-12

As many competitors know, the difference between winning and losing is often based on small factors. Using materials that reduce friction to manufacture athletic apparel increases comfort and reduces chafing and blisters. 5178-01

An upholstery textile that has the surface texture of sueded leather. This 60 per cent nylon, 40 per cent polyurethane textile is available in 137 cm (54 in) widths and in over twenty colourways. The colour has a light-fastness of five. Its abrasion resistance is 100,000 double rubs on the Martindale test and it has a shrinkage of 2 per cent. The textile is machine-washable and current applications are for contract and residential upholstery. 4996-07

Originally designed for medical applications, this textile is now used by the military. It is a thin, flexible, coated textile that protects against X rays and is used as an alternative to lead-lined materials for protection against radiation for medical radiographers and hazardous waste cleanup crews. It is a composite of polyurethane, polyvinyl chloride and organic and inorganic salt particles, and is laminated between a non-woven and a woven textile. The resulting material attenuates and disperses gamma radiation, converting it into heat. 5093-01

ABOVE + BELOW
Constructed from recycled polyester fleece and a layer of woven fibreglass coated with an outer aluminum layer, this broadband sound and heat absorbing insulation is heat-bonded in a semi-rigid sheet. It is available in a non-flammable version, and can be used for car and construction industry insulation. 5306-01

These lightweight, flexible hoses are abrasion-, heat-, chemical-, oil-, and weather-resistant. They are made of a technical textile of woven mixed polyester and polyamide yarns, lined with a nitrile elastomer and covered with a ribbed nitrile elastomer, together forming a unified lining and cover. Produced in a wide range of solid and striped colours including red, black, yellow, blue, green and grey. Applications include fire hose, cold and hot water delivery, irrigation, industrial plants and cable cover. 5219-01

Not a common occurrence, these decorative honeycomb sandwich panels may be used as flooring. Polymer-coloured panels are backed with a clear honeycomb polymer core that may be up to 2.44 x 1.22 m (8 x 4 ft) in size and 1.91 cm (¾ in) thick. Applications include vertical and horizontal surfaces in interior residential and commercial spaces. 3416-04

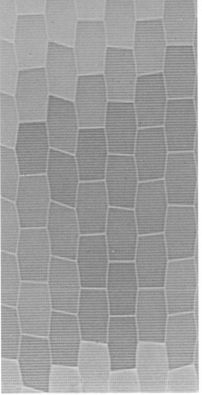

Incorporating millions of tiny microscopic glass pellets that reflect light even from low illumination sources, these woven and non-woven fabrics are available in a range of standard printed patterns and graphics. A relatively small panel can be seen from a distance of up to 120 m (131 yds) in car headlights at night. The textiles are machine-washable, dry-cleanable and are used for outdoor workwear, for footwear, clothing, backpacks and apparel accessories. 5326-03

ABOVE + BELOW
This translucent honeycomb sheet 'pixelates' transmitted shadows/images from behind it. The rigid, structural, lightweight sheet comprises an aluminum honeycomb core with two glass fibre-reinforced translucent sheets as the exterior faces. The orientation of the glass fibre within the outer sheets results in a pixelation of anything seen through the panel. Current applications include curtain walls, room dividers, cabinet doors and work surfaces. 3572-04

Similar to honeycomb, these panels have a unique, cellular appearance. They are manufactured from at least 50 per cent recycled and 50 per cent virgin polyester (PET), and incorporate two clear outer sheets and an irregular square-celled inner core. The glue used is clear. They have good UV-resistance, and provide unique visual effects and light transference. Applications are for interior curtain walls, dividers, as event structures and point-of-sale displays. 5371-01

These 100 per cent polypropylene sheets sandwich a honeycomb cell core to create this lightweight panel. Available in four opaque colours, with multiple surface textures, this rigid polymer panel is excellent for displays, as well as transportation containers, exterior signage, and model-making. 5376-01

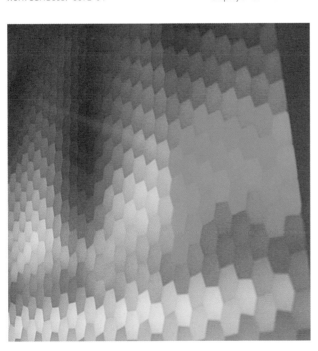

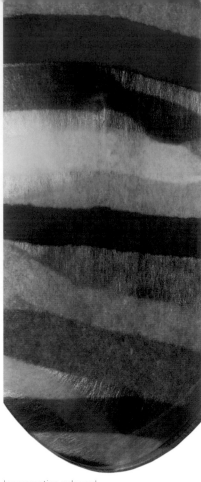

ABOVE + BELOW
This decorative
polycarbonate film allows a
printed image (on the film)
to be laminated onto an
acrylic, tempered glass or
polycarbonate sheet. It finds
applications in point-of-sale
displays, countertops,
tabletops and architectural
accents. 5342-01

Here is a low temperature
moulding process for glass
fibre-reinforced polymer
sheet. A paper-making
process that laminates
the top paper layer and
a bottom scrim in one
roll produces the sheet.
The sheet is a lightweight
composite and has a good
strength- and stiffness-
to-weight ratio. It is also
tough and ductile unlike
typical thermoset FRPs
(fibre-reinforced polymer)
composites. Decorative
surface skins may be
applied during the forming
process. Applications
include door and wall
panels, work surfaces
and seat backs. 5262-02

Incorporating coloured
acrylic (100 per cent
solution-dyed) fibres into
rigid, thermo-formable
laminates, this process is
completely customizable
by colour and pattern.
Fibres are encased in rigid
or flexible, clear PVC sheets,
and can be used for point-
of-sale displays, decorative
partitions, handbags,
accessories and interior
architectural accents.
5265-02

Available in over thirty
colours, and bacteria- and
fungal-resistant, this mesh
shading fabric for windows
is made out of glass fibre
yarn coated with 100 per
cent polyvinyl chloride (PVC)
and that is then woven.
5115-05

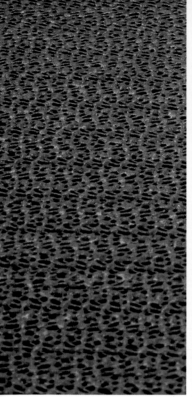

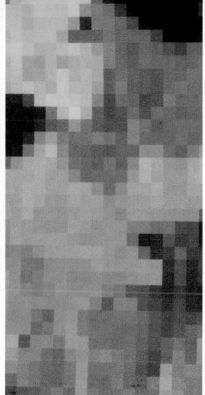

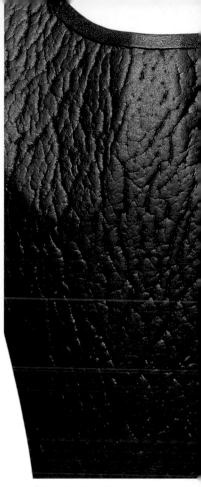

An attractive solution to a slippery situation, this rubberized flexible textile can be used for non-slip applications, including drawer and shelf liners, rug and carpet underlays and jar openers. Washable, cuttable without fraying, and both UV- and abrasion-resistant, this flexible polymer mesh is coated with synthetic rubber. 5020-01

ABOVE + BELOW
Used as a decorative surface, this moulded sculptural textile is made of closed-cell polyurethane foam fused to vinyl-coated fleece, then moulded into egg-crate forms that also possess sound-proofing characteristics. Cuttable, heat-weldable, lightweight, and durable, these sheets, available in many colours, can be used for pillows, yoga mats, headboards, apparel, accessories and architectural solutions. 5268-01

This 100 per cent polyester velour knit fleece has pebbled, or shearling surfaces, that create air pockets to trap air and retain body heat, thereby providing insulative properties. Breathable, quick-drying, and available with a water-repellent finish, the fabric is machine-washable, available in many weights and styles, and is appropriate for outdoor apparel. 0091 03

This technology allows consumer products to be 'skinned' with fabrics, hides and other films. It enables flexible materials to be quickly and easily wrapped around convex surfaces and adhered to the edges with a neat seam. Leather, suede, wood, natural and synthetic textiles, as well as patterned and coated polymer films, may be wrapped around laptop computers, PDAs and other electronic devices in order to create a distinctive visual and tactile appearance. 2048-01

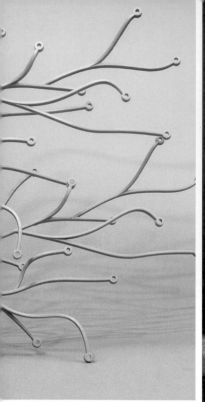

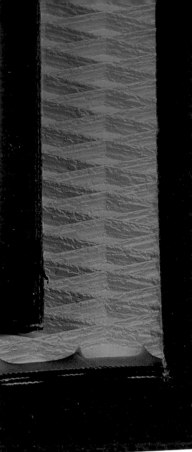

Modular and limitlessly
extendable, these 0.3 metre-
long (1 ft) moulded plastic
stem-like forms, are
injection-moulded polyolefin
plastic, and can be joined
with pegs to create
expansive partitions and
curtains that resemble
seaweed-like configurations.
They are available in red,
green, black and white, and
are perfect for interior
decoration. 5141-01

Incorporating a textured
surface, this thick, durable
sheet, typically used for
conveyor belts, can be
ribbed, diamond-patterned,
or given a high-friction
coating. It can be used
on up to a 45° incline.
Available in tan, blue and
grey, the belts are available
in continuous lengths,
in various natural and
synthetic materials.
5090-01

ABOVE
This flexible light-emitting
sheet is long-lasting, low-
power and available in large
sizes. It is similar to electroluminescent (EL) sheets but
is an LEC (light-emitting
capacitor). LEC technology
has three main components:
light-emitting phosphors,
programmable flatline
invertors and packing
materials with a low level
of heat generation. The light
comes in a flexible film that
can be graphics-printed, or
packaged in glass. It is long-
lasting and programmable
to respond to sound and
motion. Current applications
include architectural design,
floors, shop signage and
vehicle production. 5263-01

BELOW
Utilizing thin sheets of flexible
light-emitting capacitors
(LECs), Optika Scenicworks
created this unique promotion
for Coca-Cola. The trailer of
this truck was covered in
sheets of the material that
illuminated a series of 3-D
advertisements. 5263-01

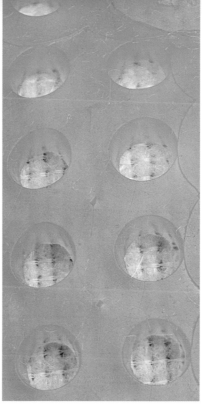

Designed for exterior use in place of lumber, this durable wood alternative is made from recycled plastic and industrial waste wood fibre. Available in colour, or as a factory-primed version (that can be painted), this flooring does not rot or deteriorate. 5333-01

This low-cost, synthetic wall covering is a recyclable alternative to vinyl, but without the associated toxicity. It is available in sixteen colours (matt), with both colour and texture fully customizable. Made from virgin polyester, it is intended for contract and institutional use, with better sound absorption than untextured surfaces. 5029-01

Polymer gels have good cushioning properties. This polyurethane gel is mouldable, colourable and comes in hardnesses as low as 2 on the Shore A hardness scale. It is lighter than other polyurethane gels and has an elongation of up to 1000 per cent. It may be incorporated into textiles (for cushioning) or moulded into custom shapes. It is available as a clear product, or in a range of colours including fluorescents. Current applications are for shoe cushioning, cycle and motorcycle seats and other anti-shock applications. 5133-01

ABOVE + BELOW
Incorporating LEDs inside non-woven insulation, this interior lighting is robust, can be bent and scrunched, is low-voltage, and has a lifetime of five to twenty years. It can be made waterproof, is available in customizable sizes, and is great for applications in interior residential and commercial lighting. 5096-01

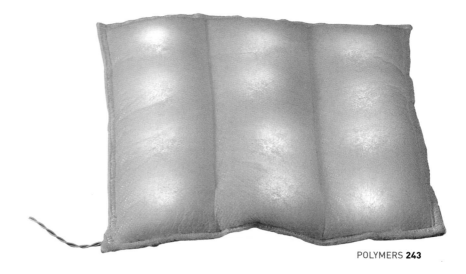

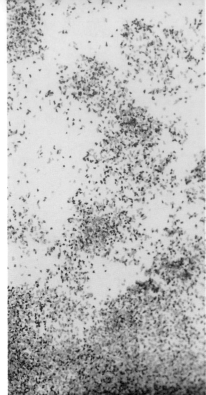

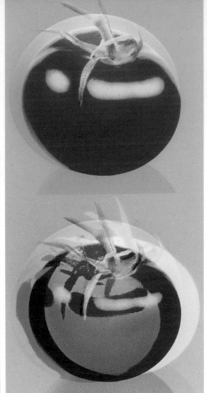

This acetal resin can be metal-plated and has high stiffness and toughness over a wide range of temperatures. Resistant to repeated impact as well as chemicals, solvents and fuels, this acetal resin may be injection-moulded, two-shot-moulded and extruded. It can be modified to be UV-resistant, low-wear, low-friction, laser-markable and mineral-filled, and the moulded parts can also be etched to allow for painting and plating.
2252-06

Originally developed as an additive to explosives to trace usage of weaponry, these additives to paints, inks, resins and coatings 'tag' the material with a unique code that can be identified by a range of methods (including fluorescence under UV light, observance of the code under an optical microscope, hand-held lasers that elicit a colour response and tag readers). Unique custom codes are created for every customer, product and application.
5441-01

ABOVE + BELOW
Setsu and Shinobo Ito used this dye sublimation printing process to great effect in these Corian® lights created for the 2006 Milano Design week. The process involves printing a substrate (such as Corian®) with sublimation dyes, and then dry heat and pressure are applied so that the image is dyed into the substrate surface. The process creates a scratch-resistant graphic and any hard solid surfacing material or complex curved surface can be printed onto.
5442-01

These optically variable-effect pigments can be incorporated into paints, resins and inks. Ultra-thin transparent flakes of a liquid crystalline polymer reflect back small amounts of incident light, changing the wavelength of the light (and hence the colour) depending upon the angle of incidence. Available in five colour combinations, and affected by the colour of the substrate, they can be used in applications for consumer products, personal electronics, as paints for cars, and in apparel, footwear and accessories.
5428-01

Flame-retardant coatings for wood and wood-based surfaces such as the these contain an iron filler, making them magnetic. A topcoat of paint is applied for protection and decoration creating a metal surface that can be used with magnets and magnetic objects for cabinetry, wall panels, cubicle dividers and as notice boards. 5444-01

As a range of low-hardness elastomers, these are tough, relatively wear-resistant, have high elongation values with high-tear strength, and excellent low temperature properties. The resins are available as a clear material and may be coloured using master-batch pigments. Current applications are for gaskets and seals as well as diaphragms in cars and industrial machinery. 5128-01

This technology allows for micro-encapsulation to be applied in the finishing stages of textile production. The capsule contents may be scented, anti-bacterial, moisturizing, deodorizing, and insect-repellent and are activated by rubbing or shaking and can withstand washing. Applications include fabric, soft furnishing or flooring. 4899-01

Colourless in the shade, these inks and dyes develop bright colours when exposed to sunlight, and are available in twenty standard colours plus several custom colours. They are formulated for offset printing, screen-printing and flexographic printing. Colour-to-colour changes are also possible with almost any colour combination possible, which is perfect for direct mail, novelty applications, security packaging and secure labels. 4379-03

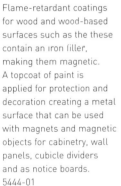

Because of their durability and impact resistance, polyurethane elastomers often perform some of material's dirty work. These materials are often used in bumper pads, coated conveyor belts, dead-blow hammers, drive belts and forklift tyres and wheels. 5128-01

These thermo-plastic elastomers can be overmoulded onto nylon and have been developed to bond onto a broad range of nylon grades including impact modified and heat-treated nylon 6,6. Suitable for both insert and multi-shot moulding processes, these elastomers preclude the need for drying or pre-heating of the part before overmoulding and allow for as much as 50 per cent reduction in cooling times compared to similar thermoplastic elastomers. Current applications are for dishwasher-safe kitchen utensils, gardening and power tools. 0186-03

The open-weave mesh above can be moulded and formed with hot water, hot air or steam at temperatures of 71ºC (160ºF) and will stretch on the bias, is self-bonding, and moulds over any porous or shiny surface to create mirror-image casts. Re-workable by applying heat again, and available in heavy, light and gauze, it is used for orthopedic splinting, masks, costumes, props, prototypes, models, sculpture and fine arts applications. 5038-01

Designed for use in high strength structural applications, these polymer composites combine nylon, polyester, polypropylene, polyphthalamide and other thermoplastics with long glass fibres using a patented pultrusion process. Frequently used as a replacement for die-cast metal, common uses include vehicle front-end modules, instrument panel substrates, battery trays, shifter bases, sunroof beams, mirror brackets and fuel rails. 0148-04

Used mainly for sports apparel, this elastic fibre is resistant to UV, chlorinated water, salt and high heat, having 20 per cent elasticity with low residual stretch. It is most effective when blended with viscose but can be used with all types of yarn and is found in sportswear (especially swimwear), outerwear and hardwearing workwear. 4992-02

Installations such as this retail display designed by Fricke Le-Royer exhibit the versatility of modern synthetic fabrics. The elasticity, translucency, light weight and fire retardancy needed for these commercial installations is elegantly achieved using these materials.

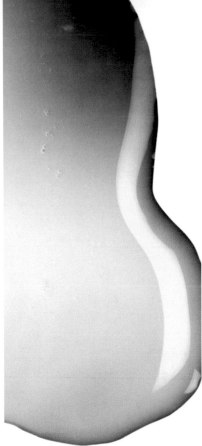

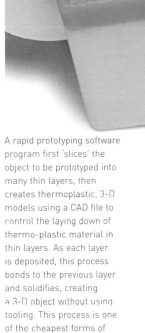

Used for soft-touch overmoulding applications, this resin has a high friction, gripping surface and is used mainly for materials like polypropylene, polycarbonates and polyamides. It is oil- and grease-resistant, colourable, and suitable for low temperature applications, as well as medical, power tool and recreational applications. 5063-01

Incorporated into wax for the skis in the 2002 Winter Olympics, and now being used in anti-fouling, and ice-repellent coatings for marine and winter sports equipment, this coating, produced by the sol-gel process, and using nanoparticulates, can be incorporated into a solution to improve corrosion, scratch-resistance and friction properties. It is also used to protect surfaces against vandalism. 4997-01

This 100 per cent polyolefin cross-laminated synthetic and printable film is impervious to air, heat vapour, water and most chemicals. It is available in no-tear and tear-resistant versions. UV-stabilized for outdoor applications, and available in coated, uncoated and laminated versions, it can be used in such applications as airport luggage tags, roll-up maps, washable garment tags and trade show displays and banners. 5324-01

A rapid prototyping software program first 'slices' the object to be prototyped into many thin layers, then creates thermoplastic, 3-D models using a CAD file to control the laying down of thermo-plastic material in thin layers. As each layer is deposited, this process bonds to the previous layer and solidifies, creating a 3-D object without using tooling. This process is one of the cheapest forms of 3-D printing and can handle acrylo-nitrile butadiene styrene (ABS). 4108-02

Arik Levy's Black Honey bowl was created using a rapid prototyping technology and polymer powders. By selecting a specific polymer, a designer can vary the performance and aesthetics of the finished product. Whether opaque or translucent, rigid or flexible, the wide range of polymers offer an almost infinite palate.

This is a unique process for the low-cost production of small silicon spheres. It relies on the surface energy of silicon, in that small solid spheres of the material are produced quickly and economically by dropping liquid silicon into a heated bath of distilled water. Variations in the sizes of the spheres are achieved by regulating the amount of each droplet, with a nominal maximum diameter of 2.54 cm (1 in). Colour and stiffness of the material is customizable and the process is made more economical by the curing speed of the silicon. This form of silicon is currently used in cushioning. 5086-05

Mainly used in low-cost, high-volume moulding applications, this thermoplastic resin has high optical transparency, good surface quality, high-impact strength and rigidity, as well as stress-cracking resistance. It offers high transparent clarity, similar to acrylic resins, and can be coloured using master-batch pigments. Current applications for the moulded resin include cosmetics, pens, cases, watches, home appliance cases and plastic stemware. 5129-01

Made from 100 per cent renewable softwood pulp, this cellulose-based, moulded resin can incorporate and retain fragrance for extended periods of time. It is tough, hard, strong, has a surface gloss and is chemical-resistant as well as warm to the touch. It is also easily moulded, extruded or fabricated and available in four colours: natural, clear, amber and black. Typically used for consumer products such as radios, telephones, toothbrushes and toys. 4780-06

Optically clear, and for low-cost moulding, this polymer resin has high-impact resistance, good UV resistance, good scratch resistance, and can be blow-moulded, extruded, injection- and compression-moulded. Minor scratches may be removed using a heat gun (unlike acrylic) and it can also be bonded using plastic welding or solvent bonding. Available in a range of colours, including fluorescent, it is approved for dry food storage, and is currently used for cosmetic containers. 4780-05

Patrick Messier designed this sensuous rocking chair for mother and child. Made from a single sheet of fibreglass, the high-gloss surface is achieved through a coating of urethane giving the chair a smooth and easily cleaned finish.

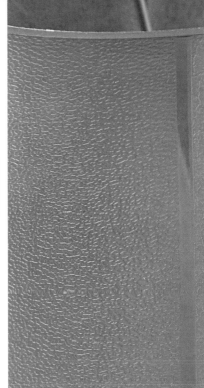

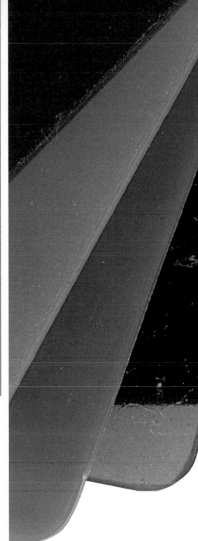

These cast polyurethane forms have excellent optical clarity, are durable, virtually unbreakable, lightweight, and can be drilled and processed without cracking. Resistant to acetone, methyl alcohol and distortion from heat, these resins adhere well to adhesives and coatings. When produced as lenses, they are available polarized and photochromic, coloured or tinted, and can be used for goggles or face shields, sunglasses, armoured vehicle and helicopter viewport, and architectural security glazing. 5500-01

Constructed from a modified polypropylene/polystyrene (PPE/PS) blend, this range of resins is available in injection-mouldable, extrudable and foamable grades. Also available are car-specific grades and special high-modulus grades capable of replacing stamped steel and die-cast metal in tight-tolerance, functional assemblies. It has halogen-free flame retardancy characteristics that make it suitable for use in public building applications. 4219-04

This range of thermoplastic polyurethane, low-hardness elastomers are tough, wear-resistant, have high elongation values with high tear strength and excellent low temperature properties. They resist fungal attack, have good hydrolytic stability, and are available in clear or may be coloured using master-batch pigments. Current applications are for gaskets and seals as well as diaphragms in car and industrial machinery. 5191-01

Used for the moulding of complex shapes by injection and compression processes, these synthetic resins are engineered for specific applications and are available in a wide range of hardnesses. 5017-01

Mass production was truly born when injection moulding came into use. This process, coupled with high-strength polymers, can be used to create anything from mobile phones to architectural modules. Here, designer Karim Rashid has created a simple but dramatic staircase by repeating the same simple plastic form slotted into a central spine.

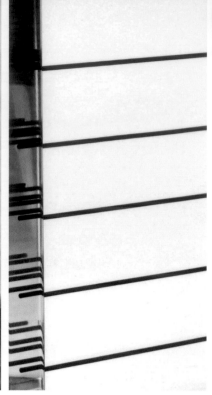

These copolymer panels incorporate a photo-luminescent pigment. The copolymer is acrylic modified polyester with transparent fibreglass reinforcement. The sheets are shatterproof and approximately half the weight of glass while being up to 7 times more insulating. Applications are for decorative panelling for interior and exterior vertical surfaces. 1012-02

Made from 100 per cent acrylic (PMMA) cast into clear sheets that incorporate thin nylon threads to ensure that slivers do not detach during breakage, this is a highly transparent polymer sound barrier. Designed to act as a noise barrier along rail lines, roadways and bridges, the cast sheet is highly ten-year guarantee. The sheets may be curved by thermo-forming and are secured using channels and bolts. 0027-03

This injection moulding process is for making small parts with high tolerance. A wide range of polymer types may be used for these micromouldings, and current parts include gears and gear housings, hearing aids, moulded interconnect devices (MIDs), bobbins, switches, sensors, lenses, catheters, gaskets, rollers and fibre-optic components, for the electronics, medical, telecommunications and car industries. 5186-01

ABOVE
Translucent, with excellent impact and UV resistance, and coloured on one face, these extruded 100 per cent polycarbonate (PC) rigid panels have square cells that diffuse light and increase the insulative properties of the panel. A wide range of colours is available, offering a range of light transmission varying with colour. They are compliant with Florida hurricane tests when correctly installed. Great for interior and exterior daylighting systems, the panels can be custom-curved for skylights. 4207-03

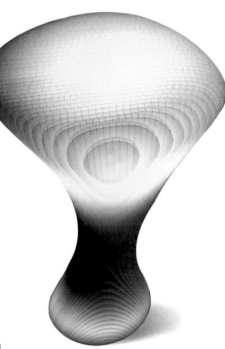

Strong, lightweight and transparent, extruded twin-walled polymer panels are a low-cost solution for a wide range of applications. Here, Shoko Cesar and Greg Ball have used the usually geometric material in topographic layers to form an organically shaped lighting fixture.

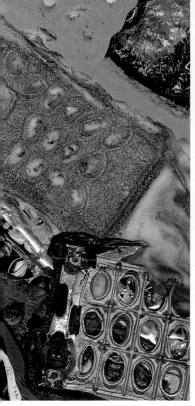

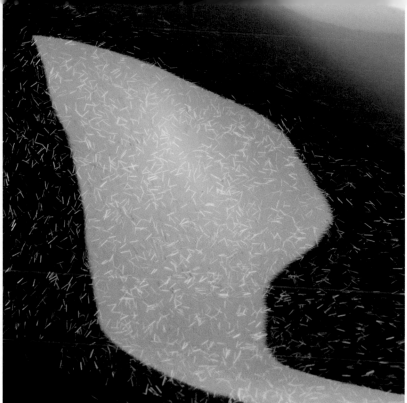

Polymer sheets like these are created from recycled waste materials such as coffee cups, CDs, production scrap, toothbrushes and mobile phone parts. These materials are added to small amounts of high density polyethylene (HDPE) and used to create distinct designs of coloured polymer sheeting. Each scrap type (in this case, old mobile phones) imparts a distinct and non-uniform colour to the sheet. The HDPE has a low melting point so care must be taken when cutting a fast speeds. 4847-02

Based on the colour illumination of the Morpho butterfly wings, this decorative glittery, self-illuminating filament is composed of 15 per cent nylon and 85 per cent polyester that have different indices of refraction. Filaments are available in rectangular and square shapes with illumination available in red, green, blue and violet and have applications for pigments for coatings on cars, sporting goods, electronics, cosmetics and printing. 5399-01

Rigid corrugated polymer sheet like the above example is made from 100 per cent polymethyl methacrylate, is lightweight, weather-resistant, versatile and easily fabricated. An impact-modified product, this sheet withstands UV light and other outdoor elements for extended periods of time, and incorporates a solar heat reflection technology (a proprietary iridescent coating that reflects UV rays). Available in customized colours, this product has applications in indoor and outdoor applications ranging from carport roofing and patio walling to office partitions, point-of-sale displays and restaurant wine racks. 1011-07

To create this striking bar, Mark Lintott Design used a polymer sheeting that incorporates scrap and waste products to create infinite colour and pattern combinations. In his design for The Lightbug Bar in Taiwan, Lintott took advantage of the material's translucent properties to dramatic effect.

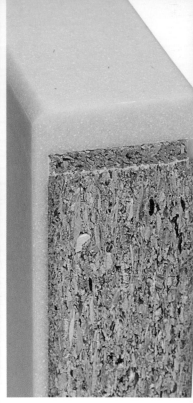

This limp-mass material made of high temperature-fused PVC, is a sound transmission blocker that reduces sound vibration from transmitting through walls, floors and ceilings. Dense mass is what allows the sheet to be so effective at reducing noise from transmitting into and out of a space; great for new construction, or to repair existing noise problems, with both reinforced (hangable) and non-reinforced versions. 5447-01

Based on the property of dilatancy, flowing when moved slowly, but stiffening up when moved quickly, this mouldable resin stiffens on impact and is moulded into flexible, elastic sheets that are designed mainly as protective padding in sportswear. The manufacturer works with the client to develop the correct shape and thickness for each application. This is limited by the size that can be cast in one mould, but pieces may be attached to each other in order to span larger dimensions. 5536-01

Predominantly closed-cell structure foams such as these have an integral surface skin, leading to very low water absorption, high compressibility and low compression set over a wide temperature range. Having good acoustic and thermal insulation properties, they are available in four densities, with different pressure-sensitive adhesive backings, in red, grey and off-white. They are also available in flame-retardant grades as well as special sizes die-cut to specification. 5054-01

Scratch and heat resistant, chemically and UV-resistant, and easy to clean, this acrylic solid surfacing sheet may be thermo-formed too. There are over fifty solid colour and stone-effect colourways available and the sheet can be moulded into basins and sinks as well as adhered to MDF. The sheets can be worked with standard wood-working tools, seams can be jointed seamlessly and minor scratches can be sanded out. Applications are for interior residential and commercial work surfaces. 5360-01

Because foamed polyurethane expands and solidifies quickly, artist Jerszy Seymour could create this freeform shelter that also provides a skate-boarding ramp. The material is also used as insulation and lightweight reinforcing fill material for doors and other hollow panels.

These predominantly closed-cell structure foams have an integral surface skin, leading to low water absorption, high compressibility and low compression set over a wide temperature range. Having good acoustic and thermal insulation properties, they are available in four densities, with different pressure-sensitive adhesive backings, and are available in red, grey and off-white for thermal and acoustic insulation. They are also available in flame-retardant grades as well as special sizes die-cut to specification. 5086-06

Approved for food contact and resistant to flames, UV, most chemicals, oil, water, bacteria and fungi, this expanded porous poly-propylene (EPP) open-celled foam can be moulded into complex shaped parts that can be laminated with a textile, thermoplastic olefin (TPO) or other material. It is lightweight, flexible, strong, buoyant and heat resistant, and is used in sports facilities, food processing plants, restaurants, offices, and gun ranges. 5381-01

ABOVE + BELOW
Expanded polypropylene solid bead foams like these can be moulded into complex shaped parts or precision-moulded into fitted parts that mate and lock. It is lightweight, has flexibility and structural strength, and provides impact protection. Applications include car components, marine applications, toys and furniture (such as the modular Q-Couch below by Frederik Van Heereveld, which requires no tools, screws or adhesives in assembly). 5381-02

Through a patented and proprietary tufting technology, this carpet presents two distinct patterns and colours depending upon the angle of viewing. Achieved by using three different layers, the carpet is no more expensive that existing tufted carpets and can be customized with logo, pattern, colour and size of effect. Also available in standard colours and patterns, it can be used for commercial and residential carpets. 4690-04

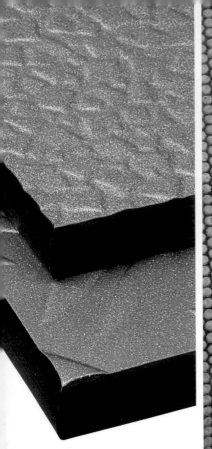

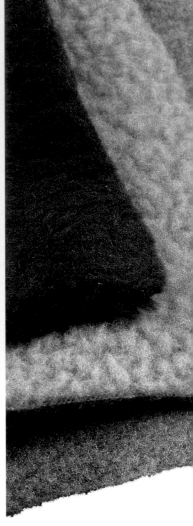

ABOVE + BELOW
Used as a chemical-, corrosion- and impact-resistant work surface, this textured composite panel is comparable to high-pressure laminates in price. Kraft paper acts as a reinforcing agent, with the natural fibres comprising up to 70 per cent of the finished product. Decoratively surfaced, it comes in a wide spectrum of colours with several textures and is used in commercial interiors.
4380-04

These micro-spheres contained within apparel either absorb or dispel heat depending upon the temperature of the wearer. The spheres may be laminated onto, or incorporated into almost any synthetic material, and the temperature of change may be engineered between -34 to 149°C (-30 to 300°F) for car, apparel, footwear, packaging, sporting goods and aerospace applications.
0139-06

Patent-pending Air Control Technology (ACT) enables this synthetic fabric to block 98 per cent of the wind, with the remaining 2 per cent allowed to circulate within the fabric, providing wind and weather protection while still retaining breathability. Featuring a breathable stretch-polyurethane membrane, these fabrics have a durable water-repellent finish and a lining inside that wicks moisture away from the body. As such, it eliminates the need for a shell, and so is perfect for sports apparel.
2691-07

This 100 per cent polyester-velour knit fleece has pebbled, or shearling surfaces that create air pockets to trap air and retain body heat, providing insulative properties. Breathable, quick-drying, and available with a water-repellent finish, the fabric is machine-washable, available in many weights and styles and appropriate for outdoor apparel.
2691-03

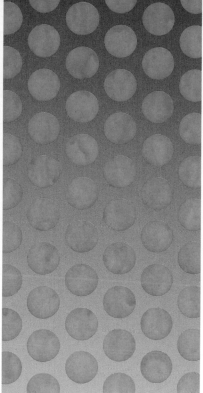

ABOVE + BELOW
Made by moulding opaque-coloured resin to create a flat sheet, this hand-poured resin surface panel is sandwiched between two clear sheets of PVC or acrylic. Available in a wide spectrum of shapes, sizes, colours and edge detailing, it has been used for counter and bar tops, tables, screens, partition walls, flooring, wall cladding and staircase construction. 4995-02

Used as decorative dividers or as camouflage for overhead lighting, these translucent rigid panels incorporate melamine-infused paper as well as perforated metal foil and are available in eight colours, four patterns and four metallic colour types. 5359-02

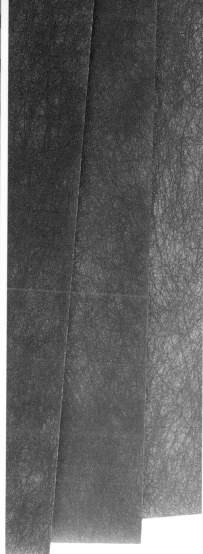

These translucent, rigid melamine sheets incorporate coloured polymer fibres that diffuse light. Available in nine colours, the sheets are used as decorative dividers or to camouflage overhead lighting, and when coupled with phenolic backing, for desktops or other horizontal applications. 5359-03

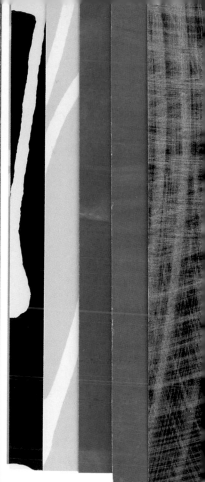

Formaldehyde-free, these rigid melamine sheets incorporate a decorative layer designed by an artist. Resistant to most household chemicals, the decorative sheets are lightfast, but intended for vertical interior surfaces that are not exposed to heavy wear. They have been used for wall and ceiling cladding, furniture, signage, retail displays, and surfacing for doors, doorframes, shipbuilding and coach fittings. 5359-05

ABOVE + BELOW
The decorative tile above incorporates an oil-based liquid, sandwiched between two sheets, that is constantly changing based on the movement or pressure on its surface. The coloured liquid and coloured translucent tile create a fluid appearance when used for flooring, table tops and other horizontal decorative surfaces. 5397-01

Designed for high traffic areas, this abrasion-resistant, high-friction, embossed flooring is made with PVC calendared into a 3-layer construction incorporating plasticizers, fillers and colour pigments. It may be cleaned with non-abrasive cleaning products, is available in ten colours with a seven-year limited warranty, and is currently used in interior commercial and institutional flooring. 0066-02

Rubber-like moulding compound like the above example has been specifically formulated for vibration and shock absorption; is an environmentally preferable, non-PVC formulation, and is currently used for small engineering parts and other confined space components that require shock and vibration absorption. The material controls shock input in limited sway space, restores system equilibrium quickly, is available in both custom mouldings and standard geometries, and can be coloured with pigmentation. 0104-05

This flooring for high traffic areas utilizes recycled PVC, has a low VOC content, and is both abrasion and high-friction resistant. Up to 50 per cent recycled PVC is calendared into a 3-layer construction, incorporating significant amounts of wood fillers, plasticizers and colour pigments. It may be cleaned with non-abrasive cleaning products, is available in twelve colours with a seven-year limited warranty, and is currently being used for interior commercial and institutional flooring. 5066-03

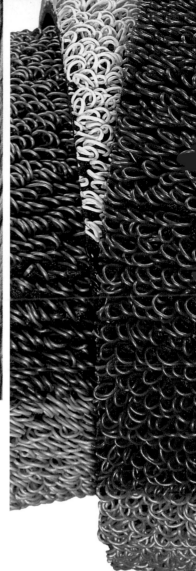

Mimicking the appearance of hardwood, this flooring for high traffic areas is available in ten colours, and is cleanable with non-abrasive products. The polyvinyl chloride is calendared into a 3-layer construction, incorporating plasticizers, fillers and colour pigments. The flooring is abrasion resistant, has a high coefficient of friction, has a seven-year limited warranty, and is currently used for interior commercial and institutional flooring. 0066-04

ABOVE + BELOW
This is a latex-based flexible rubber sheet that mimics the appearance of skin. The surface of this material has a lightly wrinkled and 'veined' appearance that is offered in various natural skin tone colours. The surface may be stitched, glued or left as a free edge. A range of standard products is available, as well as custom-designed apparel and objects. 5617-01

Made from polyvinyl chloride calendared into a 3-layer construction (the upper layer developed to withstand extreme weather conditions and air pollution), this embossed flooring for exterior flooring applications incorporates plasticizers, fillers and colour pigments. Abrasion resistant, with a high coefficient of friction, it may be cleaned with non-abrasive cleaning products, is available in ten colours with a seven-year limited warranty, and is used for exterior decking and flooring. 0066-06

This floor covering is made from PVC monofilaments that are looped and then locked into a flexible durable rubber-based layer to mimic shag carpet. Currently available in five colour options, it is used for applications in interior residential flooring. 4677-02

This handmade, hand-loomed 100 per cent recycled rubber rug is made by looping recycled bicycle tubes and weaving them into 100 per cent wool backing. Only available in black, it can be used for interior and exterior rugs, and can be cleaned by vacuuming or hand-washing with warm water and mild detergent. 5474-01

Incorporating 3-D woven fabrics that are warp knit on a Raschel machine in a single-knitting sequence, this 100 per cent polyester textile has two face fabrics independently constructed and connected by spacer yarns. The fabric properties for each face can be independently selected. The textiles have a high abrasion resistance, are soil and stain repellent and are available in eight colours, for residential upholstery. 0044-05

Printed with a range of digitally created, unique images for commercial and residential decorative wall coverings, this 100 per cent PVC calendared wallpaper has a class A fire and smoke rating. 5053-01

This 100 per cent polyurethane-coated polyester knit textile has an embossed surface that mimics the appearance of brushed metal. Available in twenty-two metallic colours, it is durable and is mainly used for seating upholstery. 0314-06

Rubber, especially vulcanized natural rubber, has been in constant use since its discovery in the 1840s. The vulcanizing process gives rubber its stable form, while preserving its natural elasticity. Katja Aga Thom creates these rubber bags from recycled tyres reclaimed from landfills, proving just how practical the material is.

Composed of 100 per cent polyethylene yarns, this woven, durable, flame-retardant textile for supporting and protecting friable fabrics is anti bacterial and stain-resistant. Its seams are almost invisible for wall coverings and it moulds easily onto furniture. It is currently being used for panels and upholstery in institutional situations such as hospitals, and also in airports and hotels. 0010-06

Woven from cotton fibres with rubber, this upholstery textile has a ridged surface that can also act as a non-slip surface. The textile is 137 cm (54 in) wide and is available in three colours (green with black rubber, white with black rubber and yellow with white rubber). 1940-11

Comprised of 100 per cent post-industrial recycled polyester, these panel fabrics are class A fire rated, and are available in eight colours, and nine patterns. Certified by the Greenguard Registry for reduced emissions, they are used for privacy curtains and wall coverings. 0314-08

This decorative, open-weave fabric is comprised of polyester, cotton, linen and nylon. It is available in 160 cm (63 in) widths and in four colours. The textile is typically used as a drapery fabric for interior residential applications. 3495-07

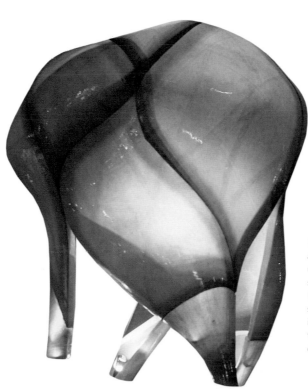

Lars Spuybroeck of the Dutch architectural practice NOX has used epoxy covered, CNC-milled styrene foam to construct his D-Tower. This lightweight, but structurally rigid material, is also translucent, allowing the structure to glow in different colours.

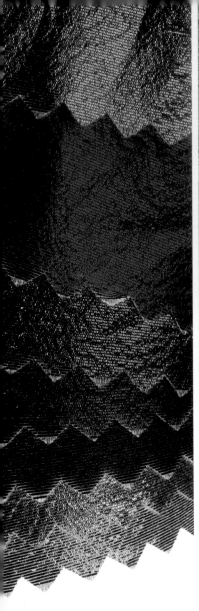

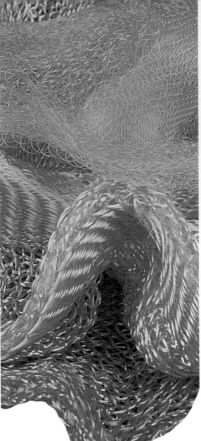

This decorative metallic textile is comprised of both polyester and various metals in seven colours, and is available in 170 cm (67 in) widths. The textile is typically used as a drapery fabric for interior residential applications. 3495-08

ABOVE + BELOW
With its 'shape memory' characteristics, this 300 denier nylon apparel textile is knitted using a doppelbed knitting machine and coarse needles to mimic snakeskin. Additional fine viscose yarns are interwoven to create further texture and evoke a metallic lustre. The material can be stretched on one axis to create a variety of shapes and to accommodate volumes, and it will retain that shape until pulled on the other axis. 4773-01

Made from 100% Trevira CS that has been coated with Teflon® (PTFE) for stain resistance, this upholstery textile is is available in 140 cm (55 in) widths and in twenty-seven colourways. The colour has a light-fastness of 5 (on an ISO scale of 1-8) and an E fire rating according to California Bulletin 117. Its abrasion resistance is 30,000 double rubs on the Martindale test and it has a shrinkage of approx 2%. 4996-05

Made from used bicycle inner tubes, this woven floor rug comprises woven inner tubes from bicycles in one direction of the mat with a high-tenacity synthetic yarn in the warp to hold the tubes together. This mat is available in only black and is for residential interiors. 4849-06

Available in five openness factors: 3, 5, 10 and 25 per cent, these non-PVC, polymer woven, window-shading textiles are resistant to bacteria and fungi, and are highly UV-resistant. The textiles are used for interior commercial window shading. 5104-01

These high-pile synthetic furs are made of microfibre polyester, and are available in ten patterns including fox, mink, beaver and lamb. They closely imitate the texture and appearance of real fur, and may be washed or dry-cleaned. They meet class 1 flammability classification in the US, and applications include apparel, upholstery, handbags, toys and accessories. 2604-15

Comparable to Charmeuse, though it is 50 per cent finer, this jersey fabric is made from Meryl® and Lycra®. The construction results in a 50 per cent reduction in thickness, and allows for support without construction and complete freedom of movement with maximum breathability. Applications include swimwear, lingerie, active wear, fashion and accessories. 4794-02

This upholstery textile is made from recycled polyester (PET) reclaimed from other textiles and water bottles. The textile contains 78 per cent recycled PET, 15 per cent virgin PET, and 7 per cent nylon woven textile that has been coated with Teflon® for stain resistance. The colour has a lightfastness of 5 (on an ISO scale of 1-8) and an E fire rating according to California Bulletin 117. Its abrasion resistance is 30,000 double rubs on the Martindale test and it has a shrinkage of approx 2 per cent. 4996-03

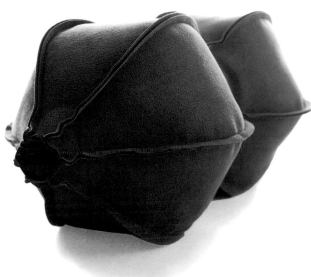

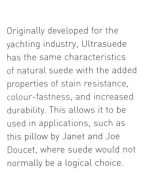

Originally developed for the yachting industry, Ultrasuede has the same characteristics of natural suede with the added properties of stain resistance, colour-fastness, and increased durability. This allows it to be used in applications, such as this pillow by Janet and Joe Doucet, where suede would not normally be a logical choice.

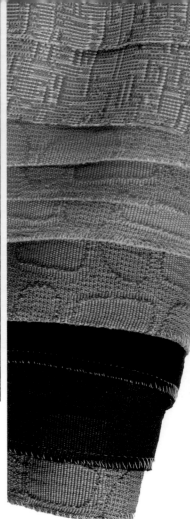

ABOVE + BELOW
This blend of patented synthetic yarn with a small proportion of natural fibres has the hang of cotton but the wicking ability of polyester. The yarn is engineered on the fibre level so that the wicking properties are not merely a surface effect that washes off. While these fabrics are typically used for sports and lingerie, other types of clothes can benefit from their abilities. 5282-01

Using steel cables for cut resistance, this woven textile is made from high-strength, drawn steel. Twelve-strand wire cable is woven into open-mesh, polyvinyl chloride-coated polyester fibres. The steel wire is tough enough to withstand box cutters. The mesh may be connected to a power source as a security alert if cut. Current applications are for flexible doors, baggage trolleys, vehicle covers, burglar-proof ceilings and safety nets. 5373-01

Made from polyester (PET) and Lycra®, this warp-knitted camouflage textile is available in black, sand and olive colours, and has a matt, scoured surface texture. It has a good bursting strength and resistance to tearing, and is currently used for military camouflage. 5396-01

Created with virtually no toxic footprint, these panel fabrics have been made from polyester that is antimony-free (heavy metal-free), these textiles are designed to be used, recovered and remanufactured safely and effectively throughout multiple product lifecycles. They have achieved a gold standard according to the MBDC Cradle-to-Cradle™ sustainability index, and are for residential and commercial upholstery. 5334-01

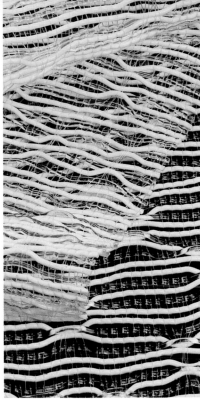

ABOVE + BELOW
This laser-cut faux fur is used in decorative applications. High-pile, faux-fur fabrics are laser-cut to create 3-D patterns. The faux fur is 100 per cent acrylic with a cotton and wool backing. The fabrics are available in five standard colours as well as custom colours. Applications include interior decoration and apparel. 5304-02

Combining monofilament and proprietary fibres to create a translucent fabric, this fabric includes a decorative Nylon monofilament and a patent-pending transparent polymer fibre woven together to incorporate additives to give increased UV-resistance. Possible applications for this textile include window treatments, as panel fabrics and for lighting. 5032-01

Produced with minimal impact on the environment, this velvet fabric is manufactured from 100 per cent wool from New Zealand and a cotton backing, both of which have been tested for pesticides and other harmful substances. The fabric is then coloured (five colours available) with dyes that contain no heavy metals and are purported to be the lowest impact dyes on the market. 5255-05

This self-supporting woven textile is used for office chair upholstery. The open weave, mesh fabric is elastomeric in one direction with the other direction providing colour and pattern. Able to withstand over 181.5 kg (400 lbs) in weight with complete recovery, the textile is comprised of 76 per cent flame-retardant polyester and 24 per cent nylon, the textile withstands 90,000 double rubs on the Wyzenbeek test, passes the California Technical bulletin 117 for flammability, and is colourfast. 5423-01

SOURCE BOOK

RICHARD LOMBARD

GLOSSARY

Abrasion resistance
The ability of the surface of a material to withstand wear. It is measured by the loss of weight when subjected to specified abrading conditions.

Accelerated delamination
A delamination test designed to produce failure (the separation of two or more layers of the laminate) caused by the same failure mechanism that would occur in normal use, but in a considerably shorter time.

Acid-free
Specifically paper that is manufactured under neutral or mildly alkaline (basic) conditions, is therefore acid-free and can maintain its physical properties for hundreds of years.

Acid-resistant
Inert to the deleterious effects of exposure to chemicals identified as acids, which turn litmus dye red, taste sour, react with certain metals and bases or alkalis to form salts, and have a pH value less than 7.0.

Aerogel
An extremely lightweight, highly porous foam with a high surface area and very low density that can be made of silica (SiO_2), alumina (Al_2O_3), carbon and other materials.

Alloy
A substance with metallic properties that is composed of two or more chemical elements, at least one of which is a metal.

Alkali- or base-resistant
Inert to the deleterious effects of exposure to chemicals identified as alkalis or bases, which turn litmus dye blue, taste bitter, have a slippery feel, react with acids to form salts, and have a pH value greater than 7.0.

Anisotropic
Having properties that are not the same in all directions.

Annealing
Subjecting glass or metals to a heating and slow cooling process that improves their properties.

Anodizing
The formation on the surface of certain metals, particularly aluminum and magnesium, of hard, stable surface coatings (an oxide of the metal) with good electrical insulating properties that can absorb dyes and pigments. The coating is deposited on the metal via an electrochemical process in which the metal is the anode, hence it is called an anodic coating.

ANSI
The American National Standards Institute is the administrator and coordinator of the US private sector voluntary standardization system.

Aramid
The generic name for a class of flame-retardant polyamide fibres, used for protective clothing, tire cord, and bullet-resistant materials (DuPont's Kevlar® and Nomex®).

Aromatic hydrocarbon
A major group of organic chemical compounds with a basic chemical structure containing one or more six-membered rings of carbon. They are largely derived from petroleum and coal tar and tend to have a relatively strong odour, hence their name.

Backstrap loom
A hand-loom that gets its name from the belt or strap support which fits around the back of the weaver, who controls the tension of the warp by leaning against it.

Barcol hardness test
This test is used to measure the degree of cure of a plastic, and directly reads (on a scale of 0–100) the resistance to penetration of a sharp steel point under a spring load.

Billet
A solid, semi-finished round or square metal product which is less than twice as wide as it is thick.

Binder
An organic or inorganic substance added to particles of a material to hold them together. In injection moulding ceramic or metal powders, the binder is a temporary agent for providing the powder with plasticity and flow.

Biocompatibility
Does not produce injurious, toxic or immunological responses in living systems.

Biodegradable
Can be decomposed by micro-organisms in the soil, weather, plants and animals.

Blanking
Punching, cutting or shearing a work piece out of stock to a desired shape.

Bulk moulding compound (BMC)
A mixture of chopped glass fibres, resins, fillers and additives, with a dough-like consistency for ease of use.

Braided textile
A textile of systems of yarns inter-twined in the bias (diagonal direction) to form an integrated structure.

Breaking load
The maximum applied force or load that results in rupture of the material being tested. Also referred to as breaking strength.

Brinell hardness test
Determines the hardness of a material by forcing a hard steel or carbide ball into the material under a specified load. The result is expressed as the Brinell hardness number (HB). Some Brinell hardness numbers are: aluminum 40; dental gold alloy 80–90; zinc 91; 410 stainless steel 250.

Brocade
An apparel or decorating fabric woven on a Jacquard loom, with an all-over ornate pattern of slightly raised floral and figure designs that are introduced by additional weft threads.

BTU
Symbol for British thermal unit, the unit for expressing quantity of heat in the English system of units.

Burst strength
A measure of the ability of a material to withstand internal fluid or gas pressure without rupturing.

Byk/Gardner mirror
A hand-held device for measuring gloss in paper.

Calendaring
Continuous method for producing plastic sheet with a smooth finish and a specified thickness and width by passing the raw materials through a series of pressure rollers.

Cal
Symbol for calorie, the unit for expressing quantity of heat in the metric system.

Candela (cd)
A unit of luminous intensity in a given direction.

Carbon black content
Carbon black improves the durability of moulding compounds for outside applications by protecting against ultraviolet degradation.

Carbon fibre
High tensile strength fibres for reinforcing composites, produced by decomposing with heat (pyrolysis) in an inert environment, organic fibres such as rayon, polyacrylonitrile (PAN) or petroleum pitch.

Carbon-based materials
Materials containing carbon, which is a nonmetallic element present in all organic compounds including organic polymers and many inorganic compounds. Carbon has three crystalline forms (diamond, graphite and Buckminster Fullerene/ 'buckyball') and several amorphous forms (coal, coke, carbon black and charcoal). Buckminster Fullerene, a recently identified form of carbon, is a molecule made up of 60 carbon atoms arranged in the shape of a soccer ball, which resembles the shape used by R. Buckminster Fuller in his geodesic dome, hence the name. These molecules combine to form nanostructures in the form of tubes and wires that are expected to become very important materials.

Carcinogen
A substance or agent causing cancer.

Carding
Disentangling fibres such as wool before they are spun using a wire-toothed brush or a machine fitted with rows of wire teeth.

Cast coating
Made by depositing a liquid plastic onto a surface followed by evaporation of the solvent.

Cast film
Made by depositing a solution or dispersion of a plastic onto a surface followed by evaporation of the liquid.

Casting
Forming a shape by pouring a molten or liquid material into a mould where it hardens.

Cement
A synthetic mineral mixture of fine-ground lime, alumina and silica that when ground to a powder and mixed with water sets to a very hard product. The water combines chemically with the other ingredients to form a hydrate, which is a stone-like mass that is resistant to compressive loading.

Ceramic casting
A forming process in which a slip (slurry or suspension of ceramic powder in water) is poured into a porous mould that absorbs enough of the water to form a fairly rigid object that after drying can be fired.

Ceramic
Product manufactured from inorganic, nonmetallic substances that are subjected to high temperature during manufacture and/or use.

Cermet (ceramic + metal)
Heterogeneous materials consisting of a mixture of ceramic and metallic components that combine the physical properties found in both components i.e., the strength and toughness of the metallic material with the heat and oxidation resistance of the ceramic.

Chemical milling
A process by which chemicals are used to remove metal from the surface of a workpiece to produce metal parts with predetermined dimensions.

Chlorine-free
Does not contain the bleaching agent, chlorine. This property is specific to pulp and paper-making where chlorine is used in the first stage of the bleaching sequence for pulp. As chlorine has detrimental environmental effects because of the formation of chlorinated organic byproducts, it is being replaced.

Chlorofluorocarbon (CFC) content
Any of several compounds composed of carbon, chlorine, fluorine and hydrogen. Their use has been restricted because of their depleting effect or ozone depletion potential (ODP) on stratospheric ozone.

Closed-loop manufacturing
Production systems that take into account manufacture, post-production recycling, post-consumer reclamation and recycling to reduce or eliminate waste and minimize material usage

Cobb size
Indicates the water absorptivity of a certain kind of paper used for labels, such as for beer and wine bottles, that are applied using a wet glue. Cobb is the name of the test that determines the water absorptivity of the labeling paper.

Coefficient
A numerical measure of a physical property that is constant for the system being tested.

Coextrusion
Several layers of material are combined using a die designed with multiple flow distribution channels so the extruded layers come together after they have been evenly distributed initially, thereby creating unique product properties compared with monolayer materials.

Colloid
Particles that when dispersed in a fluid remain suspended in the fluid without settling out or dissolving, (foams, fogs, smokes, emulsions, gels).

Commodity forms
The shapes or structures in which bulk quantities of materials are marketed, such as fibres, resin, powder, pellets and sheets.

Composite
A material produced by the mixture on a macro scale of two or more solid materials that are mutually insoluble, are different chemically and are solid in the finished state. The constituents of a composite retain their identities but act collectively.

Compressive strength
The maximum compressive stress that a material can develop based on the original area of its cross section. This property has a definite value if the material fails in compression by undergoing a shattering fracture.

Copolymer
A long-chain molecule formed by the reaction of two or more dissimilar monomers.

Corrosion resistant
The ability of a material to withstand ambient conditions without its properties being degraded (rusting and pitting in metals and fine cracks in plastics).

Creep
The change in size or shape of a material, which is under a force (load), with time, such as the elongation of a metal or a plastic.

Critical radiant flux
A measurement of the amount of exposure to heat from a nearby fire that a floor covering can withstand before it bursts into flame.

Cross-dyeing
A process for intentionally dyeing a textile that contains two or more types of fibres so that each of the various fibre types accepts a different colour. In some cases, the dye bath is planned so that certain fibres do not accept any of the colours, but remain white. The result depends on the way the fibres create the design in the textile, such as a check, a tweed, a stripe, a muted colour or some other design.

Crystal
A homogeneous solid made of atoms, ions, or molecules arranged in a 3-D repetitive pattern with fixed distances between the constituent parts.

Curing
An irreversible change in the physical properties of a material due to a chemical reaction or vulcanization, usually by the action of heat and catalysts.

Cytotoxicity
Produces a toxic effect on cells.

Damask
A firm, lustrous fabric made of silk, linen, cotton, rayon, or a combination of these fibres, on Jacquard looms, with flat patterns in a satin weave, on a plain-woven ground on the right side, and a plain-woven pattern on a satin ground on the reverse side.

Deep drawing
A process for forming deeply recessed metal parts by forcing sheet metal to flow plastically (i.e. without rupturing) between two dies.

Decatizing
A textile process for adding luster to cloth and for setting the nap and size by winding it on perforated rollers and circulating hot water/steam through it.

Delamination
Splitting or separating the layers of a laminated material.

Denier
A unit for expressing the linear density or fineness of a filament, fibre or yarn. The lower the denier, the finer the yarn.

Die cavity
A machined hollow shape for forming a metal.

Dielectric constant
An index of the ability of an insulating material to reduce the transmission of an electrostatic force between two charged bodies. The lower the value, then the greater the reduction. A good dielectric is a good insulator but the reverse is not necessarily true in every case. Dielectric constant values decrease with increasing temperature.

Diffuse reflection
The scattering of incident light by reflection from a rough surface.

Dimensional stability
Measure of the change in dimensions of an object as the result of temperature, humidity, chemical treatment, aging or stress. It is usually expressed as a change in the units of the dimension per unit.

DIN
Deutsche Industrie Normen (German Industry Standards).

Drawing (metal)
A metal forming process in which a previously rolled, extruded or fabricated product is pulled through a die at relatively high speed. Variations of drawing are wire drawing by cold drawing steel in which a pointed rod or wire is pulled through a circular hole or die; tube drawing in which a mandrel or solid bar with a blunt end is placed inside the tube to control the tube's diameter during drawing; and deep drawing (or cupping) in which the metal is passed through by a punch from the inside.

Dressing
The shaping/squaring of stone blocks.

Dry-laid
A textile that is made by carding or air-laying the fibres in a random or an oriented fashion.

Duck
A durable, closely woven heavy cotton or linen fabric.

Ductility (metals)
The ability of a metal to be deformed without fracturing.

Durometer hardness
This test measures the indentation into a plastic or rubber material of an indenter under load on a scale of 0 to 100. Several types of indenter can be used such as blunt-ended (Type A) for softer materials and pointed (Type D) for harder materials. When the indenter is pressed into the plastic specimen so that the base rests on the plastic's surface, the amount of indentation registers directly on the dial indicator.

Dyne
Symbolized dyn, it is the unit for expressing force in the metric system. Its counterpart in SI is newton (N) and in the English system is pound-force (lbf).

E-glass
A glass fibre with high electrical resistivity used as a reinforcement in plastics and for electrical laminates. Also called electric glass.

Elastic modulus
The measure of rigidity or stiffness of a material. It also known as the modulus of elasticity, E, and Young's modulus.

Elastomer
An elastic, rubber-like material that recovers approximately its original shape and size after being stretched. Elastomers include vulcanized natural rubber as well as synthetic rubbers.

Electrical conductivity
A measure of the ability of a material to conduct an electric current. It is defined as the reciprocal of the material's resistivity, which is the resistance a material offers to the flow of electric current.

Electromagnetic interference (EMI)
Undesirable interference particularly in electronic devices and equipment from radiation, from sources such as other electronic devices, electric motors, or other sources of electromagnetic energy.

Electrostatic discharge (ESD)
Static charge, which builds up usually as a consequence of rubbing effects, can generate voltages from tens of volts to as high as 30 kV. When it discharges this static charge can destroy electronic components.

Electrostatic propensity
The tendency of materials, such as carpets, to build up a static charge when a person walks across them. The amount of extension of a uniform test piece expressed as a percentage of its original length.

Elmendorf Tear test
A specially prepared sample of fabric or paper is mounted firmly in the grips of a pendulum tester. The indicator is set at 0 and the pendulum is released. After the pendulum comes to rest, the maximum force to tear the material is read on the indicator.

Emissivity
1) The ability of a surface to emit or absorb radiated energy. The lower the emissivity the more efficient the material is in emitting or absorbing the radiated energy. 2) The ratio of the radiation emitted by a surface to the radiation emitted by a black body (a theoretically perfect absorber) at the same temperature.

Enamel
A vitreous, usually opaque, protective or decorative glossy coating baked on a metal or ceramic surface.

EPA
US Environmental Protection Agency.

EPDM
Ethylene-propylene-diene-monomer.

Ester
An organic compound that corresponds in structure to an inorganic salt. Esters are considered to be derived from organic acids. For example, acetates are esters of acetic acid.

Europeen Normen (EN)
European Standards.

E-value
A measure of emissivity, which is the ability of a surface to emit or absorb radiant energy. The lower the e-value, the more efficient the material is in managing energy, therefore in increasing the savings in energy costs.

Exfoliating material
Material that breaks off in flakes.

Expanding
A process that uses a punch (the male part of a die) to increase the diameter or to change the shape of the walls from straight to cylindrical or cylindrical to spherical of metal cups, shells or tubes.

Extrusion
Shaping a material by forcing it through a die.

Fascia
In architecture, a flat, horizontal band or member between mouldings.

Fatigue
The failure of a material after several cycles of loading to a level of stress below its ultimate tensile stress (the highest stress it can sustain in a tensile test).

FDA
US Food and Drug Administration.

Felt
Non-woven, fibrous textile composed of fibres interlocked by mechanical or chemical action, moisture or heat.

Felting
The formation of a non-woven fibrous fabric from wool, mixed with fur and other natural or synthetic fibres, by interlocking the loose fibres with heat, moisture, chemicals and pressure.

Fibre
A solid fibre with high tenacity and an extremely high ratio of length to diameter. Fibres can be natura, semi-synthetic, synthetic, ceramic, metal or hollow. The terms fibre and filament are often used synonymously.

Fibreboard
Building material composed of wood chips or plant fibres bonded together, compressed or rolled into rigid sheets.

Fibreglas™
This is a trademark (Owens Corning) for products made with glass fibres.

Fibreglass
Term used to describe two different products. One product is a material consisting of extremely fine glass fibres. The other is a composite consisting of these glass fibres in various polymeric matrices such as polyester and nylon, also called glass fibre reinforced polymer (GFRP).

Filament
Continuous fibre for use as a reinforcement usually made by extrusion from a spinneret and drawing. Filaments are often very long with a small diameter.

Filament winding
Process for fabricating a reinforced plastic or composite structure in which continuous reinforcements (filament, wire, yarn, tape) impregnated with a resin or impregnated during the winding, are wrapped around a suitably shaped rotating and removable form (or mandrel).

Filled composites
A bonding material such as a resin, asphalt or linseed oil that is loaded with a flake-like or particulate filler (linoleum).

Filler
A relatively inert inorganic, organic, mineral, natural or synthetic substance added to a plastic to change its properties or to lower its cost or density.

Flame retardant
Flame retardants hinder or slow the progress of a flame and are added to materials such as plastics to inhibit their combustion.

Flame spraying
Type of thermal spraying in which the coating material in the form of wire or powder is fed into an oxygen fuel gas flame, where it is melted and propelled onto the surface being coated.

Flash ignition temperature
The temperature at which a material must be heated in order to burst into flame and/or burn.

Flash point
The temperature at which a liquid or volatile solid emits sufficient vapour to form an ignitable mixture with the air near its surface.

Flexural modulus
Commonly used as an indicator of the stiffness of a plastic material, a fibre-reinforced plastic composite or wood. Also called Bending modulus, it is the ratio of the applied stress to the strain, within the elastic limit of the material.

Flock
Pulverized wool or felt used to texture or pattern paper, fabric or metal.

Fly ash
The very fine ash produced by the combustion of coal or coke. It is a mixture of aluminum oxide, silicon dioxide, unburned carbon and various other metallic oxides. When recovered it can be used as a filler for cement or plastics and also as a constituent of some commercial products.

Foam
Cellular structure formed by a dispersion of gas bubbles in a liquid in the presence of surface active stabilizers that maintain the foam's integrity and prevent it from collapsing.

Forging
The process of working metal to a desired shape by impact or pressure via hammers, forging machines, presses, rolls and forming equipment.

Formaldehyde emission
The release into the atmosphere of formaldehyde (a carcinogen that is toxic by inhalation and a strong irritant). Formaldehyde is a gaseous chemical used in the manufacture of melamine, polyacetal and phenolic resins; for durable-press treatment of textiles; and to make foam insulation, particleboard and plywood.

Galvanized metal
Where the metal surface, usually iron or steel, is coated with zinc by various processes, to prevent corrosion.

Gas
A state of matter with very low density and viscosity compared with liquids and solids and comparatively great expansion and contraction with changes in temperature and pressure, the ability to diffuse readily into other gases, and the spontaneous tendency to occupy with almost uniformity the whole of any container.

Gel
A colloid in which the dispersed phase (particles between 1 nanometer and 1 micrometer) has combined with the continuous liquid phase to form a viscous jelly-like product.

Gesso
A mixture of plaster of Paris (calcium sulfate) or gypsum, and glue used as a base for low relief (bas-relief) or as a surface for painting.

Glass-ceramic
A devitrified or crystallized form of glass with properties that can be varied over a wide range. Corning's Pyroceram is an example.

Glass
Amorphous solids composed of a uniformly dispersed mixture of 75% silica or sand (SiO_2), 20% soda ash, and 5% lime often combined with metallic oxides such as those of calcium, lead, lithium or cerium, depending on the properties desired.

Graphite fibre
High tensile fibres made from rayon, polyacrylonitrile or petroleum pitch, produced as filament, yarn and fabric for uses such as protection clothing, flame-proof textiles, reinforcement for polyester and epoxy composites for aircraft. They are processed at much higher temperatures than carbon fibres and contain a higher percent of elemental carbon: 99% in graphite fibres compared with 93–95% in carbon fibres (see also carbon fibre).

Gray
The SI unit for measuring an absorbed dose of radiation, symbolized Gy.

Green Seal Assessment
The Green Seal is an independent, non-profit organization dedicated to protecting the environment by promoting the manufacture and sale of environmentally responsible consumer products. It sets environmental standards and awards a 'Green Seal of Approval' to products that cause less harm to the environment than other similar products.

Grit
Crushed abrasive material that is available in various mesh sizes corresponding to the number of openings per linear inch/cm in a screen through which the particles can pass.

Gunite
A concrete mixture that is sprayed over steel reinforcements in light construction, using a special type of gun.

Gypsum
A colourless mineral (calcium sulfate with attached water molecules) used to make plaster of Paris and various other plaster products.

Hand lay-up
Layers of fibre mats or woven roving are manually placed in a mould cavity to fabricate a part. There is virtually no limit to the size of a laid-up part because when properly applied, layers of resin and reinforcement build into an integral laminate.

Hardboard
Thin fibre-base panel products with densities which are higher than medium density fibreboard (MDF).

Header
A floor or roof beam placed between two long beams, which supports the ends of the tail pieces.

Hertz
Symbolized Hz, Hertz is a unit of frequency equal to 1 cycle per second.

Hologram
An optical image of a 3-D object formed when the light from a laser is split into two beams: an illuminating beam and a reference beam. The illuminating beam is aimed at the object and its reflection strikes a light-sensitive film; the reference beam meets the reflected beam at the film. The interference between the reflected and reference beams leaves a pattern of the object on the film.

HMIS–NFPA
US Hazardous Materials Identification System – National Fire Prevention Association.

Hydraulic cement
A mixture of finely ground lime, silica and alumina that sets to a hard cement when mixed with water.

Hydrophilic
Having an affinity for water thus readily absorbs or dissolves in water.

Hydrophobic
Repelling water thus does not combine with or dissolve in water.

Hygroscopic
A material that absorbs moisture from the air. Examples are calcium chloride, silica gel, paper and cotton fabrics.

Hysteresis
The lag of an effect behind its cause. For example, when a resilient material that is compressed does not return immediately to its original shape when the compressive force is removed.

IFD
Indentation Force Deflection at 25% and 65% compression. It is a measure of load bearing for flexible foam slabs.

Impact energy
The amount of energy needed to break a material. It is measured via several different tests: the Charpy impact test in which the energy required to fracture a notched sample of the material is calculated from the difference in the initial and final heights of a weighted swinging pendulum; the Izod impact test, in which a V-notched sample of the material receives a sudden blow from a weighted pendulum; the Tensile impact test that does not notch the test specimen; and falling weight tests.

Infrared (IR) radiation-absorbing
Absorbs radiant energy in the form of electromagnetic waves from the region of the electromagnetic spectrum from 0.78 micrometers to about 300 micrometers, which is longer than visible light and shorter than microwaves.

Infrared (IR) radiation transmitting
Transmits radiant energy in the form of electromagnetic waves from the region of the electromagnetic spectrum from 0.78 micrometers to about 300 micrometers, which is longer than visible light and shorter than microwaves.

Injection moulding (ceramics and metals)
Parts are formed by heating a mixture of a ceramic or metal powder plus a binder, then forcing the softened material into a closed die, processing the formed part to remove the binder, and densifying the compact by high-temperature sintering.

Injection moulding (thermoplastics)
The melted plastic is injected into a mould cavity where it cools and takes the shape of the cavity. Details such as screw threads and ribs can be integrated allowing the operation to produce a finished part in one step.

Injection moulding (thermosets)
The thermoset material is first heated until it liquefies, and then is made to flow into one or more mould cavities where it is held at an elevated temperature until cross-linking is completed. The hardened formed part is then removed from the open mould.

Inlaid
An inlaid surface has a decorative design set into it.

Inorganic chemicals
These are generally considered to include all chemicals except hydrocarbons (compounds of carbon and hydrogen) and their derivatives, or all chemicals that are not compounds of carbon, with the exception of carbon oxides, carbides, metallic cyanides and metallic carbonates, and other similar carbon-containing chemical compounds, which are classified as inorganic chemicals.

International System of Units or SI
A modernized metric measurement system that is becoming the dominant measurement system used in commerce throughout the world.

Intumescent material
A material that swells or bubbles when heated and is used for fire protection.

Investment casting
A metal shape is made by first creating a pattern for the mould in a waxy material, then making a ceramic mould by coating the wax pattern with a ceramic slurry. The wax is removed by heating and the mould is fired. Molten metal is then poured (cast) into or around the hardened mould. This is also known as the lost wax process.

Ionomer
A thermoplastic polymer that is 'ionically cross-linked' by means of the transfer of electrons between atoms (ionic bonds).

ISO
The International Organization of Standardization. Founded in 1947, it has 110 member countries and has published over 9000 ISO standards.

Isotropic
Identical or uniform properties in all directions.

Izod impact strength
A measure of the toughness of a material in which a V-notched sample of the material receives a sudden blow from a weighted pendulum.

Joule
Symbolized J, a joule is the unit for expressing electrical, mechanical and thermal energy in the International System of Units (SI).

Ketone
A class of liquid organic compounds used as solvents in lacquers and paints, and in textile processing.

Knoop hardness test
The Knoop hardness test is an indentation hardness test that uses calibrated machines to force a rhombic-shaped pyramidal diamond into the surface of the material.

Kynar
The proprietary name (Pennwalt) of the thermoplastic fluorocarbon polymer, polyvinylidene fluoride, which has good mechanical and weathering properties. Properly fabricated films are 3–5 times more piezoelectric than crystalline quartz. Uses include protective paints and coatings, insulation for high temperature wires, audio speakers, shrinkage tubing to encapsulate electronic components, sealant. Other proprietary names are: Dyflor (Dynamit Nobel), KF (Kureha), Solef (Solvay), Foraflon (Atochem).

Laminating
Joining or bonding two or more layers of material by adhesives, or by the application of heat and pressure.

Leno weave
A fabric in which the warp yarns are paired and twisted.

Light-emitting diode (LED)
An electronic device that shows electroluminescence (the production of light from electricity). The colour of the light emitted corresponds to the energy emitted when electrons move from a higher to a lower energy state.

Lignin
An amorphous polymer that comprises 17–30% of wood. Some of its uses are as a ceramic binder, a dye leveller and dispersant and for special moulded products.

Liquid
A form of matter intermediate between gases and solids that flows readily and is relatively incompressible, in which the molecules are much more highly concentrated than in gases but much less concentrated than in solids.

Liquid resin
An organic, polymeric liquid that when converted to its final state for use becomes a solid or semi-solid material (such as linseed oil).

Louvre
A framed opening in a door or window fitted with fixed or movable horizontal slats for admitting air and light; also one of the slats used in such an opening.

Lumber
Timber sawed into boards, planks, or other structural members of standard or specified length.

Lumen (lm)
The amount of light emitted by a source one candela in intensity radiating equally in all directions.

Lux (lx)
The unit of illumination in the International System of Units (SI) equal to one lumen per square centimetre.

Mandrel
A tool around which materials can be shaped.

Matrix
The continuous or principal material in which another constituent is dispersed in a composite. For example, in a ceramic particle-reinforced aluminum composite, the aluminum is the matrix, in a glass fibre-reinforced epoxy composite, the epoxy is the matrix.

MDF
Medium density fibreboard. MDF panels are made of fibrous raw material and generally have smoother surfaces and edges than particleboard.

MDI
This is the chemical compound, methylene diphenylene isocyanate. It is used in the preparation of polyurethane resin and spandex fibres, and also for bonding rubber to rayon or nylon. It is a strong irritant with fumes that are toxic if inhaled and combustible.

Melt blowing
The extrusion of a softened thermoplastic polymer through a single-extrusion orifice into a high-velocity heated air stream that breaks the fibre into short pieces.

Membrane
A thin sheet of natural or synthetic material that is microporous and acts as an efficient filter for very small molecules such as ions, water and other solvents and gases.

Metal injection moulding (MIM)
Metal powders mixed with a polymeric binder are granulated and fed into an injection moulding machine where the material is heated so it can flow into a cavity of the desired shape. After cooling and solidifying it is ejected from the die, the polymer is removed by debinding, and the shaped component is then heated to densify it.

Metal
Most materials classified as metals are opaque, lustrous crystalline solids that are good conductors of heat and electricity, are malleable and ductile, and when polished, are good reflectors of light.

Metal casting
A forming process in which molten metal is poured or injected into a mould to produce an object with the desired shape.

Metal foam
A cellular metallic structure fabricated from metal powder or molten metal with an additive that releases hydrogen during processing. A foam-like material is produced that is lighter in weight than the solid metal and can absorb shock on impact.

Metallization
A deposited or plated thin metallic film used for its protective or electrical properties.

Microfibre
Fibres with extremely small diameters in the micrometer range. Microfibres as fine as 0.001–0.0001 tex (0.01–0.001 den) and not more than 0.03 tex or 0.3 den are used to make human-made leathers with the properties and appearance of natural leather. Thicker microfibres (0.01 tex or 0.1 den) are used to make a suedelike material with a fine nap (such as ultrasuede).

Microspheres
These are hollow spheres in the micrometer size range (20–150 micrometers). They can be made of glass, silica or various polymers with high molecular weights (>5000), or proteins (for example gelatin or albumen).

Millboard
A strong, heavy, hard paperboard used, for example, in lining book covers and for panelling in furniture.

Milling (machining)
In machining, milling refers to the use of a rotary tool with one or more teeth that engage the workpiece and remove material from it as it moves past the rotating cutter.

Milling (powder technology)
In powder technology, milling refers to mechanically breaking down a material, usually in a ball mill, to change the size or shape of the individual particles, to coat one component of a mixture with another, or to create a uniform distribution of the components.

Mineral
A widely used general term referring to the nonliving constituents of the earth's crust. These include naturally occurring elements, compounds, and mixtures that have a definite range of chemical composition and properties. Usually inorganic, but sometimes including fossil fuels such as coal. Minerals are the raw materials for a wide variety of elements (such as metals) and chemical compounds.

Modacrylic fibres
Synthetic textile fibres that are long-chain polymers composed of between 35% and 85% by weight of acrylonitrile units.

Modulus
A quantity that expresses the degree to which a material possesses a property, such as the elastic modulus.

Mohs hardness
The hardness of a material based on a scale devised by Mohs listing ten minerals, each of which would scratch the one listed below it. In decreasing order of hardness these minerals are: diamond 10, corundum 9, topaz 8, quartz 7, orthoclase (feldspar) 6, apatite 5, fluorite 4, calcite 3, gypsum 2, talc 1.

Moisture vapour transition rate (MVTR)
A measure of the amount of water vapour transmitted per square metre of a material per 24 hours. Often done under two service conditions: 1) with one side of the material wetted and 2) with low humidity on one side and high humidity on the other.

Monel
Trade name for a series of corrosion-resistant alloys of nickel and copper.

Monofilament
A single, continuous length of fibre.

Monomer
A simple molecule or compound that usually contains carbon that can be converted to polymers, synthetic resins or elastomers by combining with itself or other similar molecules or compounds.

Mortar
An adhesive or bonding agent that is soft and workable when fresh but sets to a hard solid on standing.

MPa
The symbol for megapascal, an SI unit for measuring pressure or stress. Its counterpart in metric units is dyne per square centimetre (dyn/cm2) also kilogram-force per square metre (kgf/m2).

Mrad
The symbol for megarad, the metric unit for measuring an absorbed dose of radiation.

Mullen Burst test
Measures the force required to burst a sample of a material clamped between two plates when a fluid filled moulded rubber diaphragm exerts a constantly increasing pressure against the unsupported sample. A gauge indicates the pressure rise. When the sample bursts, the pressure drops, leaving the gauge pointer stationary and indicating the force required to burst the sample.

Mullen burst waterproof test
A Mullen Burst Hydrostatic Machine is used to determine how impervious to water a coated fabric is by measuring the force required for penetration by water.

Needle punching
A process in which thousands of barbed needles penetrate a stack of oriented or random layers of fibres, consolidating it by entangling the fibres and creating an integrated structure with through-the-thickness fibre reinforcement. This process is also called needling.

Neoprene
A synthetic elastomer (chemical name, polychloroprene) available as a solid, a latex or a flexible foam. Uses include rubber products and adhesive cements, seat cushions, carpet backing.

Newton
Symbolized N, it is the unit for expressing force in the International System of Units (SI).

NFPA
National Fire Prevention Association.

Noise reduction coefficient
A measure of the amount that the noise is diminished under specified conditions by a sound-absorbing material, and the effectiveness of an acoustically insulating material. It is expressed as the ratio of the noise transmitted with the acoustical insulating material in place to the noise without it.

Nonpolar liquid
The positive and negative electrical charges on the molecules of the liquid coincide. Benzene is a nonpolar liquid.

Non-woven fabric
A planar textile structure produced by loosely compressing together fibres, yarns and rovings by mechanical, chemical, thermal or solvent means, or combinations of these.

Oils
Refers to a wide range of substances that are quite different in chemical nature. Oils are classified as mineral (petroleum and petroleum-derived); vegetable (largely from seeds and nuts); animal (tallow, fish-liver); essential (complex volatile liquids from flowers and plants); and edible (from fruits or seeds of plants).

Oligomer
A polymer unit consisting of only a few monomer units (such as dimer, trimer, tetramer).

Organic binders
A binder is mixed with a ceramic or metal powder to form a uniform feedstock for moulding. The most commonly used binders are thermoplastic polymers such as polyethylene, polypropylene, and polystyrene, which are categorized chemically as organic compounds.

Organic chemical compounds
A major class of chemical compounds; over 6 million have been identified and named. They include all compounds of carbon with certain exceptions such as the carbon oxides, carbides, metallic cyanides and metallic carbonates, and other similar compounds that are classified as inorganic chemical compounds.

Oriented strandboard (OSB)
A sheet material made of long, narrow wood flakes called strands cut from small logs.

Ozone depletion potential (ODP)
The ozone depletion potential is a relative index that indicates the extent to which a chemical product may cause a reduction in the amount of ozone in the stratosphere, where it acts to shield the Earth from damaging electromagnetic radiation from the sun.

Pa
Abbreviation for pascal, a unit of pressure in the metric and SI systems.

Particleboard
A sheet material made from particles or small pieces of wood bonded together with an adhesive under heat and pressure to form sheets that have greater flexibility but lower strength than hardboard.

Particulate composites
A wide range of materials in which the reinforcement is spherical particles or particles with dimensions that are similar in all directions (such as concrete and filled polymers).

Pascal (Pa)
A unit of pressure in the metric system.

Patina
A thin, greenish layer, usually copper sulfate, that forms on the surface of copper or copper alloys such as bronze, due to corrosion. It can also mean a sheen produced on a surface.

Peel strength
The average force per unit width required to separate progressively two bonded surfaces.

Permeance
The ability of a material of a specified thickness to transmit moisture, which is expressed as the amount of moisture transmitted per unit for a specified area and differential pressure, and measured as grains (of water vapour). Materials with low permeance are used as vapour retarders.

pH
A value that represents the acidity or alkalinity (basicity) of a water-based solution. Pure water with a pH of 7 is the standard for the pH scale. Other representative pHs are: a strong acid such as hydrochloric acid 2; a strong base such as sodium hydroxide 12; blood 7.3–7.5; milk 6.5–7; sea water 7.8–8.2.

Phosphorescent
A type of luminescence in which the emission of radiation takes place after the initial excitation, and can last from a second to an hour or more. Light from the firefly and the TV tube are examples.

Photopolymer
A polymer or plastic that undergoes a change on exposure to light.

Photosensitive
A material that is responsive to light or radiant energy.

Piezoelectric material
A piezoelectric material (for example, quartz) converts a mechanical stress into electrical energy and conversely expands in one direction and contracts in another, when subjected to an electric field. Piezoelectric thin and thick film polymers and ceramics are used as transducers and sensors as well as for microphones and earphones.

Plaster
A mixture of lime (for example calcium oxide) or gypsum (which is a mineral of calcium sulfate with attached water molecules), sand and water, sometimes with added fibre, that hardens to a smooth solid and used for coating walls and ceilings.

Plastic
A material that contains as an essential ingredient an organic polymer of large molecular weight, is solid in its finished state, and at some stage in its manufacture or its processing into finished articles can be shaped by flow. Although materials such as rubber, textiles, adhesives and paints may in some cases meet this definition, they are not considered plastics. The terms plastic, resin, and polymer are somewhat synonymous, but the terms resins and polymers most often denote the basic material as polymerized, while the term plastic encompasses compounds containing plasticizers, stabilizers, fillers and other additives.

Plastic foam
A cellular plastic that can be either flexible (e.g., polyurethane, polyethylene, or vinyl polymers) or rigid (e.g. polystyrene, polyurethane, epoxy, and polyvinyl chloride) an is normally produced using a blowing agent such as sodium bicarbonate or hydrazine.

Plasticizer
A material is added to a polymer both to facilitate its processing and to increase the flexibility and toughness of the final product.

Plastisol
A dispersion of finely divided resin in a plasticizer, used mainly for moulding thermoplastic resins such as polyvinyl chloride.

Plate
A sheet of hammered, rolled or cast metal.

Ply
1) Joined materials by moulding or twisting. 2) A layer of a doubled-over cloth or paperboard. 3) A sheet of the wood glued together in plywood. 4) One of the strands in a twisted yarn or rope.

Plywood
A panel made from wood veneers that are bonded to one another. Generally, each ply is oriented at right angles to the adjacent ply, and the two face plies have the grain direction parallel to each other to increase strength.

Poisson's ratio
The elongation per unit length when a rod of material is stretched with sufficient force is the strain. At the same time as the rod is elongated its lateral dimensions contract. The ratio of the contraction per lateral unit to the elongation per unit length, which is constant for a given material within the elastic limit (below the point where further strain would result in a permanent change in its dimensions) is known as Poisson's ratio.

Polar liquid
The positive and negative electrical charges on the molecules of the liquid are permanently separated. Water is a polar liquid.

Polymers
Natural or synthetic long-chain molecules with backbones of carbon atoms. Polymers are composed of many (poly) repeating units (mers or monomers) joined together. Cellulose is an example of a natural polymer and polypropylene is an example of a synthetic polymer.

Polymerization
A chemical reaction, usually carried out with a catalyst, heat or light, in which a large number of relatively simple molecules combine to form a chain-like macromolecule.

Porosity
Fine holes or pores within a solid material. The amount of these pores, which is the material's porosity, is usually expressed as a percentage of the total volume of the material in question.

Portland cement
A type of hydraulic cement (hardens under water) in the form of a finely divided grey powder composed largely of lime (calcium oxide), alumina (aluminum oxide), silica (silicon dioxide) and iron oxide with small amounts of magnesia (magnesium oxide), sodium, potassium and sulfur.

Post-consumer recycled content
Materials that are recovered from used and discarded consumer products and then are recycled into new materials or products.

Post-industrial-production / pre-consumer content
Materials or by-products that have not reached a business entity or consumer for an intended use, including industrial scrap, overstock or obsolete inventories, and by-products generated from, and reused within, the original manufacturing process.

Pot life
The length of time that a thermosetting polymer system retains a low enough viscosity to be used for processing. It is used to compare the relative rate of reaction of various polymer/hardener combinations.

Pozzolanic
A hydraulic cement that has the properties of a pozzolana (a cementitious material formed by the reaction of a finely powdered aggregate similar to volcanic ash with slaked lime).

Prepreg
A thin sheet of a partially cured thermoset resin or a thermoplastic resin containing woven or unidirectional fibres for fabricating composites.

Processed raw materials
Raw materials (such as ores and clays) that have undergone a first level of processing such as extraction, refining and purification, followed by further processing into materials such as alloys, polymers and ceramics for fabrication into finished products.

Pulforming/pull forming
A variation of pultrusion that allows the formation of curved shapes in which the cross section varies, provided the cross sectional area stays constant.

Pultrusion
A continuous process for manufacturing composites which have a constant cross-sectional shape, that consists of pulling a fibre-reinforcing material through a resin impregnation bath and then through a shaping die, where the resin is cured.

Punching
The operation of piercing or punching a hole in which the shape of the hole is controlled by the shape of the punch (the male part of a die) and its mating die (the female part of the die, which is called the die).

Quartz
The common name for crystallized silicon dioxide (silica).

Raffia
Fibres of the leaf of an African palm tree, used for mats, baskets and other woven products.

Rapid prototyping
This is a process for quickly fabricating complex-shaped 3-D objects directly from CAD (computer aided design) models. A number of such methods have been developed based on a concept called layered manufacturing, or solid freeform fabrication (SFF), in which 3-D computer models of an object are decomposed into thin cross-sectional layers, which are then followed by physically forming the layers and stacking them up to create the object.

Raschel knitting
A warp knit fabric, usually of intricate lacy patterns that imitates crochet, net or lace.

Rayon
The generic name for a semi-synthetic fibre that is typically composed of regenerated cellulose from wood pulp.

Reflectance
The ratio of the radiant power reflected from a material's surface to the radiant power incident on it, which is usually expressed as a percentage.

Refractive index
The ratio of the speed of light in a vacuum to its speed in the medium under consideration. It depends on the wavelength of light used and the temperature.

Refractory material
This usually involves ceramics that are used where resistance to very high temperature is required, such as for use in furnace linings and metal-melting pots.

Relative Heat Gain (RHG)
RHG is a numerical indicator of the amount of heat gained through a specific glass, which is calculated according to a formula. The number is especially useful when comparing several types of glass (for example, in construction or commercial or domestic interiors). A higher number indicates a greater heat gain and thus a poorer performing glass.

Release paper
A paper sheet that serves as a protectant or carrier or both for an adhesive film or mass that is easily removed from the film or mass prior to use.

Renewable resource
A material that is abundant and easily replaceable by natural ecological cycles or sustainable management practices.

Resin
As used here, resin refers to a human-made polymer produced by a chemical reaction between two or more substances, which does not contain any additives such as plasticizers, stabilizers or fillers.

Resin transfer moulding (RTM)
This is when a catalyzed resin is introduced into a closed mould that contains a woven, non-woven, or knitted fabric reinforcement and cured. The advantages of RTM are the relatively low investment needed for equipment and tooling and the ability to mould large, highly reinforced parts that can incorporate cores and inserts.

Reticulated material
A material that contains an open network and can be used as a filter.

Retroreflectivity
A measure (using a reflectometer) of the night-time visibility of pavement markings and road/street signs.

Rockwell hardness test
An indentation hardness test in which a calibrated machine uses either a steel ball or a diamond cone with a slightly rounded point in order to indent a material. The depth of the indentation under a constant load is the final measure of the hardness. There are 15 scales of Rockwell hardness numbers (for example, A, B, C, D, E, F, G, H, K, L, M, P, R, S, V) based on the hardness of the materials to be evaluated.

Rod
A solid round, straight metal or wood piece with a length that is large in relation to its diameter.

Rolling
A process for reducing the cross-sectional area of metal stock or for the general shaping of metal products by using rotating rolls. Cylindrical rolls produce flat shapes; grooved rolls produce rounds, squares, and structural shapes.

Rotational moulding
In this process the product is formed from a liquid or powdered thermoplastic resin inside a closed mould or cavity while the mould is rotating biaxially in a heating chamber. It is most suited to produce large, hollow, products requiring stress-free strength, complicated curves, a good finish, a variety of colours, and uniform wall thickness.

Routing
Routing is a process for cutting out and contouring edges of various shapes in a relatively thin material using a small diameter rotating cutter that is operated at relatively high speeds.

Roving
A bundle of continuous filaments in the form of an untwisted strand or twisted yarn.

Rubber
A natural or synthetic high molecular weight polymer with unique elongation properties and elastic recovery after vulcanization (cross-linking) with sulfur or other cross-linking agents, which in effect converts the polymer from a thermoplastic to a thermoset.

Sandblasting
Cleaning or etching a surface with an air blast that throws abrasive particles of sand against it.

Sandwich
Usually formed of a lightweight core material (such as honeycomb or foam) adhered between two relatively thin, high-strength or high-stiffness sheets.

Saran
A thermoplastic polymer (chemical name: polyvinylidene chloride) produced as extruded and moulded products, oriented fibres and films for packaging foods, seat covers, upholstery, and bristles.

Sceleroscope hardness test
An indentation hardness test using a calibrated instrument that drops a diamond-tipped hammer from a fixed height onto the surface of the material being tested. The height of the rebound of the hammer is the measure of the material's hardness.

Scientific Certification Systems Assessment / Certified Eco-Profile
The Certified Eco-Profile labelling system, which was created by Scientific Certification Systems, is the first comprehensive environmental declaration label to provide a summary of each product's unique ecological profile. Information reported on the Certified Eco-Profile is obtained by conducting a lifecycle assessment. This environmental assessment technology measures the total environmental impacts from the extraction of resources through manufacturing, distribution, use and disposal.

SCS
Scientific Certification Systems, an organization that assesses lifecycle environmental impact.

Sealant
A paste or liquid (usually an organic substance), which hardens or cures in place, that when applied to a joint forms a permanent bond that acts as a barrier to the entry of a gas or liquid.

Selvage
The edge of a fabric that is woven so it will not fray or ravel.

Semi-interpenetrating polymer network or semi-IPN
A 3-D network at the molecular level, composed of two combined or blended polymers one a thermoset and the other a thermoplastic. The properties of a semi-IPN are different from the two constituent polymers.

S-2 glass
Commercial grade, high-tensile strength glass fibres (magnesium aluminosilicate composition) for reinforcing composites.

Shear modulus
The ratio of shear stress to the corresponding shear strain for shear stresses below the point at which a further stress will create a permanent alteration in the shape of the object (known as the proportional limit). Also called the modulus of rigidity.

Sheet Moulding Compound (SMC)
A reinforced plastic composite, usually a mixture of a thermoset with chopped continuous glass fibres plus a mineral filler. SMC is processed into a tack-free sheet that has a leather-like feel for ease of handling in compression moulding.

Shore hardness
Shore hardness measures the resistance of a rubber or elastomeric material to indentation using a spring-loaded indenter called a Sceleroscope. The higher the number the greater the resistance, therefore the harder the material

SI
The International System of Units, abbreviated SI from the French name Le Système International d'Unités

Silicone
Any of a large group of polymers called siloxanes that are based on a chemical structure consisting of alternate silicon and oxygen atoms with various organic chemical groups attached to the silicon atoms. They are liquids, semi-solids, or solids and have a wide variety of applications including as adhesives, textile finishes, lubricants and coatings.

Sintering
In the sintering process, a mass of powders (ceramic or metal) is heated at high temperatures to bond the powder particles together.

Slubby
A textile containing yarn that has soft, thick nubs that are either imperfections or purposely created for a desired effect.

Slurry
A thick mixture of solid particulate material suspended in a liquid.

Smart Wood

Smart Wood is a Rainforest Alliance programme that aims to reduce the negative impacts of commercial forestry by rewarding its seal of approval to responsible forest managers. The programme's regional experts work in tropical, temperate and boreal (northern North Temperate zone) forests in order to reduce the environmental damage caused by wood harvesting and to maximize the positive impacts of commercial forestry on local communities.

Soffit

The underside of a structural component such as a beam.

Soft magnet

A material that can be readily magnetized on the application of a relatively low strength magnetic field and loses most of its magnetization when the field is removed.

Solar Heat Gain Coefficient (SHGC)

The portion of directly transmitted and absorbed solar energy that enters a building through the window glass. It is an indicator of the ability of the window glass to affect the amount of heat from solar energy that enters a building. The higher the number, the higher the heat gain.

Solubility

The ability or tendency of one substance to blend uniformly with another. The solubility of solids in liquids varies from 0–100%.

Solvent

A substance capable of dissolving another substance (solute) to form a universally dispersed mixture (solution). Water is the most common solvent.

Sound absorption

The propagation of sound can be dissipated by converting sound energy into thermal energy.

Sound transmission coefficient (STC)

This is used to compare the relative effectiveness of panels for building partitions to dampen the transmission or reflection of sound waves.

Spalling

The chipping, flaking, fragmentation, or separation of a surface or coating.

Spin bonding

A process that forms non-woven fabrics by adhering the fibres immediately after they are extruded from the spinnerets.

Spin lacing

Spin lacing is a process that is also called hydro-entangling which forms a fabric similarly to the way spin-bonded webs are formed except that jets of water are forced through the web, shattering the filaments into staple fibres and producing a structure that resembles woven fabrics. Spin-laced fabrics have greater elasticity and flexibility than spin-bonded fabrics.

Spontaneous ignition temperature

This is the self-generated temperature at which a material will burst into flame and/or burn without the application of heat from an external source.

Spool

A spool is the name given to a cylindrical device on which thread, fibre, filament, yarn, wire or tape is wound.

Spray lay-up

Spray lay-up is the term for a wet lay-up process for producing reinforced plastic in which a stream of chopped fibres (usually glass) is fed into a stream of liquid resin in a mould. The direction of the fibres is random compared with the more regularly oriented mats or woven fabrics that are used in hand lay-up.

Spraying

In the spraying process a cloud of liquid droplets is randomly dispersed in a gas phase by an atomizer that transforms the liquid into droplets by using hydraulic pressure, electrical, acoustic or mechanical energy to overcome the cohesive forces within the liquid. Spraying is used for applications such as spray coating, spray painting, spray drying and continuous casting.

Stainless steel

An iron-base alloy containing from 10.5–25% chromium.

Steel

Steel is an alloy of iron that contains manganese and also, from 0.02 to 1.5% carbon. In addition, there are many special-purpose types of steel that contain one or more other alloying metals.

Stitch-bonding

When reinforcement materials are sewn together in plies, which preserves their planar character.

Stress

An applied force that tends to strain or deform a material or the internal resistance of a material to such an applied force.

Sublimation

The direct change of a solid to a vapour without becoming a liquid. For example dry ice (solid carbon dioxide) vaporizes at room temperature.

Surface burning characteristics

The spread of flame over a material's surface and the density of the smoke developed when exposed to a test fire.

Surface tension

The force acting on the surface of a liquid that tends to minimize the area of the surface. Its strength varies with the chemical nature of the liquid. Polar liquids like water have a high surface tension, while non-polar liquids with much lower values flow more readily than water. Mercury, which has the highest surface tension of any liquid, does not flow but disintegrates into droplets.

Swaging

Tapering or reducing the diameter of a bar, rod, wire or tube by forging, hammering or squeezing.

Synthetic resin

The distinction between a synthetic resin and a plastic is that the resin is the human-made high molecular weight polymer itself and a plastic is the polymer plus various additives such as plasticizers, colourants or fire retardants.

Taber™ Abraser test

Measures the abrasion resistance of a material's surface by a combination of rolling and rubbing that causes wear on the surface, which is quantified as a loss in weight.

TAPPI

Technical Association of the Pulp and Paper Industry

TDI

Toluene diisocyanate.

Temper

To harden or strengthen metal or glass by applying heat or by heating and cooling.

Tempered glass

In the tempering process a high permanent stress is induced in the glass by rapidly cooling the glass surfaces slightly below the softening point temperature. This creates a high degree of compression at the surfaces with the tensile forces confined to the interior. Tempering greatly increases the strength of the glass thus its impact resistance. One of the uses of tempered glass is for vehicle windshields.

Tenacity

The strength per unit weight of a fibre or filament, expressed as gram-force per denier (gpd) or newton/tex (N/tex). It is measured as the rupture load or breaking force (gram-force or newton) divided by the fibre's linear density (denier or tex).

Tensile strength

The rupture strength per unit area of a material during a test in which it is being pulled in tension.

Terne

Sheet iron or steel plated with an alloy of 3 or 4 parts of lead to 1 part of tin used as a roofing material.

Tex

A unit for expressing the linear density or fineness of a filament, fibre, or yarn.

Tg

The symbol for the glass transition temperature.

Thermal arc spraying

A coating technology in which two oppositely charged metal wires are fed through a gun creating an electric arc when they touch that causes the metal to melt. A highly compressed gas fed through an orifice atomizes the molten metal and propels the droplets spraying a thin layer of the metal on the surface of the object to be coated. The desired coating thickness is obtained by spraying multiple layers. This process does not produce any undesirable combustion by-products.

Thermal resistance

Thermal or heat resistance is the ability of a material to withstand the potentially damaging effects of exposure to high temperatures. It is expressed as the ability of a material to prevent the flow of heat through it, and is measured as the difference between the temperatures of the two.

Thermal resistance (continued)
opposite faces of the material divided by the rate at which the heat flows through it. Superalloys based on nickel, iron-nickel, or cobalt are examples of heat resistant metals developed for service at very high temperatures.

Thermal shock resistance
The tendency of materials such as ceramics and glasses to partially or completely fracture usually as a result of sudden or rapid cooling.

Thermal spraying
A coating process in which finely divided metallic or ceramic materials in the molten or semi-molten state are deposited on a surface.

Thermoforming
A thermoplastic sheet is formed into a 3-D shape after heating it to the point at which it becomes soft and flowable, and then differential pressure is applied to make the sheet conform to the shape of a mould or die.

Thermoplastic polymers
Polymers that can be repeatedly softened by an increase in temperature and hardened by a decrease in temperature. When heated, thermoplastic polymers undergo a largely physical rather than a chemical change, and in the softened stage can be shaped into articles by moulding or extrusion. Polyethylene, polyvinylchloride, and polystyrene are examples.

Thermosetting polymers
High molecular weight polymers that can be cured, set or hardened by heat or radiation, into a permanent shape. They form cross-links on heating and become permanently rigid. They do not soften when reheated but can decompose at high temperatures. Polyesters and silicones are examples.

Thermotreating
Subjecting a material to heat to alter its properties and/or appearance.

Torsional stiffness
The resistance to elastic deflection when subjected to a twisting action.

Tow
An untwisted bundle of continuous filaments, usually referring to human-made fibres, particularly carbon and graphite, but also glass fibre and aramid fibres (such as Kevlar®).

Trapezoid tear strength
Trapeziod tear strength is the force required to continue or propagate a tear started previously in woven, nonwoven, layered, knit or felt textiles.

UL
Underwriters Laboratories Inc. (UL) is an independent, not-for-profit product safety testing and certification organization that has conducted US product safety and certification since 1894. There are several types of UL Marks, each with its own specific meaning and significance. The only way to determine if a product has been certified by UL is to look for the UL Mark on the product itself. In a few, exceptional instances, the UL Mark may be present only on the product's packaging.

Ultrasonic welding
Ultrasonic welding is a process that uses high-frequency vibratory energy in order to weld a joint that is held together under pressure.

Ultraviolet (UV) radiation
Radiation in the region of the electromagnetic spectrum from just beyond the wavelength of the violet end of the visible spectrum to the border of the wavelength of the x-ray region.

Upholstered Furniture Action Council (UFAC)
The Upholstered Furniture Action Council is a US industry, voluntary programme established to help protect consumers from cigarette fires started in upholstered furniture. The Upholstered Furniture Action Council (UFAC) was founded in 1974 to make upholstered furniture more resistant to ignition from smouldering cigarettes, which are the leading cause of upholstery fires in the home. According to the latest figures (1978–1994) there has been a 77.1% decline in the number of upholstered furniture fires in households from smouldering ignition due to cigarettes.

U-value
A measure of heat transfer or thermal conductivity. The higher the U-Value, the more heat is conducted.

Vapour density
The weight of a vapour per unit volume, at any given temperature. The vapour density of air is one.

Vacuum evaporation
Drying a material by drawing off the moisture by vapourizing it under reduced pressure (less than the ambient atmospheric pressure).

Varnish
A protective coating, similar to paint, except that it is not coloured. It can be composed of a vegetable oil such as linseed oil and a solvent, or of a synthetic or natural resin and a solvent. In the case of the oil, the formation of the coating is due to polymerization of the oil; in the case of the resins it is due to evaporation of the solvent.

Veneer
1) A thin surface layer, such as a finely grained wood, glued onto an inferior wood. 2) Anyone of the thin layers that are glued or bonded together to form plywood.

Vibration damping
The loss in energy as dissipated heat when a material or system is subjected to rapid oscillations (vibrations).

Vicat softening point test (VSP)
A sample of a thermoplastic material is heated at a specified rate of temperature increase and the temperature is noted at which a needle indents into the material a distance of 1 mm ($\frac{1}{16}$ in), under a load of 10 N (36 oz-force) using a temperature rise of 50°C (122°F) per hour.

Vickers hardness test
A micro-indentation hardness test that uses a pyramidal-shaped diamond indenter and variable test loads, which makes it possible to use one hardness scale for all ranges of hardness.

Viscosity
The property of a fluid that causes it to resist flow. A liquid has a viscosity of 1 poise (P) if a force of 1 dyne per square centimetre (1 dn/cm^2) causes two parallel liquid surfaces 1 square centimetre (1 cm^2) in area and 1 centimetre (1 cm) apart to move past each other at a velocity of 1 centimetre per second.

Volatile organic compound (VOC)
Any hydrocarbon (organic compound consisting of the elements carbon and hydrogen) except methane and ethane, with vapour pressure equal to or greater than 0.1 mm mercury (Hg). The VOC content refers to the amount of these constituents that will evaporate at their use temperature.

Volatility
The tendency of a material (solid or liquid) to vaporize at a given temperature.

Vulcanization
A physical change in a rubber such as polyisoprene, which improves its strength and resiliency and reduces its stickiness, resulting from chemical reaction with sulfur or other suitable additives that cross-link the polymer chains.

Waferboard
A sheet material made of wood flakes from small logs. The flakes or wafers are large, flat sections of wood in the grain (longitudinal) direction of the wood.

Warp
In a woven fabric, the threads that run lengthwise and are crossed at right angles to the weft are called the warp.

Warpage
Dimensional distortion in an object. Usually stated as the per cent of deviation from the original dimension (for example, the diagonal or the edge of a tile).

Warp knit
One of the two categories of knitting technology in which the formation of knitted loops is along the machine or warp direction. Warp knitted structures are usually more stable than weft knit structures in which the knitted loops are introduced across the machine direction or in the weft direction.

Water Efficient – SCS
Scientific Certification Systems (SCS) certifies flow rates that are at least 10% below the federal level of 9.5 litres (2.5 gallons) per minute.

Water-column Test
Measures a fabric's resistance to the penetration of water.

Water permeability
The rate of the flow of water through a porous material.

Waterproofing
Coating a fabric and filling the pores with film-forming material such as varnish, rubber, nitrocellulose, wax, tar or plastic. Fabrics can also be laminated to films so that the total structure is waterproof or water-resistant but breathable.

GLOSSARY (continued)

Water retention capacity
The quantity of water that a material can retain per unit area.

Watt (W)
The unit for expressing power in the International System of Units (SI).

Wax Pick (Dennison)
A measure of the internal bond strength of paper. A range of calibrated waxes are used to determine whether inks with a comparable tackiness can be used without pulling off the paper. (Dennison is the name used to refer to the company that makes the waxes used for this test).

Wear rate
The amount of material removed per unit time in a sliding wear test. The reciprocal of this measurement is the material's wear resistance.

Wear resistance
Depends on the conditions under which the wear occurs hence the wear conditions must always be specified. It is expressed as the reciprocal of the wear rate.

Web
1) The structural part of a cloth.
2) A continuous length of a material as compared with a sheet.

Wedging
The measurable deviation from rectangularity and straightness of the sides of a flat, rectangular ceramic wall and floor tile.

Weft
The horizontal threads interlaced through the warp (please see the previous page) in a woven fabric are named the weft. They are also known as the woof.

Welding
Joining two or more pieces of material by applying heat and/or pressure.

Welding (thermoplastic)
Heat is used in order to soften or to melt the areas intended to be bonded together to fusion temperature. After joining, the area is cooled causing the plastic to harden and resolidify forming the joint or weld.

Wet lay-up
The fabrication of reinforced plastics by applying the resin system as a liquid when the reinforcement is put in place.

Whisker
A short, single crystal fibre used as a reinforcement for metal or ceramic matrix composites, 1 to 25 micrometers (10,000–250,000 Å) in diameter, with an aspect ratio (length/diameter) between 50 and 150.

Wick resistance
The resistance to the flow of a liquid along the surface of a fibre into a space that is known as capillary action.

Wire
A thin, flexible, continuous length of metal, usually with a circular cross section, and typically produced by drawing through a die.

Wire drawing
The reduction of the cross section of a wire achieved by pulling it through a die.

Wyzenbeek test
This is a precision test for determining the wear resistance of fabrics.

Yarn
An assemblage of fibres twisted or laid together so as to form a continuous strand that can be made into a textile fabric.

Yield strength
Indicates the onset of plastic deformation (alteration in shape) in metals such as steels and aluminum alloys. For example, the yield strength of wrought aluminum alloy for sheet metal is 24 MPa (3480 psi) and for stainless steel is 375 MPa (4375 psi).

Zahn's Cup test
A method for determining viscosity that measures the time it takes for a specified volume of a liquid to completely flow through an orifice of a specified size.

Zwick Elongation test
Measures how far a fabric can be stretched as a percent increase in the original dimension.

DESIGNER DIRECTORY

adidas America, Inc.
5055 N. Greeley Avenue
Portland, OR 97217, USA
www.adidas.com

Adjaye/Associates
23–28 Penn Street
London, N1 5DL, UK
www.adjaye.com

Ghiora Aharoni Design Studio LLC
126 Fifth Avenue, 13th Floor
New York, NY 10011, USA
www.ghiora-aharoni.com

Harry Allen & Associates
207 Avenue A
New York, NY 10009, USA
www.harryallendesign.com

Ed Annink
Ontwerpwerk
Prinsestraat 37, 2513 CA Den Haag
Postbus 45, The Netherlands
www.ontwerpwerk.com

Aoki Design Corporation
Izurricho Church Building 1F
1–3–11 Kanda Izumi-cho, Tokyo
Japan
www.aokidesign.com

The Apartment
101 Crosby Street
New York, NY 10012, USA
www.theapt.com

Ron Arad
62 Chalk Farm Road
London, NW1 8AN, UK
www.ronarad.com

Architects of Air
Oldknows Factory, Egerton Street
Nottingham, NG3 4GQ, UK
www.architects-of-air.com

Archi-tectonics
200 Varick Street
Suite 507B, New York
NY 10014, USA
www.archi-tectonics.com

Atelier Bow Wow
8–79 Suga-cho Shinjuku-ku
Tokyo 160–0018, Japan
www.bow-wow.jp

Atypyk
17 rue Lambert
75018, Paris
France
www.atypyk.com

Autoban
TatarBey Sokak
No: 1 K:1, Galata, 34425 Istanbul
Turkey
www.autoban212.com

Georg Baldele
Unit 15, The Dove Centre
109 Bartholomew Road
London, NW5 2BJ, UK
www.georgbaldele.com

Barbers Osgerby
Ground Floor
35 Charlotte Road, London
EC2A 3PG, UK
www.barberosgerby.com

Bengtsson Design Ltd
17–25 Cremer Street
London, E2 8HD, UK
www.bengtssondesign.com

Ozwald Boateng
12a Savile Row
London, W1S 3PQ, UK
www.ozwaldboateng.co.uk

Ronan & Erwan Bouroullec
12 rue Roussel
93200 Saint-Denis, France
www.bouroullec.com

Jason Bruges Studio
56 Shoreditch High Street
Unit 2.03, London, E1 6JJ, UK
www.jasonbruges.com

Bugatti Automobiles SAS
1, Château Saint Jean
F-67120 Molsheim
Dorlisheim, France
www.bugatti.com

Duangrit Bunnag Architect Ltd
81 Sukhumvit, 26 Klongtoey
Bangkok 10110, Thailand
duangrit@loginfo.co.th

Estudio Campana
Rua Barão de Tatuí, 219 Santa Cecília
São Paulo sp 01226 030, Brasil
www.campanabrothers.com.br

Louise Campbell Studio
Gothersgade 54, baghuset 2 sal
DK–1123 Copenhagen K, Denmark
www.louisecampbell.com

Hussein Chalayan
Zetland House, Block H
109–123 Clifton Street
London, EC2A 4LD, UK
www.husseinchalayan.com

Nathalie Chanin
Project Alabama
6534 County Road 200
Florence, AL 35633, USA
www.projectalabama.com

Kenneth Cobonpue
3A General Maxilom Avenue
Cebu City, Philippines
info@kennethcobonpue.com

Dan Craft
6-23-33 Jindaiji Kitamachi
Chofu-si, Tokyo 182-0011
Japan

Matali Crasset Productions
26 rue du Buisson Saint Louis
F-75010 Paris, France
www.matalicrasset.com

Derin Design
Abdi ipekçi Cadddesi No: 77/1
Maçka Istanbul, Turkey
www.derindesign.com

Design Faith
5-1-207 Aoshinke-4chome
Minoo, Osaka 562-0024
Japan
www.kisweb.ne.jp/personal/faith

Design Studio Press
8577 Higuera Street
Culver City, CA 90232, USA
www.designstudiopress.com

Design Studio S
2-16-15-502, Manami Aoyama
Minatoku, Tokyo, Japan
www.design-ss.com

Design Studio Triform
5-26-29 Nakano, Tokyo, Japan
www.triform.co.jp

Cheick Diallo
Bamako, Mali

Digitalscape
Shibuya-nomura Bldg
8F, 1-10-8 Dogenzaka
Tokyo, Japan
www.dsp.co.jp

Janet Echelman, Inc.
175 Florence Street,
Chestnut Hill,
MA 02467
USA
www.echelman.com

Fabrican
www.fabricanltd.com

Monica Förster Design Studio
Åsögatan 194
116 32 Stockholm, Sweden
www.monicaforster.se

Freedom Of Creation (FOC)
Hobbemakade 85 hs
1071 XP Amsterdam
The Netherlands
www.freedomofcreation.com

Front
Tegelviksgatan 20, 116 41 Stockholm
Sweden
www.frontdesign.se

Fujita Design Lab
www.fdl-italform.net

Naoto Fukasawa Design
5-17-20-4F Jingumae, Shibuya-ku
150-0001 Tokyo, Japan
www.naotofukasawa.com

fuseproject
528 Folsom Street
San Francisco, CA 94105, USA
www.fuseproject.com

Future Systems
20 Victoria Gardens
London, W11 3PE, UK
www.future-systems.com

GK Design International
4007 Paramount Blvd, Suite 110
Lakewood, CA 90712, USA
www.gkdi.com

GKD Metal Fabrics
Metallweberstraße 46
52348 Düren, Germany
www.gkdmetalfabrics.com

Grahacipta Hadiprana Design Consultants
Jl. Pangeran Antasari No. 12
Cipete Selatan
Jakarta 12410, Indonesia
www.grahaciptahadiprana.com

Paolo Grasselli Design
www.paolograsselli.com

Konstantin Grcic Industrial Design
Schillerstr. 40
D-80336 Munich
Germany
www.konstantin-grcic.com

Zaha Hadid Architects Ltd
66 Bowling Green Lane
London, EC1 4GH, UK
www.zaha-hadid.com

Ineke Hans
Dijkstraat 105
6828JS Arnhem
The Netherlands
www.inekehans.com

Usman Haque
www.haque.co.uk

Stuart Haygarth
Winterfeldt Strasse 1
10781 Berlin, Germany
www.stuarthaygarth.com

Jaime Hayon
Muntaner 88, 2.1A, 08011 Barcelona
Spain
www.hayonstudio.com

Heatherwick Studios
16 Acton Street, London
WC1X 9NG, UK
www.thomasheatherwick.com

Simon Heijdens
Graaf Florisstraat 23a
3021 CB Rotterdam
The Netherlands
www.simonheijdens.com

Helfand Architecture
552 Broadway 4th Floor
New York
NY 10012, USA
www.helfandarch.com

Inflate
1 Helmsley Place
London,
E8 3SB, UK
www.inflate.co.uk

Inside Outside
Eerste Nassaustraat 5
1052 BD Amsterdam
The Netherlands
www.insideoutside.nl

International Fashion Machines, Inc.
1205 East Pike Street Suite 2G
Seattle
WA 98122, USA
www.ifmachines.com

Irvine Spectrum
8001 Irvine Center Drive, Suite 500
Irvine
CA 92618, USA
www.watg.com

Toyo Ito & Associates, Architects
Fujiya Bldg. 1-19-4, Shibuya-ku
Tokyo 150-0002, Japan
www.toyo-ito.co.jp

Hanson Jay & Associates Ltd
22-B Kyoto Plaza
499 Lockhart Road, Hong Kong

Tine M. Jensen
Studio: Korsgade 16 st.th.
2200 Copenhagen N, Denmark
tinem@jensen.mail.dk

Eva Jiricna Architects
Third Floor, 38 Warren Street
London, W1T 6AE, UK
www.ejal.com

Hella Jongerius
Jongeriuslab, Eendrachtsweg 67
3012 LG Rotterdam
www.jongeriuslab.com

Claudia Jongstra
Openhartsteeg 1
NL-1017 BD Amsterdam
The Netherlands
www.claudyjongstra.com

Agence Patrick Jouin
8 Passage de la Bonne Graine
75011 Paris, France
www.patrickjouin.com

Kennedy & Violich Architecture (KVA)
160 North Washington Street
8th Floor, Boston, MA 02114, USA
www.kvarch.net

Eley Kishimoto
215 Lyham Rd
London, SW2 5PY, UK
www.eleykishimoto.com

Klein Dytham architecture
AD Bldg 2F, 1-15-7 Hiroo
Shibuya-ku
Tokyo 150-0012, Japan
www.klein-dytham.com

Matti Klenell
Heleneborgsgatan 38, 117 32
Stockholm, Sweden
www.mattiklenell.com

Kobata Design Studio
www.d1.dion.ne.jp

Anne Kyyrö Quinn
Unit 2.06 Oxo Tower Wharf
Bargehouse Street, London
SE1 9PH, UK
www.annekyyroquinn.com

Joris Laarman
Marconistraat 52, 3029 AK Rotterdam
The Netherlands
www.jorislaarman.com

FUB
www.chmielorz.de
Germany

Furniture Today
www.furnituretoday.com
USA

Furniture World
www.furninfo.com
USA

FX Magazine
www.fxmagazine.co.uk
UK

Good Housekeeping
www.goodhousekeeping.com
USA

GQ
www.gq.com
USA

Graphic Design
www.graphic-design.com
USA

Graphis
www.graphis.com
USA

GUM
www.gumweb.com
Germany

Habitat
www.ctiweb.cf.ac.uk/habitat
UK

Habitat Ufficio
www.habitatufficio.com
Italy

Harvard Design Magazine
www.gsd.harvard.edu/research
USA

Haute Living
www.hauteliving.com
USA

Hawaii Home & Remodeling
www.hawaiihomeandremodeling.com
USA

Health Care Design
www.healthcaredesignmagazine.com
USA

High Performance Composites
www.compositesworld.com/hpc
USA

HOB
www.hob-magazine.de
Germany

Home
www.homemag.com
USA

Home and Design
www.homeanddesign.com
USA

Hospitality Design
www.hdmag.com/hospitality
design
USA

House and Garden
www.houseandgarden.com
USA

House Beautiful
www.housebeautiful.com
USA

Icon
www.icon-magazine.co.uk
UK

I-D Magazine
www.idonline.com
USA

Idea
www.idea-mag.com
Japan

idFX magazine
www.magazine-group.co.uk
UK

IdN
www.idnproshop.com
Hong Kong

Inc.
www.inc.com
USA

**Industrial Fabric Products
Review**
www.ifai.com
USA

Innovation
www.innovationjournal.org
USA

Intelligente Architecktur
www.xia-online.de
Germany

Interieurs
www.interieurs.fr
France

Interiors and Sources
www.isdesignet.com
USA

Interior Design
www.interiordesign.net
USA

International Fiber Journal
www.ifj.com
USA

Intramuros
www.intramuros.fr
France

IQD
www.iqd.it
Italy

L'Arca
www.arcaedizioni.it
Italy

License
www.licensemag.com
USA

Log Home Design Ideas
www.lhdi.com
USA

Log Home Living
www.lhdi.com
USA

Manufacturing & Technology News
www.manufacturingnews.com
USA

Martha Stewart Living
www.marthastewart.com
USA

Medical Design Technology
www.mdtmag.com
USA

Medical Product Manufacturing News
www.devicelink.com/mpmn
USA

Men's Vogue
www.mensvogue.com
USA

Metal Construction News
www.moderntrade.com
USA

Metro
www.metromag.co.nz
New Zealand

Metropolis
www.metropolismag.com
USA

Metropolitan Home
www.neodata.com/hfmus/mhme
USA

Monday Morning Quarterback
www.mmqb.com
USA

Modern Woodworking
www.modernwoodworking.com
USA

Nasfm
www.nasfm.org/magazine
USA

Natural Home
www.naturalhomeandgarden.com
USA

The New Environmentalist
www.thenewenvironmentalist.com
USA

Nikkei Architecture
www.kenplatz.nikkeibp.co.jp/
building
Japan

Nikkei Design
http://nd.nikkeibp.co.jp
Japan

NonWovens Industry
www.nonwovens-industry.com
USA

Norsk Design
www.norskdesign.no
Norway

Ny Teknik
www.nyteknik.se
Sweden

OASE
www.oase.archined.nl
The Netherlands

Object
www.object.com.au
Australia

Objekt
www.objekt.nl
The Netherlands

Oculus
www.oculus.com
USA

Old House Interiors
www.oldhouseinteriors.com
USA

Old House Journal
www.oldhousejournal.com
USA

Ottagono
www.ottagono.com
Italy

Packaging News
www.packagingnews.co.uk
UK

Paper
www.papermag.com
USA

Plastics News
www.plasticsnews.com
USA

POL Oxygen
www.poloxygen.com
Australia

Pool & Spa Living
www.poolspaliving.com
USA

**Popular Photography &
Imaging**
www.popphoto.com
USA

Pure Contemporary
www.purecontemporary.com
USA

ReadyMade
www.readymademag.com
USA

Residential Architect
www.residentialarchitect.com
USA

Sculpture Magazine
www.sculpture.org
USA

SEGD
www.segd.com
USA

Southern Accent
www.southernaccents.com
USA

Southern Living
www.southernliving.com
USA

Surface
www.surfacemag.com
USA

Surface & Panel
www.surfaceandpanel.com
USA

Surface Fabrication
www.surfacefabrication.com
USA

Technical Textiles International
www.technical-textiles.net
UK

MATERIAL ORGANIZATIONS

Tema Celeste
www.temaceleste.com
Italy

Terrain
www.terrain.org
USA

This Old House
www.thisoldhouse.com
USA

Town & Country
www.townandcountrymag.com
USA

Traditional Building
www.traditional-building.com
USA

The Trend Curve
www.trendcurve.com
USA

Vedere Tech
www.vedere.it
Italy

Veranda
www.traditionalhome.com
USA

View
www.viewmag.com
Canada

View Textile
www.modeinfo.de
Germany

Vis.a.Vis
www.visavismag.com
USA

Visionaire
www.visionaireworld.com
USA

VM+SD
www.visualstore.com
USA

Vogue
www.vogue.com
USA

W
www.wmagazine.com
USA

Wallpaper*
www.wallpaper.com
UK

Wired
www.wired.com
USA

Wood Design & Building
www.woodmags.com
USA

Wood Magazine
www.woodmagazine.com
USA

A to Z of Materials
Suite 24, 90 Mona Vale Rd
Warriewood
NSW 2102
Australia
www.azom.com

**Advanced Materials & Processes
Technology Information Analysis Center**
201 Mill Street, Rome
NY 13440
USA
http://ammtiac.alionscience.com

American Ceramic Society
735 Ceramic Place
Suite 100
Westerville
Ohio 43081
USA
www.ceramics.org

American Iron & Steel Institute
WASHINGTON, D.C.
1140 Connecticut Ave., NW
Suite 705
Washington, D.C. 20036
USA

DETROIT, MICHIGAN
2000 Town Center
Suite 320
Southfield
MI 48075
USA

PITTSBURGH, PENNSYLVANIA
680 Andersen Drive
Pittsburgh
PA 15220
USA
www.steel.org

American Plastics Council
1300 Wilson Blvd
Arlington
VA 22209
USA
www.plastics.org

**American Composites Manufacturers
Association**
1010 North Glebe Road
Suite 450
ArlingtoN
VA 22201
USA
www.acmanet.org

Associazione Italiana di Metallurgia
Piazzale Rodolfo Morandi 2
I-20121 Milano
Italy
www.metallurgia-italiana.net

**Austrian Society for Metallurgy
& Materials**
Montanuniversität Leoben
A-8700 Leoben
Austria
www.asmet.at

Benelux Métallurgie
Génie Metallurgique CP 165/71
Université libre de Bruxelles
50 ave. F. D. Roosevelt
B-1050 Brussels
Belgium
www.beneluxmetallurgie.be

British Ceramic Confederation
Federation House
Station Road
Stoke-on-Trent
ST4 2SA
UK
www.ceramfed.co.uk

Bond voor Materialenkennis
Postbus 70577
NL-5201 AE s-Hertogenbosch
The Netherlands
www.materialenkennis.nl

**Conservation & Art Material
Encyclopedia Online**
C/o Museum of Fine Arts, Boston
Avenue of the Arts, 465 Huntington Ave
Boston, MA 02115-5597
USA
www.mfa.org/_cameo/frontend/home.
asp

Copper Development Association Inc.
260 Madison Avenue
New York, NY 10016
USA
www.copper.org

**Czech Society for New Materials
& Technologies**
Karlovo nam. 13., C Z-121 35 Prague 2
Czech Republic
http://csnmt.fme.vutbr.cz

Danish Metallurgical Society
C/o The Technical University of
Denmark, Dept of Manufacturing,
Engineering & Management
Kemitorvet b. 204, DK-2800 Lyngby
Denmark
www.d-m-s.dk

**Deutsche Gesellschaft für
Materialkunde**
Senckenberganlage 10
60325 Frankfurt am Main
Germany
www.dgm.de

**Deutscher Verband für
Materialforschung**
Unter den Eichen 87
D-12205
Berlin
Germany
www.dvm-berlin.de

**Environmental Design Research
Association**
Post Office Box 7146
Edmond, OK 73083 7146
USA
www.edra.org

Estonian Materials Science Society
C/o Tallinn Technical University
Chair of Semiconducting Materials
Technology Ehitajate tee 5
EE-0026 Tallinn
Estonia

**European Council of Vinyl
Manufacturers**
Av E van Nieuwenhuyse 4
Box 4
B-1160 Brussels
Belgium
www.ecvm.org
www.pvcdesign.org

European Steel Industry Confederation
1 Carlton House Terrace
London
SW1Y 5DB
UK
http://www.iom3.org

**Federation of European Materials
Societies**
The Institute of Materials,
Minerals and Mining
1 Carlton House Terrace
London
SW1Y 5DB
UK
www.fems.org

Fibrous Materials Research Center
Drexel University
Philadelphia, PA 19104
USA
www.materials.drexel.edu/fml

GlassOnWeb.com
Visual Communications S.r.l.
Via Generale Cantore N. 2
34170 Gorizia - GO
Italy
www.glassonweb.com

The Graphite Page
www.phy.mtu.edu/%7Ejaszczak/
graphite.html

MATERIAL ORGANIZATIONS (continued)

**Hellenic Society for the Science
& Technology of Condensed Matter**
Institute of Materials Science
NCSR 'Demokritos'
15310 Aghia Paraskevi
Attiki, Athens
Greece

Institute of Materials, Minerals & Mining
1 Carlton House Terrace
London
SW1Y 5DB
UK
www.iom3.org

Knovel – Science – Technology
13 Eaton Avenue,
Norwich, NY 13815
USA
www.knovel.com

Library of 3-D Molecular Structures
www.nyu.edu/pages/mathmol/library

Liquid Crystal Database
www.eevl.ac.uk/lcd

Lithuanian Materials Research Society
Sauletekio 10,
LT–2040 Vilnius
Lithuania
www.ltmrs.lt

Material Data Management Consortium
www.mdmc.net

Material Data Safety Sheets – MSDS Sheets on the Internet
www.ilpi.com/msds/index.html

Material Handling Industry of America
8720 Red Oak Blvd, Suite 201
Charlotte, NC 28217–3992
USA
www.mhia.org

Material Research Society
506 Keystone Drive
Warrendale, PA 15086–7573
USA
www.mrs.org

MATPRO – Materials & Processes Database
ammtiac.alionscience.com/MATPRO

MatWeb – Database of material data sheets
www.matweb.com

MEMS Materials Data – From the MEMS & Nanotechnology Clearing house
www.memsnet.org/material

Metal Science Society of the Czech Republic
C/o Charles University Prague
Faculty of Mathematics
& Physics
KE Karlovu 5
CZ–12116 Prag2
Czech Republic

Minerals Information – From the US Geological Survey
minerals.usgs.gov/minerals

Nano, Quantum & Statistical Mechanics & Thermodynamics – Data & Property Calculation Websites
http://tigger.uic.edu/~mansoori/
Thermodynamic.Data.and.Property_
html

NanoHub – Resource for online Simulations
www.nanohub.org

Navy Metalworking Center
www.nmc.ctc.com/index.cfm?
fuseaction=about

Nickel Page – Nickel Institute
www.nipera.org/index.cfm/ci_id/
13597/la_id/1.htm

Norsk Metallurgisk Selskap (NMS)
C/o SINTEF
Materials & Chemistry
Richard Birkelands vei 2B
N–7465 Trondheim
Norway
http://materialteknisk.no

Optics InfoBase – Optical Society of America (OSA)
www.osa.org/pubs/infobase

Országos Magyar Bányászati és Kohászati Egyesület (OMBKE)
Fõ u. 68
H–1027 Budapest
Hungary
www.ombkenet.hu

Photonic & Sonic Band Gap Bibliography Compiled & Maintained by Jonathan P. Dowling, Department of Physics & Astronomy, Louisiana State University
http://phys.lsu.edu/%7Ejdowling/
pbgbib.html

Polish Society for Materials
ul. Woloska 141
PL–02–507
Warsaw
Poland

The Rematerialise Project
School of 3D Design
Knights Park Campus
Kingston University
Kingston-upon-Thames
Surrey
KT1 2QJ
UK
www.kingston.ac.uk/rematerialise

Royal Society of Chemistry
Thomas Graham House
Science Park Milton Road
Cambridge
CB4 4WF
UK
www.chemsoc.org

Scirus – Science–specific search engine
www.scirus.com

Slovensko Drustvo Za Materiale
Lepi pot 11
SL–1000
Ljubljana
Slovenia

Sociedad Española de Materiales
Av. Gregorio del Amo 8
E–28040 Madrid
Spain
www.semat.info

Sociedade Portuguesa de Materiais
INETI–DMTP
Estrada do Paço do Lumiar
P–1649–038
Lisbon
Portugal
www.spmateriais.pt

Society Argentina de Materiales
Av. Gral. Peace 1499
(B1650KNA) – San Martin
Buenos Aires
Argentina
www.materiales-sam.org.ar

Société Française de Métallurgie et de Matériau
250 rue Saint Jacques
F–75005
Paris
France
www.sf2m.asso.fr

Society for New Materials & Technologies in Slovakia (SNMTS)
C/o Slovak University of Technology
Dept of Materials & Technologies
Pionierska 15SK– 831 02
Bratislava
Slovak Republic

**The Sol-Gel Gateway
Site for Exchanging & Gathering Information on Sol-Gel Related Areas**
www.solgel.com

Spanish Society of Ceramics & Glass
Calle de Valdelatas
s/n. Campus de Cantoblanco
28049 Madrid
Spain
www.secv.es

Svenska Föreningen för Materialteknik
C/o Dept of Materials Science
& Engineering
Royal Institute of Technology KTH
SE–10044 Stockholm
Sweden

TechStreet – Standards Information
www.techstreet.com

US Advanced Ceramics Association
United States Advanced Ceramics
Association
1800 M Street N.W.
Suite 300
Washington D.C. 20036–5802
USA
www.advancedceramics.org

Utilise Gold – Online Resource for Industrial Gold Products, Materials & Chemicals
www.utilisegold.com

COMPETITIONS + AWARDS

Aga Khan Award for Architecture
(Architecture)
www.akdn.org/agency/akf.html

AR Awards for Emerging Architecture
(Architecture)
www.arplusd.com

American Institute of Architects
Young Architects Award
(Architecture)
www.aia.org/awp_youngarch

Archprix International
(Architecture)
www.archiprix.org

BraunPrize International
(Product Design)
www.braunprize.com

Composites on Tour
(Composite Materials)
www.compositesontour-2.be

Cooper Hewitt National Design Awards
(Multiple Disciplines)
www.ndm.si.edu/NDA

Design & Business Catalyst Award
(Multiple Disciplines)
www.idsa.org

Electrolux Design Lab
(Appliance)
www.electrolux.com/designlab

Frederick Kiesler Prize for
Architecture and the Arts
(Architecture)
www.kiesler.org

Harvard Design School
Excellence in Design Award
(Design)
www.gsd.harvard.edu/inside/
registrar/register/educational_
resources/fellowships_prizes.html

I-D Magazine Annual Design Review
(Multiple Disciplines)
www.idonline.com/adr

Index Award
(Multiple Disciplines)
www.indexaward.dk

Industrial Design Excellence Award
(Industrial Design)
www.idsa.org

International Bauhaus Award
(Architecture + Design)
www.bauhaus-award.de

International Forum Design
Competition
(Multiple Disciplines)
www.ifdesign.de

International Interior Design
Association Competition
(Interior Design)
www.iida.org

JPMA Student Design Competition
(Children's Products)
www.jpma.org

Lighting for Tomorrow Contest
(Lighting)
www.lightingfortomorrow.com

MATERIALICA Design Award
(Multiple Disciplines)
www.materialicadesign.com

NASA's Great Moonbuggy Race
(Transportation + Engineering)
www.nasa.org

The Observer Ethical Awards
(Multiple Disciplines)
www.observer.guardian.co.uk/
ethicalawards

Peugeot Design Contest
(Transportation)
www.peugeot-concours-design.com

Pritzker Architecture Prize
(Architecture)
www.pritzkerprize.com

Prix de Rome
(Art + Architecture)
www.prixderome.nl

Red Dot Design Award
(Multiple Disciplines)
www.en.red-dot.org

Royal Institute of British Architects
Stirling Prize
(Architecture)
www.riba.org

Taiwan International Design
Competition
(Ideological)
www.boco.com.tw/2006Competition

US Green Building Council Natural
Talent Design Competition
(Architecture + Design)
www.usgbc.org

FELLOWSHIPS

American Institute of Architects
Fellowship
(by nomination only)
www.aia.org/awp_fellowship

Berkeley Maybeck Fellowship in
Architecture
www.arch.ced.berkeley.edu/news/em
ployment/maybeck_fellowship.htm

Beverly Willis Architectural Foundation
Grants
www.bwaf.org/grants.html

Boston Foundation for Architecture
Grants
www.bfagrants.org

Enterprise Foundation, Frederick P.
Rose Fellowship, for Architecture
www.enterprisefoundation.org/majori
nitiatives/rosefellowship/index.asp

Harvard Design School:
Arthur W. Wheelwright Traveling
Fellowship in Architecture
www.gsd.harvard.edu

Harvard Design School:
Loeb Fellowship
www.gsd.harvard.edu/professional/
loeb_fellowship

Jan Van Eyck Academie
Post-Academic Institute for
Research & Production, Fine Art,
Design & Theory
www.janvaneyck.nl

LEF Foundation Grants
www.lef-foundation.org

National Endowment for the Arts
Grants in Design
www.nea.gov/grants/apply/Design.html

New York Foundation for the Arts
Artist's Fellowships
www.nyfa.org

New York State Council on the Arts
Architecture, Planning & Design
Program
www.nysca.org

Royal Ontario Museum Research
Fellowships in Textile & Costume
History
www.rom.on.ca

Skidmore, Owings & Merrill
Foundation Fellowships
www.somfoundation.som.com/
fellowships_awards.htm

Steedman Fellowship
www.steedmancompetition.com

University of Michigan Architecture
Fellowships
www.caup.umich.edu/arch/
fellowships.html

Whitney Museum
Independent Study Program
www.whitney.org/www/programs/
isp.jsp

PICTURE CREDITS

The materials illustrated in this book were photographed by Eugene Gologursky. The authors would like to acknowledge the following for permission to reproduce images of objects, interiors, installations and buildings:

p. 1: Materialise.MGX
p. 4: Wilsonart International
p. 6: 1 Vucciria & Flux Design
2 Guy Wenborne
3 Stephan Böhm, Jürgen Flohre, Maria Mocanu & Arne Hofmann
4 Rinaldo DeSantis
5 Lovegrove Studio
p. 7: 6 Mathieu Lehanneur
7 Colbond Inc.
8 J. Mayer H.
pp 8–9: DEDON GmbH
p. 10: 1 Dan Howell
2 David Joseph
3 Terrence Kelleman for the Museum of Modern Art
4 Edra & Peter Traag
p. 11: 6, 7 + MAIN Nigel Young/Foster and Partners
5 Bengtsson design limited
8 Christa Winter
p. 12: 1 Boora Architects
2 Architecture of Israel Quarterly
p. 13: Arne Hofmann, Stephan Böhm, Jürgen Flohre & Maria Mocanu
p. 14: 1 CHISTA
2 James Owen Design
ABOVE Bathsheba Grossman
p. 15: 3 Massimiliano Adami
4 Raoul Kramer & Paul D. Scott
BELOW Thomas Duval
p. 16: Ferrari Group
p. 17: BELOW Wilsonart International
ABOVE Barend van Herpe
p. 18: 1 castordesign.ca
2 Cornerstone Garden, Sonoma
BELOW David Jacquot
p. 19: BELOW Akemi Tanaka
4 Robert Rausch / Gas Studio
p. 20: 1 © Undine Prohl
2 Richard Lombard
p. 21: 3, 4 + OPPOSITE Guy Wenborne
p. 22: Thomas Malmberg
p. 24: 1, 2 + 3 Teijin Fibers Ltd
4 GE-Advanced Materials
p. 25: 5 Bathsheba Grossman
6 Eugene Gologursky
7 TFL COOL SYSTEM® by TFL Leather Technology Ltd
8 © Geoff Hardy/Shutterstock
MAIN Ingmar Lindewall
p. 26: Colbond Inc.
p. 27: © Chris Fourie/Shutterstock
p. 28: © Volkov Ilya/Shutterstock
p. 29: © Orlov Mihail Anatolevich/Shutterstock

p. 30: 1 PHILKNOT Anthology
2 Designtex
p. 31: 2 Colbond Inc.
4 L. Duffy
p. 32: Colin Williamson
p. 33: 2 © Nadezda Igorevna Firsova/Shutterstock
3 Rubbersidewalks, INC
p. 34: 1 bambu
2 Ivan Frederiksen
p. 35: Greg Anthony
p. 36: 1 © Richard Goldberg/Shutterstock
2 Greg Anthony
p. 37: 3 © Marcus P. Turner/Shutterstock
4 © Arlene Jean Gee/Shutterstock
p. 38: 1 CFF-Germany/Design Kay Thoss
2 © Bruce Amos/Shutterstock
p. 39: 3 Michael Skott
4 © Bateleur/ Shutterstock
p. 40: 1 Fielitz
2 © sgame/Shutterstock
p. 41: 3 Ilvio Gallo
MAIN Interstuhl
p. 42: 1 Fielitz
2 SUN-TEC Co. Ltd
pp 44–45: Mathias Bengtsson, Bengtsson Design
p. 46: 3 Usman Haque
p. 47: 5 Usman Haque
6 Anne Kyyrö Quinn Design
7 Louise Campbell
8 Dan Lecca
MAIN Mathias Bengtsson, Bengtsson Design
pp 48–49: 1 NOX Architecture
2 J. Mayer H.
3 Inflate
4, 6 + MAIN veech.media. architecture
pp 50–51: 1–6 Mark West
BELOW courtesy Testa & Weiser
p. 52: 1–5 Kennedy Violich Architecture
p. 53: J. Mayer H.
p. 54: 1 Longchamp
2–4 India Mahdavi
5, 8 + MAIN Sybarite
p. 56: Heatherwick Studio
p. 57: Longchamp
p. 58: The Apartment
p. 59: India Mahdavi
p. 60: 1 Mathias Bengtsson, Bengtsson Design
2 Mathieu Lehanneur
3 Poltona Frau
5, 8 + MAIN Mathieu Lehanneur
pp 62–63: 1 Front
2 + 3 Nendo
4 Autobahn
MAIN Paolo Grasselli
p. 64: 1 + BELOW Mathias Bengtsson, Bengtsson Design
2 Readymade Projects Inc.

p. 65: Naoto Fukasawa Design
p. 66: Louise Campbell
p. 67: Ontwerkwerp
p. 68: 2 + 4 Anne Kyyrö Quinn Design
p. 69: MAIN Lama Concept
p. 71: 2 Patrick O'Connor
3 Lama Concept
MAIN Schoeller Switzerland AG
p. 74: Anne Kyyrö Quinn Design
p. 75: Helena Hietanen
p. 76: 1 Johannes Worsøe Berg
2 Freedom of Creation
3–4 Marc Fluri
p. 77: 5, 8 + BELOW Johannes Worsøe Berg
p. 78: 1–2 Freedom of Creation
p. 79: 3–4 Fabrican/Manel Torres
pp 80–81: 1, 2 + MAIN Marc Fluri
p. 82: Dan Lecca
p. 83: International Fashion Machines
p. 84: 1 + 3 Yamagata Studio
2 Usman Haque
p. 85: 5, 6 + 8 Yamagata Studio
7 + MAIN Usman Haque
pp 86–87: Usman Haque
p. 88: Valerie Vivancos
p. 90: Design Studio Press
p. 91: Bugatti Automobiles S.A.S.
p. 92: 1 Design Studio Press
BELOW Lovegrove Studio
p. 93: Design Studio Press
pp 94–95: Greg Anthony
p. 96: 1 Moroso Spa
2 Sergio Chimenti
3 Tim Soar & Adjaye Associates Ltd
4 Kartell
p. 97: 5 Nacasa & Partners Inc.
6 Kartell 7 Maarten Van Houten
8 Piero Fasanotto for Miss K
MAIN Lovegrove Studio
pp 98–101: JongeriusLab
p. 102: 1 + BELOW Marcel Wanders Studio
p. 103: 2 Marcel Wanders Studio
BELOW Maarten Van Houten
p. 104: BELOW Maarten Van Houten
1 Edland Man
pp 105–108: LOT-EK
pp 109–111: Lovegrove Studio
p. 112: ABOVE B+B Italia BELOW Driade
p. 113: BELOW Moroso Spa
p. 114: ABOVE Kartell
BELOW Foscarini Murano
pp 115–117: Zaha Hadid Architects
pp 118–119: Tim Soar & Adjaye Associates Ltd
pp 120–121: Adjaye Associates Ltd & Studio Toni Yli Suvanto
pp 122–125: Nacasa & Partners Inc
pp 126–129: Sergio Chimenti
pp 130–131: 1 + 5 Dan Lecca
2–4 + BELOW Target Corporation
p. 132: 1–8 Chris Moore
BELOW Swarovski
p. 133: Swarovski
p. 133: 6 Chris Moore

pp 134–135: Swarovski
p. 136: 1 Kartell
BELOW Piero Fasanotto for Miss K
p. 137: 2 Patricia Bailer
3 Claude Weber
p. 138: Kartell
p. 139: Patricia Bailer
pp 140–141: PadLab
p. 142: 1 Furst and Bartosch
2 DuPont
p. 143: 1 + BELOW Herman Miller, Inc.
4 Victor Innovatex
p. 144: Nicolas Zurcher – IDEO
p. 146: 1 DuPont
2 DuPont Fluoroproducts
BELOW DuPont Tate & Lyle Bio Products, LLC
p. 147: DuPont Tate & Lyle Bio Products, LLC
p. 152: 1 Furst and Bartosch
2 Darrin Haddad
3 Rinaldo DeSantis
p. 153: MAIN Lama Concept
p. 154: 2, 6 + 7 Altus Group
p. 156: BELOW Chapman Innovations
p. 157: BELOW Altus Group
p. 158: 3 material raum form
8 material raum form
p. 160: BELOW LiTraCon Bt
p. 161: BELOW material raum form
p. 162: 1, 4 + 6 Dominic Crinson Designs
3 + 5 Keith Carlson
p. 163: 11 Courtesy of Keronite PLC
12, 14 + 16 Dominic Crinson Designs
p. 164: BELOW Courtesy of Keronite PLC
p. 164: BELOW Dominic Crinson Designs
p. 166: BELOW Rinaldo DeSantis
p. 167: BELOW Keith Carlson
p. 168: 2 Murano Due
3 + 5 Darrin Haddad
6 Joel Berman Glass Studios
8 Artwork in Architectural Glass (AAG)
p. 168: 1 Trend USA
3 Darrin Haddad
5 Vitrics
6 Trend USA
7 Joel Berman Glass Studios
p. 169: 16 Darrin Haddad
p. 170: BELOW Christian Yakowlef
p. 171: BELOW Michael Weber
p. 172: BELOW Vitrics
p. 173: BELOW © gruppe RE/ECKELT GLAS GmbH
p. 174: BELOW Artwork in Architectural Glass (AAG)
p. 175: BELOW Joel Berman Glass Studios
p. 176: 1 Joe Hutt
3 Forms+Surfaces
5 © Sophie Mallebranche
p. 177: 9 TECU® Classic. Photograph © KME/ Christian Richters
11 © Sophie Mallebranche

ACKNOWLEDGMENTS

12 Mads Lauridzen
14 Forms+Surfaces
15 AmberStrand™ by Syscom Technology, Inc.
8 Forms+Surfaces
p. 178: BELOW BLUESTEIN SRL
p. 179: BELOW Dr-Ing. Meywald GmbH & Co. KG
p. 180: BELOW TECU® Classic
p. 181: BELOW Joe Hutt
p. 182: BELOW © GKD / A.M. van Treek
p. 183: BELOW ARCHICHURA architects
p. 184: BELOW Mads Lauridzen
p. 185: BELOW Raoul Kramer & Paul D. Scott
p. 186: BELOW O. Oettel/S. Schneider
p. 187: BELOW CFF-Germany/Design Kay Thoss
p. 188: 1 Vam Cheung
2 Guido La Puca
3 + 4 EFFEPIMARMI SRL
5 Matthew Septimus
6 Marco Alberi Auber
7 Kerex SRL
8 James Silverman
p. 189: 10 + 11 Elena Moretti Credits
12 Guido La Puca
13 Raffia Fabric
14 EFFEPIMARMI SRL
15 Gerard Minakawa
16 Robert Hakalski/STUDIO PHOTOS
p. 190: BELOW Gina White
p. 191: BELOW VILLANI LEONELLO
p. 192: BELOW Lama Concept
p. 193: BELOW Teragren Bamboo Flooring, Panels & Veneer
p. 194: BELOW The Milano Group
p. 195: BELOW Mr Rene Malcorps
p. 196: BELOW Andreas Keller
p. 197: BELOW ERPACKUNSZENTRUM GRAZ
p. 198: BELOW Kyouei Design
p. 199: BELOW Guido La Puca
p. 200: BELOW Furst and Bartosch
p. 201: BELOW Greg Anthony
p. 202: BELOW Alastair Jardine
p. 203: BELOW Creadesign Co.
p. 204: BELOW Richard Salas
p. 205: BELOW Interlam Inc.
p. 206: BELOW Russell Gera
p. 207: BELOW Robin W. Plume
p. 208: BELOW VD Werkstätten GmbH & Co. KG
p. 209: BELOW Claus Peuckert Fotografi
p. 210: BELOW EFFEPIMARMI SRL
p. 211: BELOW Two-Lux®
p. 212: BELOW BlastGard International
p. 213: BELOW James Silverman
p. 214: BELOW Raffia Fabric
p. 215: BELOW Kyra & Robertson Hartnett
p. 216: BELOW UONO
p. 217: BELOW Matthew Septimus
p. 218: 4 www.silentium-online.de

5 Teijin Fibers Limited
7 Lama Concept
8 Kinnasand GmbH
p. 219: 9 AO/GCL. Product & Photograph by Panelite
10 S.V. Gomma
13 S.V. Gomma for MIZAR & Tobias Scarpa
16 Fossil Faux Studios
p. 220: BELOW Design by Mark Daniel of Slate. Graphic Design by Sean Seninger of Bamboo Worldwide
p. 221: BELOW Stephen Johnson
p. 222: BELOW CPI Daylighting, Inc.
p. 223: BELOW assaashuach.com
p. 224: BELOW Russell Gera
p. 225: BELOW Nishimoto Photography
p. 226: BELOW Fulcrum Composites Inc.
p. 227: BELOW PHILKNOT Anthology
p. 228: BELOW 3M DI-NOC™
p. 229: BELOW RENOLIT
p. 230: BELOW Fabrice Covelli
p. 231: BELOW Citizen : Citizen
p. 232: BELOW Bob Lukeman
p. 233: BELOW S.V. Gomma for LUCEPLAN
p. 234: BELOW E4/Bruce Talbot
p. 235: BELOW Lux Elements
p. 236: BELOW Material ConneXion Bangkok, Thailand Creative & Design Center
p. 237: BELOW Mark Cosslett
p. 237: BELOW www.silentium-online.de
p. 239: BELOW Vucciria & Flux Design
p. 240: BELOW Lumigraf
p. 241: BELOW Patrick O'Connor
p. 242: BELOW CeeLite
p. 244: BELOW PadLab
p. 245: BELOW assaashuach.com
p. 246: BELOW DuPont™ Corian®
p. 247: BELOW Bayer Material Science LLC
p. 248: BELOW Hal Strata
p. 249: BELOW Materialise.MGX
p. 250: BELOW www.messierdesigners.com
p. 251: BELOW Arash Moallemi
p. 252: BELOW Greg Ball & Shoko Cesar
p. 253: BELOW Colin Williamson
p. 254: BELOW Jerszy Seymour
p. 255: BELOW Greg Smolders (Studio Positive)
p. 256: BELOW Debbie Franke Photography, Inc.
p. 257: BELOW Fossil Faux Studios
p. 258: BELOW B.lab Italia
p. 259: BELOW Olivier Goulet
p. 260: BELOW Peter Riddihough
p. 261: BELOW NOX/Lars Spuybroeck
p. 262: BELOW V. Groß
p. 263: BELOW Russell Gera
p. 264: BELOW Leigh Webber
p. 265: BELOW Lama Concept

I want to thank Jamie Camplin for supporting us, once again, in our efforts to spread our thoughts and ideas. He, along with the entire team at Thames & Hudson, has been instrumental in making this second edition a wonderful follow up to the first book.

Here at home, my colleague Andrew Dent and I have also, once again, had a wonderful time in producing this book together. Our thanks also to Bradley Quinn, whose experience has provided the project with a fresh new voice.

We have also enjoyed the support of a number of people here at Material ConneXion: Andrew's colleagues on the library staff, most notably Jake Remington who spearheaded a highly effective and successful image gathering campaign; along with our Public Programs team, Richard Lombard and Benjamin Rosenthal, whose behind-the-scenes efforts touched many parts of the book. We could not have done this project without Richard Lombard's ardent and vigilant effort to put all the pieces together in addition to his valuable running commentary.

In the end, there were dozens of people to whom we owe a debt of thanks – and you know who you are – and we hope that the book you hold in your hand fills you with the inspiration of all of those who are featured in it and who worked on it.

George M. Beylerian
Founder and President
Material ConneXion, Inc.

Many designers and architects share my enthusiasm for the new materials, and I especially appreciated those who were able to contribute to this project by sharing their knowledge, ideas contacts and visions of the future.

I'd like to thank David Adjaye, Hussein Chalayan, Naoto Fukasawa, Zaha Hadid, Charles Holliday, Toyo Ito, Hella Jongerius, Ross Lovegrove and Mohsen Mostafavi for making time for an indepth interview, and Akushika Akiwumi-Thompson, Kathleen Forte, Hiromi Hosoya, Roger Howie, Milly Patralek and Miki Uonon for making those interviews happen.

Other designers also gave generously of their time – in particular I'd like to thank Ed Annink, Mathias Bengtsson, Louise Campbell, Janet Echelman, Monica Förster, Paolo Grasselli, Usman Haque, Helena Hietanen, Tine Jensen, Sheila Kennedy, Matti Klenell, Anne Kyyrö-Quinn, Mathieu Lehanneur, Jürgen Mayer, Simon Mitchell, Pia Myrvold, Yeohlee Teng, Stuart Veech, Valerie Vivancos, Mark West and Zeynep Yener.

Last, but not least, I'd like to thank Rebeka Cohen, the book's editor, for her unwavering commitment to the project, and Anna Perotti, the book's designer, for creating an outstanding design.

Bradley Quinn